GNOSTIC MYS
of SEX

"Gnostic Mysteries of Sex takes us on a wild ride through the secret, enigmatic and heretical world of Gnostics, medieval troubadours, the visions of Blake, and the counterculture of the 1960s—all united in their quest for union with God. The reader should not be fooled by Tobias Churton's inimitable style of writing, because beneath his humor and provocative statements, there's a profound understanding of one the greatest mysteries of all time—the power of sexual *gnosis*."

HENRIK BOGDAN, ASSOCIATE PROFESSOR IN
RELIGIOUS STUDIES, UNIVERSITY OF GOTHENBURG

"In *Gnostic Mysteries of Sex*, Tobias Churton works to heal Western civilization's deepest wound—the millennia-old divorce of sex and spirit. Revealed herein are the dangerous and radical sexual secrets that the Church could not eradicate, kept hidden by the occult underground through long centuries of persecution, torture, and crusade. And here is the radical message of the Gnostics, as shocking and critically important now as it was in the second century—that sex is the gateway of liberation, and the kingdom of heaven is within."

JASON LOUV, AUTHOR OF *GENERATION HEX* AND
COAUTHOR OF *THEE PSYCHICK BIBLE*

"If you think the last word has long since been said on the subject of sex, then you need to read this book. The question of how to reconcile sex with spirituality has long preoccupied the religious culture of both East and West. Churton explores how the Gnostics had their own approach to this issue, an approach that he traces down the centuries through the Rosicrucians and the work of poets such as Andrew Marvell and William Blake. Their message, Churton shows, points the way to a glorious synthesis of the sexual and the spiritual."

CHRISTOPHER MCINTOSH, PH.D., HONORARY UNIVERSITY FELLOW
AND WESTERN ESOTERICISM LECTURER AT THE UNIVERSITY
OF EXETER AND AUTHOR OF *THE ROSICRUCIANS*

"One of the world's greatest scholars of what Blake calls the 'excluded' tradition, Tobias Churton brings together a profound knowledge of Western esotericism with extensive new research to weave a rich and multifaceted tapestry detailing the long-hidden mysteries of sexual gnosis. Including in-depth analysis and detailed commentary on select sacred and heretical texts from Epiphanius, Hippolytus, Valentinus, Blake, Crowley, and more, *Gnostic Mysteries of Sex* is an illuminating volume filled with passion, truth, fascinating detail, and dynamic historical perspectives."

JOHN ZORN, MUSICIAN

"Churton brings to this frank and deeply insightful study a surprisingly personal and moving narrative. The late scholar of Gnosticism Ioan Couliano once said the Gnostics were the champions of free thought—asserting a freedom to explore every logical possibility of their complex demiurgic estrangement from God and nature. It's not so surprising then that sexual metaphysics and practices in all of their permutations were explored, along with the big questions they pose, and the gnosis they transmit. As Churton observes, 'The new heaven and new earth result from an improvement of sensual enjoyment. There was, and is, need of it.'"

STEPHEN J. KING (SHIVA X°),
GRAND MASTER, ORDO TEMPLI ORIENTIS

"Readable and hugely informative, Churton makes a solid case that explains the Christian teachings on sex as reactive to the non-canonical texts. As Churton writes, sex is the 'essential battleground between heresy and orthodoxy.' I suspect this may be a totally new branch of scholarship."

VANILLA BEER, ARTIST

"An erudite view of a fascinating subject. Highly recommended."

DONALD TRAXLER, TRANSLATOR OF THE WORKS
OF MARIA DE NAGLOWSKA

GNOSTIC MYSTERIES of SEX

Sophia the Wild One and Erotic Christianity

TOBIAS CHURTON

Inner Traditions
Rochester, Vermont • Toronto, Canada

Inner Traditions
One Park Street
Rochester, Vermont 05767
www.InnerTraditions.com

Text stock is SFI certified

Library of Congress Cataloging-in-Publication Data
Churton, Tobias, 1960–
  Gnostic mysteries of sex : Sophia the Wild One and erotic Christianity / Tobias
Churton.
     pages cm
  Includes bibliographical references and index.
  ISBN 978-1-62055-421-0 (pbk.) — ISBN 978-1-62055-422-7 (e-book)
  1. Erotica—Religious aspects—Christianity—History of doctrines—Early
church, ca. 30–600. 2. Gnosticism. 3. Sex—Religious aspects—Christianity—
History of doctrines—Early church, ca. 30–600. 4. Christian heresies—
History—Early church, ca. 30–600. 5. Wisdom (Gnosticism) I. Title.
  BR195.S48C47 2015
  299'.932—dc23
                                                              2015003025

Printed and bound in the United States by Lake Book Manufacturing, Inc.
The text stock is SFI certified. The Sustainable Forestry Initiative® program
promotes sustainable forest management.

10 9 8 7 6 5 4 3 2 1

Text design by Priscilla Baker and layout by Virginia Scott Bowman
This book was typeset in Garamond Premier Pro and Gill Sans with Trajan Pro,
Parisian, and Gill Sans used as display typefaces

To send correspondence to the author of this book, mail a first-class letter to the
author c/o Inner Traditions • Bear & Company, One Park Street, Rochester, VT
05767, and we will forward the communication, or contact the author directly at
www.tobiaschurton.com.

Contents

Acknowledgments

I should not have made my way down this intriguing road to the future—a possible future anyway—had it not been that Jon Graham, Acquisitions Editor of Inner Traditions, kindly suggested that I write a book about the "lascivious one," or "Prunikos" (spellings vary): the Virgin-Whore goddess of wisdom, also known among some Gnostics as "Barbelo," the real Mother, according to Sethian Gnostics, of Jesus, and all redeemed children of the "knowledge of the heart." This grew into the present attempt to cover the entire aspect of sexual practices and erosophies of the first great Gnostic movement, with a mind to some of the inheritors of those extraordinarily daring traditions that answer the question: *What is the true meaning of sex?* Without Jon, this book would not exist.

I should also like to thank, for their help and encouragement, Samantha Roddick, who reminded me of the significance today of the Gnostic concept of androgyny for sexual freedom, and Jean Luke Epstein, for his generous, thoughtful spirit.

Trying to fathom the mystery of Barbelo provided happy cause to contact again the insightful David Tibet, this time in his role as Coptologist. He very astutely passed on my initial forays into the etymology of *Barbelo* to Coptologist and scholar of esotericism Professor Dylan M. Burns at Leipzig University and to fellow Coptologist

Professor Hugo Lundhaug of Oslo University's theology faculty. Their thoughtful, critical comments I found most helpful in focusing my research. They may still not approve of my conclusions—time will tell—but these conclusions are better presented and thought through thanks to their generous responses to David's inquiry on my behalf.

I must make special mention of Paul Bembridge, my colleague at Exeter University's Department of Western Esotericism. His response to an inquiry I put to him concerning William Blake's golden riddle (as I have called it) was truly fabulous, and kick-started an even deeper probe into the startling world of seventeenth-century esoteric symbolism than I had anticipated. Thank you, Paul.

This book extends my work on the Gnostics, which now stretches back over thirty years and which has taken many forms: essays, books, TV documentaries, lectures, DVDs, music, and a number of movie scripts. In all that time, I have wonderful memories of conversing in depth with some of the greatest scholars on this subject who have ever lived. I am thinking of Hans Jonas, Gilles Quispel, Elaine Pagels, James M. Robinson, R. McLachlan Wilson, Kathleen Raine, Nicholas Goodrick-Clarke, Frank van Lamoen, and Christopher McIntosh.

In trying once more to understand the mystery that persists in understanding the Cathars and the troubadours, I think with fond affection of past conversations with Joost Ritman, Esther Ritman, Gérard Zuchetto, Anne Brenon, Michel Rocquebert, R. I. Moore, Columba Powell, and Heinz Reinhoffer. For Sasha Chaitow's ready response to inquiries concerning the wonder that was Joséphin Péladan, I am truly grateful.

This book is really about the secret meaning of love, so I dedicate it to my wife, Joanna, and daughter, Merovée Sophia, for though I have written much, I could never find the words to express what you mean to me.

The Gnostic Sex Book

Oh Gawd—Not another sex book! The oldest game in the world and yet another twist on a tired old thread: Is that what we have here? Well, I'm bound to say no! But having said so, I must confess to sharing the reservations of many who might see a title like this and think it is merely another sex guide we can all do without. You know the kind of thing: *Domestic Tantra for Nonbelievers* or *The Ultimate Secrets of Sacred Sex.* God forbid!

Let's face it, most of us have some kind of problem with sex somewhere down the line, whether it be quality, quantity, cultural inhibition, disability, or something else, but we can't honestly say that the plethora of sex guides have helped all that much. For starters, the pictures don't have quite the resonance they did back in the 1970s! Experience, on the other hand, is a great teacher, but her fees can be very high. As for the price of wisdom—unlike our contemporary tsunami of Internet porn—wisdom's price is far above rubies, coming, unlike rubies, from far above.

In short, this is not a how-to-do-it/experiment-at-home-with-your-partner manual. Rather, it is a book for those, like me, who want to understand and come to grips with the authentic sexual practices and doctrines of the Gnostic movement for spiritual revolution.

CONFESSIO CHURTONATIS

I have written more than a few books on the Gnostic tradition in the last thirty years. But I have to say, there is a specific area that, like many other scholars, I have tended to shy away from, or even—horrible expression—to deemphasize. That area has been called on occasion "radical Gnosticism." In a way, that is a shame because there is arguably quite a lot of fun as well as thought-provoking stuff in radical Gnosticism.

What "stuff" am I referring to?

Picking up for a moment the tired and seldom-helpful term *Gnosticism,* I am referring to disparate groups of Christian believers who, from the second century CE onward, held to doctrines promoted by a series of teachers who, with some core tendencies in common, saw life in the following terms: The human soul has been thrown into a dark world ruled by dark powers. This spiritually dark world is our world. Escape from this fatal world requires secret knowledge. In modern terms, humanity's very being-in-the-world constitutes an aching existential crisis—for those who can see it, or come to see it, this way.

If Jesus's kingdom is "not of this world" (John 18:36), can the same be said of humanity?

Is our essential being truly at home in a world men and women have to be taught to accommodate: a natural world that while often appearing indifferent to our presence, yet remains a world that is deeply attractive and one to which we feel bound irresistibly by a thousand and more ties—or chains—not the least of which is sexual desire and the ceaseless cycle of reproduction and death.

Radical Gnostic Christians did not believe that the Almighty God of the Old Testament or of the New Testament ruled the cosmos of which we appear to be a part. They believed the visible world was estranged from the highest God. Unlike heaven, the cosmos followed the law of a "craftsman" god, a "Demiurge," who had built the universe with deficient means, stealing—and garbling—ideas from a higher reality, a spiritual reality of which the strutting Arch-Egotist was jealous. The craftsman power was, in effect, the Ego of the Universe, its carnal mind, its Big I AM—ignorant of a spiritual grandeur beyond itself, capable only of turning binary harmony into perpetual opposition.

One name Gnostics gave to this figure was *Saklas,* which means "Fool," in the sense of a tragicomic stage impressionist, impersonating Being beyond him and his comprehension. Like the man who identifies his soul with his ego, he just *gets in the way:* not unlike perhaps the way exiled Jews might have seen the divinized Emperor Hadrian after that living god leveled the Temple Mount and forbade Jews to enter Jerusalem following the devastating Bar Kokhba rebellion (135 CE). After that, it seems the main Alexandrian and Roman Gnostic sects began to appear.

Along with innumerable variants of this fundamental and disturbing insight of estrangement from God and nature, groups described by their enemies as "Barbelo Gnostics," "Sethians," "Ophites," "Borborites," "Valentinians," "Marcosians," "Naasseni," "Simonians," "Carpocratians," among other names derived from their teachers or from derogatory nicknames, were accused of disgraceful—that is, "filthy"—practices, where sex and sexual fluids were allegedly used by adults within ostensibly religious ceremonies, along with magical rites, secret signs of recognition, and an undefined palette of pharmacological products conducive to dream states.

I don't think it was really squeamishness, skepticism, or acculturated embarrassment that relegated my interest in these dimensions of Gnostic experience to the outskirts of essential concern. There was another reason for emphasizing the philosophical and purely spiritual outlook that thrived in Gnostic traditions over the many hostile reports of extreme or curious practices apparently observed among numerous "heretical" coteries in late antiquity. In introducing the Gnostics to the general public, in liberating their story from the cloisters of academic scholarship, it was first necessary to redress a historical calumny.

Since time immemorial, both Catholic and Protestant churches have dismissed Gnostic traditions as dangerous heresies. In modern times, they have waved the issues aside as mere matters of past history, unworthy of serious consideration. In 2006, for example, when the Sethian Gnostic *Gospel of Judas* was first published in English, Rowan Williams, then archbishop of Canterbury, Primate of all England, dismissed Gnosticism as "exotic," irrelevant to the "real issues" of faith in the world. As a result of such nervous, hostile attitudes, the questions I have frequently addressed have been these: *Do these ancient traditions have anything to say to us today? And if they do, what is it?* Did these so-called Gnostics see something we have lost sight of in our thoroughly materialistic culture—a steely culture in which religion is largely divorced from natural philosophy (science), confined to agendas of democratic ethics and "subjective" idealism, leaving spirituality an unwanted stranger, rejected, and often despised, by the West's mainstream media mêlée?

In negotiating a new position for the Gnostic tradition in the modern world, it was first necessary to rebalance the terms of debate, to liberate Gnostic traditions from arguments between entrenched batteries of theologians, concerned consciously or otherwise with the welfare of their historic masters and contemporary patrons. Needless to say, I am convinced that Gnostic traditions are of global and individual, not solely ecclesiastical, significance.

Unlike the orthodox structures of the three so-called great religions of Judaism, Christianity, and Islam, Gnostic experience does not rely on faith alone. Being based on experiential knowledge, *gnosis* can stand as the bridge between science and religious belief. Understood this way, Gnostic experience can bring harmony where currently there is opposition and fear.

One area where opposition and fear have been most manifest in broadly orthodox religious circles has been the idea of a spirituality linked to sexuality; God is not to be regarded as "sexy" in any respect among proponents of the predominantly male, but apparently sexless, God. The idea of linking sex with worship is utterly anathema to mainstream religion—a veritable nightmare for those encouraged to be suspicious of female sexuality. Are not women temptresses, corrupters of male purity?

Any idea of erotic love in relation to God is basically taboo. Yet, history records that such a linkage was the stock-in-trade of circles of Gnostic believers. Given the taboo nature of this linkage, we are therefore unsurprised to discover that wherever such a link has been proven to exist, it has always been dismissed by mainstream religious leaders as fundamentally perverse, pagan, pornographic, wanton, satanic, and sinful. In an insightful, highly suggestive observation, Dutch scholar Wouter Hanegraaff has asserted that while orthodox theology has always looked with favor on a loving bond between the male and the male God, whenever such a relationship has been posited between a male and a female divine figure, the accusation of heresy has always followed. This provocative picture becomes more interesting still when we consider Catholic attitudes to the (pure and sexless) Virgin Mary. Just whose sperm swam in the Virgin's womb?

Modern scholars have not been ready to acquiesce in the automatic denigration of erotic religion, sexualized spirituality, or spiritualized sexuality. Long experience of the sources of Gnostic belief has led this author to share contemporary scholarly circumspection regarding church authorities' stories of immoral sexual practices—stories aimed at discrediting what early church father Irenaeus, in circa 180 CE, called "gnosis [knowledge] falsely so-called."

We need to investigate whether the evidence arrayed against *gnosis* is trustworthy, especially in a field where symbolism is vulnerable to misinterpretation, where signifiers mean different things to people of different levels of awareness and experience. While rarely dismissing unfavorable accounts of Gnostic practices wholesale, most modern scholars who have examined the original accusations against proponents of the gnosis have concluded that we cannot take one-sided, invective-drenched accounts at face value. If there is truth behind the stories, we are going to have to try to dig it out.

It is my sincere hope that this adventure will not leave readers languishing in a dive of "filthy Gnostickes," but rather upon an upright trajectory that may yet enable us to raise sexuality from the gutter of modern life to its portal into the New Jerusalem.

PART I

THE SEX GNOSTICS

ONE

THE
"FILTHY GNOSTICKES"

For centuries, our only information regarding the Gnostics of late antiquity came from their enemies, the church fathers. Having done everything they could to discredit the Gnostic movement, it took until the publication of Gottfried Arnold's *Impartial History of the Church and of Heresy (Unparteyische Kirche-und Ketzer-historie)* in Frankfurt in 1700 before any theologian had anything good to say about the so-called heretics. Gottfried Arnold (1666–1714), himself dedicated to the feminine figure of the divine Sophia ("Wisdom"), connected the Valentinian Gnostics of the second century and the followers of spiritual genius Jacob Böhme (1575–1624), as well as the Rosicrucians in his own time, and believed the heretics belonged in Christ's church. What they all had in common was a personal spiritual devotion to Sophia, the mirror of God. It took two more centuries, however, before biblical historians became more aware of their duty as scholars to take into account the Gnostics' own point of view, a task precipitated by the appearance of authentic Gnostic works.

Carried from Egypt to London in 1774 by explorer James Bruce (1730–1794), the Gnostic *Books of Jeu* ("Bruce Codex") were joined at the British Museum in 1794 by the Coptic *Askew Codex*. The *Askew Codex* contained the Gnostic work *Pistis Sophia* (*The Faith of Sophia* or

Faith-Wisdom). While interest in these particular works was confined to specialist scholars and to theosophical circles, the discovery in 1945 of the Nag Hammadi Library eventually brought the Gnostic phenomenon to the wider public. Published in English in 1977 under the aegis of Professor James M. Robinson, and popularized in works by Elaine Pagels, myself, and others, the appearance of the Gnostic Gospels initiated a process of enthusiastic assimilation that continues to proceed apace. There's something about these Gnostics that many people like.

This has all greatly affected our understanding not only of the origins of Christianity, but also our sense of what religion is and ought to be. Certainly, the one-sided accounts of Gnostics by patristic writers (church fathers) now have to be placed beside new bodies of knowledge in a spirit of objective inquiry, free from the old paymasters of theological studies. This author happens to be one of the first *professional* theologians engaged with the subject not to be on the payroll of any religious institution whatsoever, directly or indirectly (including church funding of academic institutions or posts). Gnostic studies require both independence of thought and a sense of humor.

Not surprisingly, most scholars nowadays tend to doubt many of the conclusions of the heresiologists—those who wrote against heretics. This doubt stems partly from the fact that we now have at our disposal copious remnants of the Gnostics' authentic voices. From such discoveries, we have learned that the authentic testimonies themselves do not generally support many anti-Gnostic accusations, particularly as far as condemnations of sexual libertinism are concerned. We just don't seem to find libidinous Gnostics in the Nag Hammadi codices. Indeed, many authentic documents veer toward antisexual "Encratism" in orientation or influence, holding theological positions favorable to celibate monks attempting to live in closed communities. That is to say, far from giving in to lusts, numerous Gnostic writers expressed, in no uncertain terms, horror and disgust at the body's tendency to overwhelm the call of the Holy Spirit to a life beyond this world. *The Book of Thomas the Contender* is particularly marked in this respect. The "one who is awake," the "one who knows himself," is the one who has come forth from the flesh and left the world of pollution behind. Sex for this Thomas is filth.

Rather than being honored as a vehicle for spiritual ecstasy, the fleshly body, for numerous advocates of gnosis, is denigrated emphatically as a tomb of the soul. For these Gnostics, flesh was to be regarded contemptuously. Flesh was the means by which the "god of this world" imposed his dominion over the will of spirit.

Of course, it could be counterasserted that this view of the flesh could easily promote indifference as to what one did with the body. The word *ecstasy*, after all, means being "beside oneself," an experience that might be considered to intimate an out-of-body experience—the breaking of the bonds of the flesh—if only momentarily, in a spirit of joyful exaltation or extreme pleasure, or a state "beyond" pleasure and physical sensation. Immoral indifference to the body was certainly an accusation leveled at the heretics: they didn't care what they did with their bodies, their enemies insisted, since the bodily life was held to be fundamentally unreal of itself ("dust to dust") from the spiritual perspective. This sharp distinction between flesh and spirit explains why Gnostics are often, confusingly, described as "dualists"; it is not a confusion I wish to promote further. The insight behind the distinction is simple enough: the highest God creates eternities, while the flesh, like wood without sap, rots. As rot-in-the-making, flesh *of itself* can be of no special interest to eternity: flesh is a temporary "billet" of the soul, not its proper home. Flesh is chaff, to be cast out and destroyed: mortally dangerous then for the soul to be attached, or too attached, to it. When the "word becomes flesh" to "dwell amongst us" in the prologue to St. John's gospel, the act is plainly a condescension, and the "word" (logos) overcomes the corruption of the flesh being absolutely superior to it, doing the "will of the Father" absolutely. Christians are to cleave to the spiritual "word" not the flesh, for the flesh inherits the lot of things in this world: Jesus's kingdom is not of this world.

The radical teacher Carpocrates (early to mid-second century CE), based in Alexandria and a follower, apparently, of the Simonian gnosis first attributed to Samaritan Simon Magus and his alleged followers— Menander, Dositheus, Cerinthus, and Saturnilus—was particularly condemned for his indifference to the flesh, since Carpocrates believed the Gnostic Christian was one "above the law" in spirit, so that, first, what the body (below) did was of no spiritual concern, and, second, apparent licentiousness could be practiced as a means of asserting contempt for the god of the law and his fleshly dominion: a kind of progressive "redemption by sin." This general approach to conduct is sometimes called "antinomian"; that is, "in opposition to law." It is also quintessentially "Tantric," reminiscent of the hero of Tantra, who, at specific points and for specific purposes, flauts convention in order to expand his consciousness and his command of existence.

According to Irenaeus and the considerably later anti-Gnostic bishop Epiphanius of Salamis (fourth century CE), Carpocrates believed that unless the soul experienced, while being above, the temptations that beset it below, it could not demonstrate its mastery of the flesh, a failure that would compel it to reincarnate, falling back into the munching jaws of the Demiurge and his fatal universe. This systemic return cycle, akin in its essence to aspects of Buddhism and its close cousins, occurred because the soul had not been sufficiently spiritualized to overcome the attractions of this world.

Something of a psychologist, Carpocrates did not share the view of the prohibitionist that you overcome risky things simply by avoiding them or by being denied them; such, he appears to have believed, only adds to their fascination, empowering lusts and attractions to work a subconscious, corrupting influence, easily hidden from the eyes of the world, but spiritually demeaning and obstructive all the same. Suppressed lusts could generate obsessional consequences. Release from obsession might involve enacting, in a somewhat ironic spirit, scenarios that ordinarily might disgust. Returning to one's right mind afterward, with the attraction having been literally drained away, one might see the former obsession's hollowness or irrelevance, and one could mock the insidious attraction, and consciously dispense with the obsession. The theory is still current. It was widely employed during the great pornography debates of the 1970s and 1980s: fascination for the forbidden, it was asserted, lasts only so long as the activity is forbidden; remove the prohibition, and free choice becomes possible in a spirit of "adult" objectivity and self-knowledge. A pitfall of the theory is of course that the fascination may continue, albeit in a more ironically detached form, promoting an interior double-mindedness that may become unsustainable. Carpocrates might blame the "world creator" as we today might attribute questionable behavior to "nature." Taking half a tip from the gospels, Carpocratians decided that hypocrisy was "dirtier" than wantonness. "Veil not your vices in virtuous words," as the antinomian advocate Aleister Crowley expressed his ironic, decadent scheme of "redemption by sin."

According to this countercultural theory, legal or moral inhibitions are basically external and arbitrary, applied without respect to one's ultimate spiritual welfare. That is why Carpocrates held that what was believed to be right or wrong merely reflected either uninformed or unexamined opinion or else the state of consciousness of the perceiver: the ultimate goal was what mattered. The value of a thing was to be judged by whether it helped or hindered divinization. In William Blake's words: "If a fool would persist in his folly, he would become wise." So it was not only a question of spiritual indifference to the flesh. Such indifference had to be proved; rather like taking up smoking to exhibit mastery by kicking the habit at will: a perilous but not impossible feat. Carpocrates proclaimed the spiritual charter for the libertine.

Teaching that mere fear of the flesh was no basis for moral and spiritual triumph, Carpocrates advocated the showing of superior contempt for ordinary morality (the law) by overcoming the fear of sin, the fear of attraction. The hypothetically freed spirit could then demonstrate a true liberation from the world, commanding angels and demons (i.e., mastering his life and mind), rather than exhibiting a cowering fear of them disguised as prim righteousness, or self-righteousness. Jesus forgave the sinner, not the self-righteous. He looked at the despised prostitute and tax collector and loved them for what they had in them that they knew not.

For all its interest, however, this antinomian point of view, which may have been the specialty of the Carpocratian Gnostics, is in fact practically absent from the Nag Hammadi Library, whose texts nowadays tend to be looked upon as a kind of collective Gnostic orthodoxy—a misleading situation, to be sure, for Gnostics have their secrets, only open to those able to perceive them.

Besides, the libertine conduct ascribed to Carpocratians also appears to have been a feature of Christian groups subject to St. Paul's censure in the mid-first century CE. Antinomianism may not necessarily be regarded as specifically Gnostic behavior. Paul suffered theological headaches trying to explain to his converts that simply because Gentiles were not under the "curse of the [Jewish] law," that did not mean they could "sin" in order to experience "grace" (Epistle to the Romans 6). Paul said that, freed from the bonds of the law by Christ, selfless love should guide conduct, and many Gnostics took their cue from that belief. One wonders how many Jews took up Paul's prescription for Gentiles of a new covenant with God without law.

It is not only a question of the incompatibility of authentic Gnostic literature with the hostile picture painted by orthodox critics. Aggressive reports of allegedly heretical practices often lack intrinsic consistency and accuracy, frequently—though not always—demonstrating scant interest in locating the truth behind hearsay reports of deviant behavior allegedly proceeding independently of episcopal control. The aim of the heresiologists' writings was to turn the curious right off the heretics, to give those at risk a nasty jolt, and make them feel grateful that there was a good, safe, tried and trusted, socially respectable and morally decent, apostolically approved alternative. Even where some effort was made to interpret Gnostic symbolism (Irenaeus was fairly diligent in this respect), such symbolism was almost always judged from a cynical, even on occasion *comedic* perspective. Heresiologist Irenaeus, bishop of Lyon, made every effort, writing in circa 180 CE, to portray adherents of the gnosis as simply bonkers, knowing that no one likes to be taken for a fool. Ridicule was a more effective repressive tool than theology alone, though, to be fair, Irenaeus did bring out in great detail his theological objections to Gnostic thought and practice as well.

Since it was taken as an a priori fact that Gnostics were perverting the orthodox (straight-teaching) gospel with an archcynical view of the world and its Creator, then their sexual practices could only be judged from the perspective of focusing on salacious details that outraged moral norms familiar to orthodox churches. According to their enemies, these cocky, perverse, and perverting people were simply scurrilous abusers of respectable religion, using Christian terminology as paper-thin, sophistical excuses to sate their lusts, laziness, and fantasies, aiming to exploit the vanity of women (in particular) and to lead innocent Christians into what Irenaeus described as "an abyss of madness and blasphemy." The price was not only sanity; the price was salvation itself.

Fortunately, we do not ourselves have to take sides, especially where the evidence is, by modern standards, inadequate to form a definitive judgment of what is surely a remarkably complex, if colorful, case. Our ability to judge this case is anyway hampered by the fact that we still live in the shadow of nearly two millennia of hostility toward and persecution of Gnostic traditions. Just how influential that policy of outright condemnation has been, and how persistently the image of sexual excess has served as its primary propaganda weapon, may be glimpsed in the writings of two very brilliant men, neither of whom, interestingly, were clergymen, and who both wrote over a thousand years after the Christian Gnostic heyday.

GREAT MONSTERS OF HERESY

The first example comes from a rare book by the brilliant German magus, theologian, lawyer, and philosopher, Henry Cornelius Agrippa (1486–1535): *Of the Vanity and Uncertainty of Arts and Sciences,* published in English in 1569. It is thought that Agrippa's thoroughly skeptical survey of existing knowledge may have been composed not only to assert his purified Christian evangelical credentials having embraced Lutheranism, but also to preserve him from censure as a dangerous black magician (he was the author of *Three Books of Occult Philosophy*). Chapter 47 dismisses as "vanity" the mystical tradition of the Jews known as Kabbalah or, as he refers to it, "Cabala":

> From this Jewish heap of Cabalisticke superstition proceed [I suppose] the Ophites, the Gnostickes, and Valentinian heretickes, the which also with their disciples have invented a certain Greekish Cabala, turning toplet [*sic*] down all the mysteries of the Christian faith, and with heretickal wickedness drawing them to Greeke letters and numbers, do make of them a body, which they call of truth, showing that without these mysteries of letters and numbers, the truth in the Gospel cannot be found out, because it is so diverse, and in some places contrary to itself, and written full of parables, that they which see it do not see, and they which hear it do not hear, and they which understand it do not understand, but to be set before the blind and ignorant, according to the capacity of their blindness, and error: and that the pure verité hidden under it is believed of the perfect sort alone, not by writing, but by a successive pronunciation of a lively voice, and that this is that Alphabetarie, and Arithmantical divinity, which Christ secretly shewed to his Apostles: and which Paule saith that he speaketh but amongst perfect men.
>
> For whereas these be very high mysteries, they have not therefore been written, nor are written but are privily searched out by wise men, which secretly keep them in their minds. And among them none is accompted wise, but he which can forge very great monsters of heresy.

It should be observed that while Agrippa seems to attack Jewish Cabala as a source of heresy (does one hear the crackling flames about

the inquisitor's stake?), he is also preserving a point about an understanding only available to the spiritually enlightened, while secreting
that point, in true cabalist fashion, beneath its apparent opposite point
of view! It all depends how you read it. Agrippa's smart and politically
adroit textual duplicity is further evident in chapter 48, "Of Iuglinge"
("Juggling"), a general section on magic that appears, note, before a
disturbing chapter on the vanity, cruelty, untruthfulness, and perverse
excesses of the Catholic Inquisition.

> Of the Magitiens also is sprung in the Church a great route of
> heretickes, which as Iamnes and Mambres* have rebelled against
> Moses, so they have resisted the Apostolick truth: the chief of these
> was Simon the Samaritaine [Simon Magus], who for this Arte had
> an image erected at Rome in the time of Claudius Ceasar with this
> inscription, to Simon, the holy GOD. His blasphemies be written
> at large by Clement [of Alexandria], Eusebius, and Irenaeus. Out
> of this Simon as out of a seed plot of all heresies have proceeded
> by many successions the monstrous Ophites, the filthy Gnostickes,
> the wicked Valentinians, the Cerdonians, the Marcionites, the
> Montanians, and many other hereticks, for gain and vaine glory
> speaking lies against God, availing not profiting men, but deceiving
> and bringing them to ruin and destruction, and they which believe
> in them shall be confounded in God's judgment.

The paramount image of the heretics here is built around their
alleged monstrousness, wickedness, and filthiness, that is to say, their
supposed sexual, orgiastic abandonments. Agrippa concludes the chapter with a confession that his original *Three Books of Hidden Philosophy*
(he reworked them later) were the product of a wayward and curious
youth, having taken a path to knowledge he now recants utterly, lest

---

*Egyptian magicians who, according to "Paul" in the apocryphal *Passio,* or *Passion of the
Holy Apostles Peter and Paul,* led Pharaoh to destruction: mentioned in II Timothy 3:8
as "Jannes" and "Jambres."

others follow Simon Magus, Iamnes, and Mambres "to the paynes of everlasting fire," such hellish punishments being the inspiration for the inquisitors' auto-da-fé, imposed on heretics before judicial burning by civil authorities.

We now leap from a leading sixteenth-century Protestant magus to the greatest seventeenth-century Protestant scientist. Living in England under a reformed Church of England, and not therefore subject to the Catholic Inquisition, Isaac Newton (1643–1727) was more or less free to publish his theological studies.

It may come as a surprise nevertheless that this father of modern science devoted more time to the study of biblical prophecy and alchemy than he did to the mathematics of gravity, but it is so. The reason was basically because Newton believed that the original religion was the original science, and vice versa, and he was concerned with restoring both as one. For Newton, science would reveal the divine majesty in its austere purity, demonstrating God's divine alchemy of nature, according to the most reasonable laws and harmonies of mathematics. Newton believed that the original truth had been corrupted over history and that the Bible gave ample evidence of the process by which this had happened. While Newton believed Jesus had come to restore knowledge of the "true Temple of God," even his work had been corrupted by the deviancy of the Catholic and Orthodox churches in *having absorbed heresies.*

Chapter 13 of Newton's *Observations upon the Prophecies of Daniel and the Apocalypse of St. John. In two parts* (1733) describes how Daniel's prophecy of a king who would magnify himself above every God, honor "Mahuzzims" (taken by Newton to refer to the souls of dead men, that is, saints), and who "regarded not the desire of women" had been fulfilled with the spread of Encratism in the church, backed by the emperors (the prophesied king), especially after the third century CE, which corruptions manifested in virginal clergy, saint worship, and a profound suspicion of the natural order. An Encratite held to a sectarian position constituted of the self-controlled, practicing temperance in all sexual matters.

It is fascinating to read Isaac Newton attacking the Gnostics, not, in this case, for alleged sexual libertinism, but rather for the opposite: body-denying Encratism that made them promoters of "monkish superstition":

> Thus the Sect of the Encratites, set on foot by the Gnosticks, and propagated by Tatian and Montanus near the end of the second century; which was condemned by the Churches of that and the third century, and refined upon by their followers; overspread the Eastern Churches having a form of godliness but denying the power thereof, came into the hands of the Encratites: and the Heathens, who in the fourth century came over in great numbers to the Christians, embraced more readily this form of Christianity, as having a greater affinity with their old superstitions, than that of the sincere Christians; who by the lamps of the Seven Churches of Asia, and not by the lamps of the monasteries, had illuminated the Church Catholic during the three first centuries.

Newton examined prophecies regarding the Antichrist from the Revelation of St. John the Divine and found his "Antichrists" among the heretics:

> It [Apostasy] began to work in the disciples of Simon [Magus], Menander, Carpocrates, Cerinthus, and such sorts of men as had imbibed the metaphysical philosophy of the Gentiles and Cabalistical Jews, and were thence called Gnosticks. John calls them Antichrists, saying that in his days there were many Antichrists.

So, in Newton's ocular perspective, the same movement that led to the dominance in the Eastern and Western churches of monks, monasteries, virginity, saint worship, and sex loathing, was the same movement of apostates from the "sincere Christians" who engaged in the spiritually inspired sexual freedom of Carpocrates on the basis of a metaphysical philosophy exemplified by Jewish Kabbalists. It sounds contradictory, of course, but Newton may have a point, once we recognize that Carpocratian sexual liberties were likely a function of the belief that the body, being matter, did not really matter, that flesh was inherently corrupt, transitory, and not subject to resurrection; and that when the spirit had been through all possible traumas of physical life and thus proved its monarchy, it would be happily free of nature altogether. For Newton, on the other hand, God created the natural world and saw that it was good. Newton intended his scientific works to demonstrate this article of faith to reason: for Newton, faith had become knowledge. Atheist believers in modern science might take note of this.

It was statements akin to those made by Agrippa and Newton that kept all but the boldest minds off the "filthy Gnostickes" until the early eighteenth century. However, we should note that just as Agrippa and Newton used the vast inherited body of condemnation of Gnostics to support their own philosophical positions, regardless of how diverse or contradictory those positions might be, so also did those who took up the Gnostic cause after 1700 tend to paint Gnostics in their own ideological colors. The view of Gottfried Arnold's *Impartial History of the Church and of Heresy,* for example, was influenced by Arnold's seeing the Valentinian Gnostics' kinship to the "philo-theosophy" of Giordano Bruno, Meister Eckhart, the Rosicrucians, and, above all, the Teutonic theosopher Jacob Böhme, whom Arnold greatly admired. Arnold's contemporary, Johann Georg Gichtel (1638–1710), who led a band of mystical Christians from his base in Amsterdam, joined Arnold in his concern for opening up spiritual and undoubtedly spiritual-erotic relations with the heroine of the Valentinian gnosis: Sophia, or Lady Wisdom.

Such studies of the Gnostics as appeared in the eighteenth century were almost always used for self-legitimization. William Blake, artist, poet, and autodidact (1757–1827), probably got some of his ideas on Gnostic emanations or aeons (which color and shape his own myths of the human psyche) from works by the radical Joseph Priestley (1733–1804).

Priestley used his limited knowledge of the heretics to justify his own heretical religious position: that of the Unitarians, the church to which he belonged and which he served. The use and abuse of Gnostic traditions continued throughout the nineteenth century among continental, mystical Freemasons and among Catholic anti-Freemasons among whom there developed the myth of a long-running conspiracy of Gnostic perversion of truth, running from the early heretics to the Manichaeans and on through the Middle Ages (the Knights Templar!) and into the Age of Reason (Freemason revolutionaries!), to the detriment of the "true faith."

A highly creative exception to the self-legitimizing tendency was the work of a brilliant Catholic scientist and philosopher, Munich-born Franz von Baader (1765–1841), who, while personally devoted to the whole immensely rich concept of the Sophia, put that interest out of pure Pietistic inwardness and into action in direct service of humanity. Von Baader's writings on the importance of erotic love, to unite men and women through mutual self-giving, discovering in each other and through each other the androgynous unity of spirit that helps humanity grow, deserve wide attention and dissemination. As Professor Arthur Versluis has maintained, von Baader's works on society, the Catholic Church, nature philosophy, and the overall meaning of human life and the philosophy of time are important not only to a Germany that has neglected him, but to the dilemmas of the modern world in general.[1]

After 1875, the launch of Madame Blavatsky's influential Theosophical Society, with its numerous offshoots, used the limited available knowledge of the Gnostics as part of a vast occult historical scheme: the passage of an antediluvian tradition of scientific spirituality through time. Theosophy's mythic superstructure and speculative embellishments, however, alienated not only adherents of mainstream religion from sane consideration of Gnostic traditions, but also more objective historians of religion. On the other hand, without theosophical studies (especially those of G. R. S. Mead [1863–1933]), many in the period would probably have never heard of the Gnostics.

The twentieth century saw the beginnings of a more rigorous, scientific approach to Gnostic thought, with the emphasis on *thought*. Hans Jonas's *Gnosis und Spätantiker Geist (Gnosis and the Spirit of Late Antiquity,* 1934–1954) marked a seminal moment in the development of serious philosophical studies regarding Gnosticism. However, it was evident from my own numerous interviews with Professor Jonas in the mid-1980s that his approach was more than a little influenced by the existentialist philosophy of his teacher Martin Heidegger at Marburg University in the last years of the Weimar Republic.

For Jonas, the phenomenon of gnosis signaled a world-historical event, when humanity for the first time experienced "otherness" or existential alienation. For some, this alienation involved a disturbing rupture in our traditional relationship with the natural world; for others, it marked the end of the grip of pagan naturalism and of what the intellectual part of humankind had long considered "natural" assumptions about the cosmos. The "Gnostic religion" (as Jonas described the phenomenon) marked a kind of evolutionary epoch wherein humankind suffered an acute awareness of the distress of the human condition, a sense of estrangement from the cosmos: a terrifying rift had opened up between humanity and the world. The ensuing alienation was dramatized, Jonas believed, in the myths of the most radical Gnostics, those who, in his words, "made the flesh creep," and which represented for him the most compelling aspects of the Gnostic "movement" by virtue of their radical, almost modern, cosmoclastic consciousness. For Jonas, the radical Gnostics are the ones who really matter; the softer and more Hermetic ones, he told me, added little to Plato. From Jonas's point of view, if you wanted a real Gnostic text, then read the *Apocryphon of John* with its jaw-dropping account of the Demiurge's treating Adam in the mythical manner of a hostile alien who has kidnapped a human being from Earth only to throw him on his mother ship's operating table for a bit of casual dissection, without anesthetic or pity!

Professor Jonas had little to say about alleged sexual excesses; they did not really concern him. He had his philosophical priorities, and he continued to feel until his death in 1993 that while the discovery of the Nag Hammadi Library in 1945 (after his first Gnostic studies were published) had revealed the authentic voice of the Gnostics themselves, his essential philosophical treatment of gnosis had stood and would continue to stand the test of time. Reading *The Gnostic Religion,* his condensed version of his Gnostic studies today, is a thrilling experience for the intellect and should not be avoided by newcomers to the subject.

Jonas was not the only person who saw the extraordinary modernity of the Gnostic challenge to the consciousness of their times, which, though long distant, suddenly came into focus with fresh relevance and cultural urgency. Carl Jung, former colleague of Sigmund Freud, also seized on the startlingly modern aspects of the Gnostic vision. Jung's ideas, however, were far less linked to the development of philosophy and the existential heart of religious thought, than to the modern science or would-be science of psychology, informed by immersion into Eduard von Hartmann's *Philosophy of the Unconscious* (1869). When Jung received a copy of the Nag Hammadi *Gospel of Truth,* a long-thought-vanished Valentinian work, he famously declared to church historian and theologian Gilles Quispel: "All my life I have been looking for the secrets of the psyche, and these people knew already." (Quispel told me this story himself at Bilthoven near Utrecht in 1986.)

When we hear the word *archetypes* in psychological jargon, we are hearing a word Jung picked from the flora of Gnostic traditions. Archetypes live in the unconscious. They make us: we do not make them. Jung compared the Gnostic *Pleroma* (or "Fullness" of the Godhead) to his conception of the Unconscious, liberating that idea from the Freudian model of an unconscious functioning primarily as an attic or even dungeon of repressed, taboo, or forbidden and denied thoughts and images. Shortly before his death, Jung shocked John Freeman's audience on the BBC's *Face to Face* TV show when, in answer to Freeman's question: "Do you believe in God?" Jung replied: "I don't need to *believe.* I *know.*"

Apart from the worlds of respectable academe and new sciences, interest in Gnostic practices continued apace through the esoteric schools that have flourished quietly and occasionally under persecution in the Western world. Among the jungle of little bodies that have sprung from the world of the French Occult and Gnostic Revival, from Freemasonry, and from theosophical variegations in America, British and European colonies, and on the Continent itself, many have taken aspects of the Gnostic tradition as have suited their philosophical outlook. Few, however, have been quite so bold as Theodor Reuss, Aleister Crowley, and E. C. H. Peithmann (1865–1943) in concentrating on the sexual lore and supposed practices of Gnostic radicals. Theodor Reuss (1855–1923) took his and Carl Kellner's (1851–1905) idea of an *Ordo Templi Orientis* (Order of Oriental Templars, or Order of the Eastern Temple) to Crowley, along with Reuss's conviction that, as with Carpocrates, the secret Jesus imparted to his disciples at the Last Supper was the occult mystery of sexual fluids. According to Reuss (and Carpocrates, according to Clement of Alexandria), Jesus practiced a kind of magical and spiritual holy sex with at least one beloved disciple and Jesus's semen (*logos spermatikos*) in this context could be considered a potent sacrament: "This is my body which I give to you."

Aleister Crowley (1875–1947) famously experimented with what was prosaically termed "sex magick" for many years between 1912 and the end of World War II. German theosophist Peithmann, author of *The Gnostic Catechism* (1904), was party to a tiny parallel body of sacred sex enthusiasts (the Old Gnostic Church of Eleusis), whose purpose was, Peithmann declared, "to liberate the seed from servitude": an idea we shall explore fully in the context of authentic Sethian and Valentinian sex gnosis.

Taking from Gnostic traditions what suits the commentator seems endemic to the case. Perhaps this has something to do with the curiously emotional appeal of the subject. Even John Lennon voiced his partiality to the Gnostics in 1980 as being the authentic holders of the true Christian flame.[2] This is not something to be found delineated in many a fan site devoted to the late Beatle, but those in the mainstream media never like to sully their hands with spiritual matters, unless they're issuing warnings against cults, celebrity excess, or the like. Journalism can easily function as a form of cultural censor.

From the perspective of objective study of Gnostic traditions, it is perhaps unfortunate that the Nag Hammadi Library appeared in English during the long post-1960s twilight, in the wake of hippydom, antiestablishment activism, sexual revolutionary fervor, psychedelicism, neotroubadours (rockers and singer-songwriters), science-fiction TV, and revived interest in occultism, mysticism, paganism, and various skeins of Sufism, Hinduism, and Buddhism. (*My!* What exciting times we have lived through!) Gnostics are again painted in colors to suit the case. This time, however, Gnostics may be presented as remarkably cool. The new vision of them is a fairly innocent, even sanitized, vision of Gnostics as advanced modernists, with strong feminist (the "divine feminine"), sex-positive, freethinking leanings. From Lynn Picknett and Clive Prince's *Templar Revelation* to Dan Brown's *The Da Vinci Code* and the recrudescence of Mary Magdalene–oriented feminine spirituality literature, we find a gnosis thoroughly purged of elements discordant to the New Age narrative with its strong neopagan, goddess-worshipping, user-friendly features, set against an authoritarian, corrupt, patriarchal evangelism or scientism of one kind or another.

It is fascinating to observe how even once-taboo elements of Gnostic sexual mysticism can be co-opted into new or revived spiritualities. For example, Marnia Robinson's harmonious relationship sex guide *Cupid's Poisoned Arrow* quotes selectively from the Nag Hammadi *Gospel of Philip* and *Exegesis on the Soul* to suggest that the famous Gnostic bridal chamber refers to some nice safe-sex practice to bring harmony into an oversexed, modern marriage–threatening scenario. That is to say, the Gnostics performed "carezza" or "caressing": orgasm-free or penetration-free sex, where the loving Christian couple celebrates a union reflecting Christ's love for his church, or the love of the Gnostic, or Jesus for Sophia, or some undefined union with God or Spirit, generated by controlled sexual excitation and immediate sublimation. One may applaud the notion that, rather than living a life of emotionally pain-ridden serial sexual encounters, stable couples might opt instead for sacred sex and long-term relationship stability.

The author offers a good dose of required neuroscience theory and experiment to suggest that repeated orgasm can increase frustration and dissatisfaction with a partner on the biological basis that nature and its supposed evolutionary imperative wants us to mate with new partners and increase the genetic stock of variant possibilities, regardless of damage to our sense of security or romantic yearnings for long-term unions. The implication from this questionable premise is that a secret of spiritual romanticism between couples was known to Gnostics (and Taoists) and that this restraint constituted a divine secret of happiness and personal fulfillment. It is, as they say, a nice, even neat, idea, but while it has its place in the canon of modern sex and relationship guides, I am not sure it is a valid interpretation of actual Gnostic practices and attitudes, where the emphasis, as we shall see, with regard to the bridal chamber is very much on quality of seed, that is, sperm, and you don't obtain that precious substance by holding back as a matter of persistent practice. Indeed, the nearest thing to restraint in the third century (when the *Gospel of Philip* was composed) would be the Encratites, whose name, as we have seen, means "self-controlled." However, Encratite self-control meant, among other things, the permanent eschewing of sex and marriage altogether. Encratites discouraged contact with the opposite sex as a matter of principle. Absolute virginity was deemed vital to salvation; there was no such thing as "safe sex." To Valentinian Gnostics, on the other hand, quality of orgasm was essential among those wedded by Christian commitment to the tree of wisdom and thus to one another.

Put more simply, as spiritual counselor Rita Louise exclaimed to me recently: "Sex without orgasm isn't sex!" To which I should only add: yoga means "union." Let's not beat around the bush!

IS AN EROTIC CHRISTIAN RELIGION
REALLY POSSIBLE?

I discussed in the introduction why I have not focused on the alleged sexual excesses of the numerous Gnostic schools before. There is probably an additional reason, less easy to express. To be honest, I don't know about you, but I find the idea of communion with God through sexual communion very difficult to conceive of clearly, either as an idea or in a practical sense, unless, that is, one takes it that there is something profoundly godly about sexual intercourse in the first place. While familiar with the crossover between romantic yearning, deep love, passion, desire, and spiritual feelings—feelings where physical acts are experienced as far more than mere sense experiences and where more appears to be involved than a physical exchange of energy or emotion, however intense—something in my thinking is still inclined to balk at the prospect of applying a sense of reality to expressions such as *sacred sex,* which fall too easily, it seems to me, from the lips of moderns.

We know what was understood by this expression in the ancient, pagan world. Religion, then, being based on nature (cycles of birth, death, and rebirth), could be very sexy indeed, even when rhetorically elevated. Their idea of the sacred might appear to us as strangely tainted with literalist vulgarity. We might find their sacred sex neither sacred nor sexy. Priests and priestesses performed sexual rites as ways of magically imitating the *hieros gamos,* or sacred marriages, between deities, as ways of magically invoking divine powers. Sex, being so closely linked to the mysterious powers of actual creation, of life itself, as well as inspiring music, poetry, plastic arts, and dance, was felt to be intrinsically magical and mysterious, with connotations of mysticism, initiation, and esotericism. To yearn to know a god or goddess was inherently erotic, where to *know* was to have erotic relations with. Intimate knowledge was intimate eroticism. Pagans found nothing surprising in this; it was natural to them. Erotic love made the world go round. A pretty face could launch a thousand ships. Gods could be attracted to human beings and even disguise themselves as humans to experience human love.

Children might be a by-product of fertility and mystery rites, but that would not have been intended necessarily, unless, say, one wanted the god, or the virtue of the god, to dwell in the child.

However, the Christian religion shot straight out of a Hebraic womb, at least to begin with, and much of the prophetic wisdom of the Jews was aimed precisely at denying the delights and conceits of the pagan world of polytheism and anthropomorphic deities (because they were so popular). Today, we are inclined to see ancient Judaism as uniquely patriarchal, gravel-voiced, overbearing, and bass-booming; sex in the Jewish Bible, where not tied to the blessing of marriage and children in the strictly natural order, is almost always the cause of disaster: David and Bathsheba, the priestly lust for Susanna in the Book of Daniel, Samson and Delilah, Jezebel; the list goes on. When Adam and Eve discover their nakedness, it betokens the absolute loss of innocence. Guilt holds mighty sway over those covenanted to Jahveh ever afterward: *Thou shalt not!* There is sacred love dotted about the scriptures, but out-and-out erotic demonstrations such as the Song of Solomon are rare, and where they do occur, the love is always sublimated by commentators into realms of symbolism that extend all the way to today's Christian marriage ceremony where marriage symbolizes the love of Christ for his church.

In first-century synagogue life, menstrual blood is considered dirty; women need to be covered lest they shame the congregation with filth and lust. The first thing a baby boy can expect on entering this world is for religion to take hold of his penis and cut it with a knife.

It was the perception of primitive Christianity being thoroughly Jewish with regard to sex that led German theologian Adolf von Harnack (1851–1930) to characterize Gnosticism famously as "the acute Hellenization of Christianity." All that tolerance of menstrual blood, sperm, and worship of a female deity (Barbelo) could not have been original; something had contaminated Jewish Christianity: Greek-speaking pagans had gotten their greasy hands under the skirts of the virgin faith and started messing around with what they found. Von Harnack's precise view is not one popular with scholars today, but it challenges us nonetheless to account for the phenomenon of Christian groups practicing some kind of sacred sex.

From the generally understood Christian perspective, is there not something contradictory in the expression?

Sacred . . .

Sex . . .

Are not those who talk blithely of such a thing today simply kidding themselves? Are they not trying to have their cake and eat it too? Is there not a confusion of worlds in this expression? This world and the next, purity and the corrupt body? Of course, in a pagan worldview, everything may partake of God. We find echoes of this idea in Christian liturgy, where our sacrifices are regarded as forms of return to source: "All things come from you, O Lord, and of your own do we give you" (I Chronicles 29:14). (Some Gnostics, as we shall see, would apply this idea to sacramentalized semen.) Catholic believers in transubstantiation "eat the flesh of the dear Son" through the form of a wafer.

In pagan philosophy, and in common practice, God (*theos*) or gods constitute the invisible aspects of the visible world. Everything has a god or an angel behind it: bodily organs, too, even pleasure itself. Church father Clement of Alexandria (ca. 150–215 CE) referred to sexual intercourse simply as "Aphrodite," she being the tutelary deity of the act; such was normal in educated Alexandrian circles in the second century. We make nothing ourselves. God has created everything, sex included.

Arguably, and from a pantheistic point of view particularly, sex is always *potentially* sacred; is it our ignorance that prevents us from realizing this? Gnostics substituted gnosis for ignorance, and this fundamental adjustment seems to have involved a revaluation or even a transvaluation of sex, away from the primitive church's Judeo-Christian point of view. As a redeemed spirit, you had to understand what sex really meant, so as not to be dragged about by it like one caught in the jaws of a hunting hound.

However, we should, I think, be making an error if we thought distinctly sex-positive Gnostic practice was simply a transposition of sensibilities from the pagan world. Pagans were also scandalized by Gnostic worldviews, as is demonstrated by the great Egyptian Neoplatonist philosopher Plotinus (205–270 CE) in his treatise *Against the Gnostics* (Enneads II, 9). Though Plotinus did not mention Gnostics by that generic name, his pupil Porphyry's title for his master's polemic, "Against those who say the maker of the world is evil and that the world is evil," indicates clearly enough what Plotinus found objectionable in the writings friends of his chanced upon. For Plotinus, Gnostics indulged in obscure mythologizing to excess and made the error of confusing the deficient aspects of manifest existence—when compared to the perfect ideas of heaven—with actual malevolence and positive evil. Plotinus would tolerate no rupture in continuity between the One and the created order, a position characteristic of Christian Platonism. Nevertheless, Plotinus's invective against Gnostics is suggestive that in many respects, his thought was not as far from theirs as he might have hoped, and that, in fact, Plotinus recognized in them an arguably open flank in his own philosophy of spiritual emanations from the One and the Good. People who liked what he had to say liked the Gnostic stuff too! This is still the case.

Gnostic *mythology,* however, was determinative in giving the heretics distinct ideas that Plotinus, like other philosophers, could not have arrived at by strictly logical means. Gnostics took as their launchpad the sacred books of the Jews (Genesis, the Psalms, and Proverbs, in particular), as well as traditions—written and otherwise—associated with Jesus. Gnostics have been called brilliant exegetes. Indeed, their thought culture did come from books, but they brought to the texts distinct sensibilities and highly characteristic, and original, attitudes, inspiration and tropes, almost as if they shared a gag—a special, liberating esoteric gag with a touch of ironic comedy—that gave those "hip" to it a key to

understanding all inherited religion, capable of giving the whole disparate body of religious ideas a unity within a greater scheme of cosmic
conspiracy against the truth of their freedom attained via transmundane redemption.

To the hard-core Gnostics, the world was a fraud; it could be laughed
at from the heights of exalted realization. Once this was recognized,
things taught to be taboo could be revealed, au contraire, as gateways to
knowledge, as symbols denied and forbidden by the repressive pseudo-
deity. Gnostics penetrated into disturbed territory of the psyche where,
we may suppose, Plotinus feared, or had more sense than, to tread.

Where would it end?

Gnostics departed from the very essence of paganism—acceptance
of nature. And here, almost paradoxically, we can see the startling face
of Jewish religion's historic objection to the pagan world: graven images
of God were blasphemous; the Creator is not one with the creation.
God must never be confused with the visible world or with objects and
substances within it; the essential message of the Jewish prophetic tradition was upended by everything the Greeks and Romans did: statues,
statues everywhere!

THE ESSENTIAL MYTH

A constant idea, arguably *the* constant idea, of Gnostic exegetical
schools, was the transposition of the Genesis Eden/Fall of Adam and
Eve myth from Earth to heaven. Edenic perfection is placed in heaven
(the Pleroma, or divine Fullness-Plenitude). However, just as in Eden,
a critical drama of temptation messes up a preexisting, possibly unconscious, harmony. The villainess is not Eve here, but the "Heavenly
Eve." The Fall *to* Earth would be an out-birth resulting from problems
in heaven and the aberrant heavenly female's subsequent exile. The
Gnostic is one for whom a "house," or home, has been prepared . . . *on
the other side.*

According to contemporary Jewish lore, God's Wisdom, called

Hokhmah in Hebrew (*Sophia* in Greek), dwelled with Him in eternity. Picking up on certain suggestions as to Sophia's peculiar nature, Gnostic writers took this primal bliss to its next logical stage, and—well, not to put too fine a point to it, they envisioned a scenario wherein she got herself into trouble. Why *she*? Surely God was not a partnership; he had no consort. Perhaps not, but *Sophia* is a feminine noun, and as far as the Gnostics knew from Jewish scripture in Greek translation (the Septuagint), she was all female, and her home was with God, for God and his Wisdom are inseparable (she being his First Thought), at least, until . . .

According to the common Gnostic myth, shared among different groups, with their own variants and emphases, Sophia allowed a *passion* to get the better of her; she desired to *penetrate* the mystery of the Divine Being of the Father (*Bythos:* Abyss, or "Depth"), even to know the unknowable, incomprehensible Father: an urge, unless we mistake, that had seized philosophers from the times of Plato at least, and with analogous results, that is, the production of an intellectual world that would prove inadequate either to critical thought or to application to the world as commonly experienced. The ones seeking absolute wisdom find themselves exiled from ordinary consciousness, with a fear of madness either in the self or from those now "outside" the experience of the seeker. The knower or would-be knower is the "outsider": the outsider, a knower. Gnosis unites metaphysical effect with metaphysical cause.

When we say that Sophia wants to know the Father, we glimpse the essence of the Gnostic accommodation with sex, for this knowledge that Sophia seeks is a taboo uncovering of the nature of the Father; symbolically, it is sexual, an erotic urge generated by attraction for what is unpossessed. The result of this precocious movement within the Pleroma is that Sophia, unsettled, falls outside of her eternal place, just as Eve and Adam are banished from Eden in Genesis. Eve tasted the fruit of the tree of knowledge of good and evil, just as Sophia is seeking to know the Father's depth, so disrupting her relationship with the Father's will.

God's will with respect to Sophia is present to her as her true syzygy, or male consort, called *Theletos* (from the Greek *Thelema* for "Will," denoting here God's will). The Fall of Sophia involves a breach of a divinely ordained pair, once united harmoniously, as were Adam and Eve, before losing their unified innocence and bliss, when Eve disregarded God's will for her own whereafter the man and woman's days were, from then on, numbered with all the horror entailed therein.

Harmony was two functioning as one, or even two in one. This idea brings us to the truly distinctive idea of Gnostic sexuality.

ANDROGYNY

In the Hermetic *Asclepius III,* attributed to ancient Egyptian sage Hermes Trismegistus (a considerable extract from which was found in the Nag Hammadi Library), we are informed plainly: "God is bisexual." Not only God the Father and Master of all generative power may be so described, but also the manifestation of his spirit as life everywhere: "For either sex is filled with procreative force; and in that conjunction of the two sexes, or, to speak more truly, that fusion of them into one, which may be rightly named Eros, or Aphrodite, or both at once, there is a deeper meaning than man can comprehend."

The unique speech that follows this introduction is found in Coptic in the Nag Hammadi Library: a rare, if not unique, paean to orgasm and its wonders presented as a holy mystery. That is why, Hermes assures his pupil Asclepius (or *Asklēpios* in the original Greek), the act is performed in secret, as an esoteric rite is performed away from prying eyes, lest the amusement of the rabble profane a holy mystery, a sacred rite of itself. Uniquely, startlingly, Asclepius lifts sexual love to the spiritual plane. The implication is one of theurgy: the Neoplatonic art of combining magic with religious fervor to generate rites attracting the light and power of heaven into the mind of the sanctified philosopher or priest.

While the hardcore Gnostic myth of Sophia's disruption of the Pleroma is foreign to the Hermetic corpus, the theme of androgyny of the spirit-that-animates is common to Hermetic and radical Gnostic material, and we must remind ourselves that there was never a Gnostic orthodoxy about any single doctrine: something for which they were taunted by opponents.

To say that God is bisexual does not mean God experiences sexual attraction to males and females, though it may well account for that attraction *in* males and females. The Hermetic (Latin) text means the form of God contains both sexes (*Utriusque sexus*): "He, filled with all the fecundity of both sexes in one, and ever teeming with his own goodness, unceasingly brings into being all that he has willed to generate; and all that he wills is good." God encompasses the original ideas of masculine and feminine and is, in a sense, then Mother and Father of life, operating in perfect, incomprehensible union. God is one, but spiritual oneness is not one dimensional, as it must appear to materialists who take their flat-Earth vision to a supposed heaven, devoid of spiritual life.

Gnostic belief in the original, divine idea of humanity (*anthrōpos*) being androgynous or even hermaphroditic follows, for did Genesis not say that woman was drawn from man (Adam) while he was asleep, that is, they thought, when Adam lost consciousness of his former androgynous divinity in the divine mind?

Expressed in the material world, God's unity becomes a duality, so man also is divided from himself, which is the divine pneuma, or spirit of life. Pneuma—Spirit—being divine, was androgynous. It was therefore the divine seed's fall into matter that led to the appearance of man and woman separated, or pared, into distinguishable beings. The body alone determines sex. The spirit of humanity remains androgynous. Gnostics of all hues are expressly warned not to worship or become enamored of the body qua body (flesh), as Jews were taught never to make graven images or material forms of the God they had never seen.

Following a Platonist philosophy, matter divides because its nature is to objectify ideas: to turn ideas into objects, that is, to separate them from their former harmony (the life of the aeons or, as we translate the concept, eternal life) and subject them to the vagaries and flux of time and space. What is harmonious in mind (*nous*) is unstable in matter. Hence, Jesus's parabolic teaching is to build one's house not on sand (unstable, transitory matter) but on rock, an image of a supernatural stone that comes from heaven. We shall discover more about the transformative stone in due course.

Male and female, then, while *natural* as far as the world of time and space is concerned (the creation, according to most Gnostics, of a misbegotten Creator derived from the out-birth of Sophia's primal precociousness)—"male and female created he them"—it was in fact a catastrophic rupture of the spiritual being, a suffering of the spirit, mirroring the wound in the divine being when the suffering, passionate Sophia exceeded her proper boundaries, resulting in an abortion that is the cosmos. This wound corresponds to the human spiritual heartache for God or a lost world, the loss of God: a profound nostalgia, experienced also as the desperate need for love, which, if perennially frustrated, turns to hate, generating evil.

While the Hermetic corpus in general does not recognize the Gnostic Sophia speculation, we nonetheless find in the Coptic extract from *Asclepius* 21–29 recognition that gnosis is the means by which ignorance is cured. This ignorance is regarded as an incurable sore of the soul that grows with incurable passions until it generates all evils. These evils, Hermes says, cannot then be laid at the door of God, for God wills that humanity accept the gift of knowledge, a grace or gift. Only this gift can cure what to humanity in ignorance remains incurable.

If he accepts the gift of gnosis, he can become pious and avoid sinking into the passions of matter: "For," as Hermes asserts in a powerful phrase, "the knowledge of the things which are ordained is truly the healing of the passions of matter." This line constitutes pretty much the essential itinerary of the Valentinian Egyptian gnosis. The myth of the passionate Sophia, suffering to know, but generating only deficiencies of her disharmonized self, was formulated precisely as a means of pointing the way to "the healing of the passions of matter." Furthermore, we are at liberty to recognize that such also must be the essential aim of the arrow of desire that is Gnostic sex. Spiritually oriented sex heals the passions of matter, subjecting the organism to spiritual and harmonious lordship. This is a healing prefiguring of the restoration of the exiled, fallen spirits to the divine Pleroma, through love and elevating knowledge of the heart. The joy of union, the dissolution of separation, is all. Thus sex becomes the great gift, a divine grace to the Gnostic man or woman whose soul is in love with God.

Incidentally, Hermes, for one, is adamant that those who cannot recognize the holy mystery of the sexual act are impious, thus condemning the larger part of official church teaching from at least the fourth century CE to our own revelatory times: "Therefore wickedness remains among the many, since learning concerning the things which are ordained [by God] does not exist among them." Sex is holy for the holy; for the wicked, it is as groping in the dark. Instead of the church teaching the gift of gnosis, it has suppressed and persecuted it—and don't we know it!

The Spirit longs for union; the flesh (divided) is weak. To repeat: *Yoga* means "union." *Samadhi,* the supreme trance in raja (royal) yoga may be expressed, from the Gnostic point of view, as: "I and my Father are one" (*cf.* John 10:30). Whether Gnostics got their ideas from India in this regard is unknown, but it is fairly obvious that once you allow that the division of the sexes, the pains of childbirth, and the life-and-death cycle are a catastrophe for the spirit of God, then the practice of a sacred reunion of the bodies can be seen as sacramentally prefiguring, or as an intimation or anticipation of, the exiled soul's reunion with its heavenly, spiritual, or angelic counterpart still at home in the heavenly world. Such is the spiritual blessing of the sacrament of marriage. A sacrament takes something of the Earth and raises it to its heavenly correspondent. To use poet Samuel Taylor Coleridge's fascinating phrase, a sacrament *disembodies the soul of fact,* which is also the function of the imagination in its highest phase.

So far, so good. Taking a Gnostic perspective, we can see a serious reason for a sacrament of sexual intercourse aimed toward realization of spiritual union with God, or at least with one's estranged angel or *daimōn* (protective transmundane spirit): that part of the human being (the crown) not entirely swallowed up by the deluge of time and space— the Pythagorean psychic non-ego, beloved as the dawning, or *augoeidēs,* of Syrian Neoplatonist philosopher Iamblichus, and known in high magical circles today as the Holy Guardian Angel.

The theory here works well enough. Conceive of sex not as a lustful descent into pleasurable stimuli in a largely inhibition-free romp, but rather as a loving discipline of minds and bodies combined and focused on a higher reality and you have, well, something like sexual mysticism. In Hindu Tantric ritual, such unions are prefigured in the love-embrace of Shakti (the feminine cosmic creative energy) and Shiva (the supreme masculine god, patron of yoga, worshipped in the form of the lingam), whose orgasm generates the universe eternally: *AUM!* The god and god-dess thus become, after considerable ascetic rehearsal, in-personated by the Tantric worshippers: *see me as Shiva and I'll see you as Shakti: thus become we One.*

In terms of creative energy, the *union* of Shakti and Shiva corre-sponds somewhat to the bisexual Hermetic God, generator of life and goodness. In this context, orgasm can be a physically registered expe-rience of God—so long as physical experience is not the condition or wished intention of the rite—and for this to have spiritual meaning, the mystical couple needs to be in a mind above the downward-tending physical consciousness. If we may employ alchemical terms, orgasm-as-sensation is ideally the *parergon* (by-product) of the *ergon* (essential work) of spiritual union.

But is it the sex itself that gets them there? I fear the theory is largely mute on this point, though we may say that the good will and right intention are primary requisites.

Again, we have a grand metaphysical theory, and we know that the theory has enjoyed many practitioners, but is such a thing *in itself* really possible or realistic? Well, nobody said it was not *rare.* However, the realization of such a state might still seem inherently contradictory if we analyze our experience. Apart from the fact that when I was in my learning stage in my teens, my first sexual experiences promoted the word heaven to come spontaneously to my lips to describe them, since orgasm seemed, to begin with, the closest thing to an overwhelming heavenly feeling I could recall—save visions of God experienced as a child—(I can hardly be alone in this!), it was of course not long before the practice fell into an appetite for more because it felt good.

Harmonious relations with the partner took second place to what was now something like a raw need. It's almost as if the mind is permitted its first spiritual delight, and then the body takes over, muscling in on the scene to get its fix and get that DNA stirring up into the great cycle in which we may lose ourselves.

Soon enough, what promised liberation, love's alleged fulfillment, became necessary, a condition of mutuality, a pang, and the delightful Edenic Adam and Eve pulsing wonder of it all became the frustrated, morbid, longing cycle that depresses youth, bound up as it is with inchoate ideas of love, marriage, security, self, peer pressure, confusion of needs with wants, and all the rest of it. What began as heaven would become an awful pain one way or another! Though, I have to say in my own case, as one fell unconsciously from the Pleroma to planet Earth's reality, the sense of romance never entirely died under the asphyxiating erotic hunger of the senses. But I had certainly lost my glimpse of heaven: innocence lost forever perhaps. I am optimistic.

We can probably agree that to enjoy sex at its best, we need to be in love with our partner and/or be very horny and aroused physically by an agreeable or more than agreeable lover. The idea of purity (which we associate with God) or lustless love as an ideal, when applied to sex, is for many of us counterintuitive. I might want in spirit to reach for divinity or celebrate divinity with, in, or through another, but to be candidly frank, to "get it up" (enthusiasm, that is) I need to think (if that's the right word) of something sexy and/or be confronted with someone who irresistibly arouses lustiness.

Alternatively, one might simply feel sexually frustrated and anxious for a fortuitous outlet for sexual emotions and physical pangs. Many who associate guilt with sex, need alcohol to get over their inhibitions. Such persons need very little reminding that "sin" can be very enjoyable, for a time. Then there's set and setting, romance, and all the other means we know to let Venus radiate in our lives. We need the right partner, and if God is love, and good sex helps us to admire our partners and cements our dependence on them, then we may say sex has a spiritual dimension, though we'd be at a loss to indicate where exactly or know what to do with it. Isn't sex problematic enough without bringing God into it?

I remember when I was about ten, my father took an interest in the local Mormon community in Birmingham (in the English Midlands). Eager representatives from Utah visited us regularly. Along with promises of root beer to substitute for forbidden coffee came a series of colorful pamphlets. One I well remember was the suggestion that membership in the Church of Jesus Christ of Latter-Day Saints entitled one to consummate one's marriage in Salt Lake City in a marriage chamber specially designed for that purpose, where it was guaranteed (if I recall correctly) that angels would be present to make that first night really something special. I found this detail laughably naive, even in my tender years, for one couldn't help wondering whether there was anywhere you could go where you might not be observed by angelic visitants. Now I think of Friedrich Nietzsche's line that "Strong beliefs are prison houses of the mind" and wonder if these angels were not so much cheerleaders of a divinely ordained nuptial as foreshadowers of a life of custodial observation to come! I also can't help wondering if the obscure origins of such beliefs might lie with some of those advocated by Swedish visionary Emanuel Swedenborg (1688–1772), who held that sexual joys and feelings of married Christians could actually be felt in heaven. If I read this right, our dear departed (and others) could sensually benefit from our nocturnal lustrations. This notion strained the tolerance and credibility of many of Swedenborg's London followers after his death, and I suspect this curiously materialistic vision would turn many off the whole notion of linking too closely our earthly amours with any heavenly scheme.

Returning to the psychology of sexual experience, I think it is generally the case that the moment we think of or concentrate on that which stimulates us physically, any spiritual aspiration or dimension of awareness splits off like the section of a *Saturn V* rocket, plunging back to Earth or jettisoned into space. In short, feelings, however temporarily uplifted, become earthbound in quality though pleasurable—in the sense of stimulating—at the sensory level and pleasurably dreamy perhaps.

Conversely, however, if you try to concentrate *solely* on receiving physical pleasure *as* physical pleasure, or the sensations of nearing and achieving orgasm itself alone, you can feel strangely cold and empty afterward, or even at the supreme moment. Self-loathing may result, along with a sense of having strangely bungled something potentially significant. The greater pleasure, its essence, may not be purely sensual at all. The deepest pleasures may be seen as simply registering something that is truly good; and I mean by *deepest* the highest. Revenge is only the highest pleasure to the lowest kind. The essence of the thing is not pleasure itself. The greater pleasure transcends pleasure. The transcendent moment may not be possessed by the ego and, therefore, is not, properly speaking, a moment at all, being timeless. Effort to possess the ultimate joy, to hold it to oneself, can lead to a very dark feeling, or lack of feeling at all: a road to be avoided at all costs. One may experience a mighty fall. Indeed, sacrifice of the ego is properly involved in sex consummated, quite unlike many of our imagined pleasures. I am reminded of Friar Lawrence's speech in Shakespeare's *Romeo and Juliet,* Act II, Scene 6:

> These violent delights have violent ends
> And in their triumph die, like fire and powder,
> Which, as they kiss, consume. The sweetest honey
> Is loathsome in his own deliciousness
> And in the taste confounds the appetite.
> Therefore love moderately. Long love doth so.

Alleged incompatibility of the physical sexual experience and the life of the spirit, which requires a surrender or transcendence of ego and wanting (anything but spiritual desires), has appeared to many observers to preclude any idea other than that sex should be seen as nothing more than nature's crafty way of establishing the conditions for reproduction, and while we may steal some temporary gratification or tantalizing glimpse of a transitory and arguably counterfeit heaven from the process through nature's slippery incentive of orgasm, that too is part of the trick. The "selfish gene" idea is not really an original thought of Richard Dawkins, but the fundamental suspicion of the Encratites of late antiquity! If orgasm is the snare that leads spirit down into the grip of the sinful world or the power of the Demiurge (which, by the way, could easily become another word for *evolution*), then orgasm and childbirth are to be avoided like the plague: the vulva is hell's gateway! This is the creed of the Encratite, both in late antiquity and today, where it might help to sustain the celibate monk and nun through the long renunciation of sex.

According to this fatal view of nature, we are enjoined to think of the Venus flytrap and think of ourselves as the hapless fly: Oh, those pretty flowers! And what is in there? Oh succulent, perfumed bliss! Oh, what if I taste it? *Snap!* Snap and crunch go the jaws of devouring nature, whose teeth, ever hungry, thrive on death: dog eat dog. Nature eats herself for breakfast; she is no vegetarian! Why, even romance itself can be seen as a ruse of nature to drug us into the great cycle to which most of us acquiesce, sooner or later—or wish we could!

In practical terms, how could one overcome the obvious dichotomy? We have all read about Tantric practitioners training for years to isolate the mind from the mundane instincts, to be able to enter a sexual union that is a spiritual exaltation as self is surrendered in a cosmic zero that annihilates subject and object. We have read about this, but it seems very far from Acacia Avenue: though Catholics are taught that God approves of children born in wedlock, and if that be not exactly ecstasy in itself, it is doubtless pleasant to know one is at least doing the right thing, even if it be a sin to enjoy it too much.

I once heard a very sensible female Anglican marriage counselor advocate—in the face of confused, delicately sensitive wives who could not equate Christian decency with sexual appetites—that Christian women should feel that it is OK to "be a whore in bed"; to give their husbands the things that, if they let themselves relax, they could really enjoy giving and not be ashamed of. In other words, they shouldn't be afraid of enjoying themselves with their husbands to the full. Good sex requires lust, and if God made the world of nature, God respects happy, lusty marriages. I hope the counselor's advice loosened up a few over-tight blouses and brought some harmony into troubled marriages. As it was *Woman's Hour* (a BBC radio show), I did not hear her advice for Christian men. It is often presumed that men are quite lustful enough, but who can say? The angels at the foot of the bed aren't telling! One sees many disappointed women whose efforts may have been wasted.

The problem of the "lust brings the spiritual exaltation down" scenario might be solved if we could find the idea of God sexually arousing, but here Western religion has a distinct problem. The root of it may be expressed in the story in Genesis (9:22) of Ham seeing his father Noah's naked genitals after Noah gets drunk in his tent, and Noah's subsequent curse of Ham's son, Canaan, for having apparently taken advantage of his condition. The father is not to be seen as sexual by the children; in Genesis, the result can be incest, as in the case of Lot's daughters (Genesis 19:30–35). One might conclude, from the Freudian perspective, that while the father might be killed (Oedipus complex), he must not be penetrated.

Western men would have to make an enormous leap to get an erection from imagining God (images anyway are forbidden), though some women might experience suppressed delights from serving an attractive Jesus image. If men want a female image to worship—and really love in the flesh—they would need to join an Isis-worshipping or other neopagan group. Nevertheless, it is well reported through the ages that mystics have been sexually excited as a by-product of high trances, where they felt transported among divine powers regardless of any overt sexual aspect within the vision itself: spiritual ecstasy can manifest in physical ecstasy, though the reverse order is more problematic. No wonder orthodoxy has always been, at best, suspicious of mystics! *Is that a pistol you got in there, or are you talking to God?*

As for the controllers of religion, are they not likely to be affected by prevailing ideas of God? If God is defined by qualities that are sexless, sex-repressive, dull, square, boring, oppressive, and so on, are his ministers not likely to appear likewise, with all the usual human failings thrown in as well, if obscured from the public eye?

Just why are horns and horniness applied to images of Satan? Well, we know the horns came originally from the god Pan (the "All"), associated with country rites and the resonant power of sacred groves. Pan has about him the physical characteristics of the lusty goat. It was William Blake who turned all this on its head when he declared in his *The Marriage of Heaven and Hell* (1793) that "The lust of the goat is the bounty of God." Bounty means a free gift: a grace, in fact. But Blake identified the New Age with its corollary: the necessary "improvement in sensual enjoyment." For Blake, as we shall see, the vulva was not the gate of hell, but of the New Jerusalem!

So, if we are to be aroused by God, we need a God who is arousing. Now, here is where Egyptian religion really "scored." And, let us not forget, Egyptian religion provided set and setting for the Gnostic schools of Alexandria. It is arguable that for Christianity or Judaism to transform into gnosis, it must be transplanted into a culture of intellectual pagans as well as mystical exegetes. It needs, I think, a sensual environment with the right climate. In Egypt, we get a real sense of the froth of Wisdom related to the foaming spirit of creation: the divine prerogative itself. By contrast, Western Christianity has, arguably, sterilized God. He only created once, apparently. His primary duty done, he spends eternity in reposeful semiretirement: more a grandfather than a father. The Father engenders, but without sex. He is, after all, the Father!

Unlike Shiva, what might be held his natural symbol is strictly, absolutely taboo. When Mary the Virgin becomes pregnant, it is not the Father but the Holy Spirit that fertilizes the ovum, passing through her hymen like light through glass as an early church father put it. Bearing this in mind, the reappearance of the Divine Feminine—both whore and virgin—will continue to raise a tremor to shake the great religions to their foundations.

An erotic religion may now be extremely rare and is perhaps for most people practically impossible, but it continues to be a consummation devoutly wished.

However, before we approach the true object of Gnostic desire, we need to establish precisely where the image of the "filthy Gnostickes" came from and specify precisely what it was that made Gnostics "filthy" in the minds of their opponents.

TWO

HERESY STARTS IN EDEN

The Accusers

I t has been little and seldom understood that as far as the dominant heresiologists of late antiquity were concerned, heresy did not begin after Jesus departed this world in the flesh. It was not simply a question of church authorities being upset at Jesus's apostles' words being twisted to suit the predilections of later heretics; heresy, as far as Christian authority was concerned, had existed since the beginning of the human story on Earth. Heresy began in Eden with the serpent's temptation of Eve.

Orthodox Christian guardians, with the possible exception of Clement of Alexandria, had no truck whatsoever with any notion of parallel cultures developing innocently around the world, each to be respected and generously compared. Any conception of cultural relativity or liberal tolerance would have appeared incomprehensible to most heresiologists: a dangerous heresy in itself, in fact. No, it had rather to be understood that the fathers of the entire human race derived from the adventures of Adam and his children, while the different races of the world descended from Noah, whose children restocked the Earth after God wiped out sinful humanity in the Great Flood. The Jewish scriptures told the essential history of humankind—all of it. For what was essential in that history was God's saving plan, evolved through covenants with his chosen people and with all humankind (God's promise to Noah after the Flood).

There had always been an ark for the elect and oblivion for the rest. The plan's eventual dénouement—the arrival of God's Son in the flesh—was a secret hinted at by the prophets of Israel and dimly by the odd Gentile soothsayer, but whose crucial mystery was the most closely guarded secret of the visible and invisible worlds. Its success would entail the lord of this world (Azazel, among other names) being duped into thinking he could get away with assassinating Jesus as he had many another outspoken prophet. According to Paul, the wooden cross or tree was the key component of the snare that trapped the "princes of this world" (I Corinthians 2:8), and which subsequently would bring the evil empire of "the rulers of the darkness of this world" (Ephesians 6:12) crashing down, for "At the name of Jesus, every knee shall bow" (Philippians 2:10).

Everything that deviated from God's will, as revealed to Noah, Abraham, and Moses, in the law and in the Prophets, and interpreted finally and definitively by Jesus and his Holy Spirit–guided apostles, was heresy. That is why, when you look at Hippolytus's *Refutation of All Heresies,* it begins with a refutation of every dominant pre- and post-Socratic Greek philosopher. These men, wise as they may have appeared, apparently did not know that they were heretics, such defense being anyhow of little avail; they stood corrected and could be rejected. Hippolytus throws in the thoughts of the Brahmins of India and the Druids of Gaul and Britain as well. Had he known of Lao Tzu or Confucius, they would doubtless have been included.

In Bishop Epiphanius's *Panarion,* the heresies begin with Barbarism, and proceed to encompass Scythianism (all non-Hebraic cultures stemming from the sons of Noah), Hellenism, Epicureanism, Stoicism, Platonism, Judaism, the Pharisees, the Sadducees, the Scribes, the Herodians, the Ossaeans, and the "Nazarenes" or "Nazoraeans" (Jewish Christians who did not believe Jesus was God incarnate). Not until section 2 of his work does he get to work on the Gnostic-type sects.

The cultures of the world, where they did not agree with apostolic truth, were all deviant and substantially heretical in thought and act. Such a thorough, blanket condemnation was hardly surprising to those who had inherited something of the outlook of Jesus and his first followers, the authentic Nazarenes (Hebrew: *Natsarim* = "Watchers" or "Guardians" in the sense of "keepers" or even "shepherds": those who faithfully stand for and maintain holy tradition as guards and guides). Jesus followed the prophetic tradition of Jeremiah 4:16 in seeing these *Natsarim* as guardians of a commission to judge those who had corrupted holy Israel. The Nazarenes constituted the core remnant that had resisted foreign and homegrown contamination and that had kept faith with God's will of righteousness (*zedek,* or "tzedek") with respect to his worship and loving-kindness or compassion (*hesed,* or "chesed") with respect to one's neighbor.

As is made clear in the canonical *Epistle of Judas* (I:14–15), probably written by Jesus's brother of that name, the prophet Enoch had announced the judgment of the "Father of Lights" on the evil, or fallen, Watchers. In this belief, Judas followed the contemporary "hot" *Book of Enoch,* wherein the prophet Enoch, based at Dan for the purpose, announced God's condemnation of the evil Watchers, bound to Earth. These rebellious Watchers, who fell from heaven as the Nephilim of Genesis 6:4 to corrupt the beautiful daughters of men and to reveal arts and sciences, which humanity was not mature enough to handle, were believed by early Christians to be the angels who governed the nations of the Earth. Anti-Gnostic church fathers declared *them* to be the sources of heresy, for the fallen angels knew that man's salvation triggered their damnation and vice versa. This theory explained the mortal position of the heresiarchs. According to heresiologists, Gnostic teachers were themselves the dupes of fallen angels, puffed up into blindness by their own pretended knowledge. Such may surprise those who have understood that it was a primary teaching of Gnosis to liberate spirits from the grip of hostile angels ("archons"), a belief clearly rooted in the *Book of Enoch* and in the teachings of St.Paul!

Thus, it could be held that the pantheons of gods worshipped by the heathen multitudes represented their secret captors, the fallen Watchers whose evil seed persisted in the generations to pervert the minds of those whose remote antecedents had once joined Noah in thankful praise of the Almighty Father of all humankind. It is for this reason that the commission came to the *faithful* Watchers, keepers of the Way (or vineyard), and guardians of the truth (see my book *The Missing Family of Jesus*), to go forth into the world and announce to all and sundry that the evil game was up.

The orthodox interpretation was that until Jew, Greek, Roman, and all peoples accepted Jesus as Lord, they all operated under heresy, laboring vainly in thrall to the evil angels whom only the cross of Jesus, promised messiah and Son of God, could nullify. If they wished to be saved from impending judgment, they had better heed the apostolic call to repentance and salvation.

Now, perhaps, readers may grasp the stakes involved in the struggle between the heretics and the orthodox. As far as orthodox Christian teachers were concerned, deviation from the apostolic message on any point rendered the deviant outside the ark of salvation. The faithful had to be saved from contaminating influences at all costs. Since the second- and third-century church did not envision having the means of coercion, the state would in due process of history provide for the persecution of heretics; the church could only preach, excommunicate, and disseminate books and letters. In this matter, some remarkably able writers gave their services to the church. In this chapter, we shall rely upon their testimony.

THE HERESIOLOGISTS

The patristic heresiologists, whose contemporary records of Gnostic beliefs and practices have survived, are as follows: Justin Martyr (ca. 100–165 CE), Irenaeus (ca. 130–ca. 202), Clement of Alexandria (ca. 150–ca. 215), Tertullian (ca. 160–ca. 225), Hippolytus (ca. 170–ca. 235), and Epiphanius (ca. 310–ca. 405).

Born circa 130 CE, Irenaeus (whose name means "Peace") grew up in or around Smyrna in Asia Minor (now Izmir in Turkey). There he heard the martyr Polycarp preach. Polycarp had received the apostolic word from one "Presbyter John," identified traditionally as John the Evangelist: a doubtful ascription as there was a confusion of "Johns" active in the late first-century church in Asia Minor. As far as Irenaeus was concerned, the authentic message had come to him unbroken from apostolic sources and had been consistent in essentials from the beginning. There is an interesting and significant caveat to that remark, however.

Irenaeus castigates heretics for eating meat sold in the marketplace that had first been offered to pagan idols. This is a common accusation made against the heretics and was considered to indicate lax morals and pro-pagan, backsliding tendencies. The problem is that St. Paul himself explicitly stated that for the understanding Christian who was not weak, as he calls spiritually immature members of the church, meat was just meat, as the gods of the idols did not exist and the idols were simply wood and stone and part of God's creation, as were the animals. A Christian whose conscience was clear on the issue need not be bothered, unless (see I Corinthians 8) his eating meat in company made a weaker brother feel his abstention from his former sin (paganism) was compromised and he might slip back into his old ways by thinking of the now-rejected gods. In that case, love for the brother must override personal wants. Better, says Paul, to give up meat altogether than generate a rift or give offense to the brotherhood and sisterhood. Nevertheless, there remained a cloud over the issue and the general line taken officially had been established in Jerusalem (Acts 15) that eating meat offered to idols was a no-no, even for Gentiles.

After the destruction of Jerusalem as a viable center for the Jesus messianic assembly in and after 70 CE, the grip of Jewish Christianity (championed until 62 CE by Jesus's brother James) had weakened considerably as the Gentile churches of Asia Minor, North Africa, Rome, Gaul, Spain, and Britain grew. Gnostic communities' outspoken practice of the sin does suggest that Paul's more nuanced teaching on this subject, and his whole scandalous stance against applying the Torah to Gentiles—surely weakening the law's hold on Jews also by implication—had taken deep root in Gnostic circles and may even have been a first point and means of differentiating themselves from "weaker brethren." Gnostics thrived on this distinction, as Irenaeus was at pains to make loud and clear.

Irenaeus became bishop of Lugdunum (now Lyon) in Gaul after the persecutions of Marcus Aurelius in 177 CE had deprived by martyrdom the see of its bishop, Pothinus. Irenaeus entered a ravaged community. It was important to know what Christians had been dying for. Irenaeus composed his detailed book series against "the gnosis falsely so-called" (*Adversus Haereses*) in about 180 CE, when followers of the Gnostic magician Marcus, a student of Valentinus, were active in Rome and in the Rhône Valley,[1] while Valentinus's student Ptolemy's teachings were also penetrating the Church in Rome. In his preface, Irenaeus writes: "I refer especially to the disciples of Ptolemy, whose school may be described as a bud from that of Valentinus." It was against Marcus and Ptolemy that Book I of Irenaeus's work was primarily aimed, and this should be borne in mind, even though Irenaeus has significant things to say about all the related movements he knew of and of their antecedents as he understood them.

Irenaeus makes many interesting generalizations about the types of people advancing the "gnosis falsely so-called"; they appeared slippery, cocky, and at times strangely insecure. The preface refers to the heretics' "plausible system." This plausibility he proceeds very cleverly and often wittily to undermine, unafraid to go into detailed exposition of Gnostic theosophical superstructures, even to the point of boredom—part of his method for undermining the grip of the Gnostics' plausibility. One thing he wants his readers to recognize is that "Their language resembles ours, while their sentiments are very different." This is still a resonant observation and subverts the notion, often held today, that, *well,* they were all *Christians,* weren't they? Not in the view of Irenaeus! They were outsiders to the communion of the apostolic faithful and should repent of their blasphemies before seeking reentry to the fold. The orthodox majority, under such leaders as Irenaeus, would never allow an esoteric branch of the faith with superior tendencies to thrive: too much like competition, to say the very least.

Irenaeus believed that the essence of the Marcosian and Ptolemaean heresies was derived from Simon Magus, a remarkable contemporary of Jesus and the apostles. Irenaeus was familiar with the brief, doubtless propagandist, account in the Acts of the Apostles that pictured a converted Samaritan magician, named Simon, marveling at the Holy Spirit baptism of Peter and John on account of its more visible effects on converts than the water baptism Simon had himself received from the apostle Philip. Simon offered money for knowledge of how the magic—as he saw it—was effected. For this sin, Peter condemned Simon, giving us the word *simony* for the sin of obtaining ecclesiastical preferment with money. Acts does not, however, have anything to say about Simon in the context of theosophical speculation, only that the Samaritans worshipped Simon, who had been active in Samaria for a long time, as "the great power of God."

Irenaeus is at pains to show that *true gnosis* is knowledge of Christ: Christian knowledge that redeems, rather than escapes from, bodily existence. Here, however, he was pitting himself against such writings as St. Paul's first letter to the Corinthians 15:50, in which Paul states that "flesh and blood cannot inherit the kingdom"; how, asked Paul, can the perishable inherit the imperishable? Irenaeus seems to have held an orthodox view that the body had the objective role in the miraculous resurrection of the faithful. It was, in Irenaeus's view, at least the failure to understand the proper apostolic relation of body to God's creation and purposes that accounted in part for what he saw as Gnostics' outrageous sexual libertinism.

Irenaeus's accounts established the basic heresiological template, and his work was copied and drawn on in different ways by Tertullian, Hippolytus, and, much later, by Epiphanius. It must be said that, of those men, Irenaeus was probably the most conscientious in getting his information basically right before turning on the sarcasm and invective.

It should also be noted, for it seldom is, that the persons and systems Irenaeus described predated the composition of much of what we know as the Nag Hammadi Library, the majority of whose works were probably composed in the third century and possibly the early fourth century, before being buried in Upper Egypt around the year 367 CE. This is an important consideration when we come to compare the second-century heresiologists' view of Gnostic sexual misdemeanors, as they saw them, with the express contents of the so-called Gnostic Gospels. It has become a tendency in Gnostic studies and public exposition to imply that the Nag Hammadi Library shows that men such as Irenaeus did not really understand what they were writing about, being exclusively concerned with tarring the whole range of ideas with a thick, blackened brush because, above all, the gnosis constituted a threat to church authority. This is something of a prejudice in itself and should be guarded against.

Encratism, rather than stemming directly from Gnostic groups, as Isaac Newton believed, may have impacted Gnostic circles similarly, the way it did mainstream orthodoxy in the late third and fourth centuries, altering the malleable essence of the gnosis. That is to say, some Gnostic groups may have partially wilted from former extravagances under the pressure of orthodox criticism and Encratite influence and become markedly less sexy or even antisex by the end of the third century and the beginning of the fourth. Such would explain why the Nag Hammadi Library itself found its probable original home within a Pachomian monastery near Nag Hammadi at Faw Qibli: an epicenter for the fourth-century birth of Christian monasticism under St. Pachom and his celibate successors.

CLEMENT OF ALEXANDRIA

While Irenaeus is known chiefly for his antiheretical work, Clement of Alexandria is best remembered for works that attempted to show Christianity both in the context of philosophy and as a respectable, indeed, superior philosophy in its own right, against the common jibe that Christianity was a superstitious religion for slaves and the uneducated proletariat. Clement was therefore considerably more open-minded where subtleties were concerned than any of the other famous heresiologists. Nevertheless, as an Athenian successor to Pantaenus's headship of Alexandria's Catechetical School, Clement aimed a good deal of his criticism at what H. A. Blair's excellent book on him describes as "cultured thinkers, captured by magic and the wrong kind of mysticism [. . .] eclectics captivated by the intellectual snobbery of the 'gnostics.' Clement out-bid them with his claim that he was himself a gnostic, and taught the full gnosis of the Christian faith."[2] Clement's breadth of understanding did not go unnoticed by Catholic authority in the years after his death; Pope Sixtus V had Clement's name removed from the Roman martyrology on the advice of Baronius in 1586.

Gnostics of various hues came under Clement's learned and critical gaze in his *Protrepticus* (*Exhortation,* ca. 195), *Paedagogus* (the *Tutor* of the title is Christ the Logos; ca. 198), and *Strōmateis* (*Patchwork,* ca. 198–ca. 203). He also preserved the words of the Valentinian-type heretic Theodotus in his important *Excerpta ex Theodoto.*

Clement of Alexandria had great insight into the idea of all archetypes (divine formative ideas) converging on their source and central principle: the Logos, God's wisdom. This principle guided his view of moral perfection, away from extremes. Thus the *Paedagogus*'s view of sex is that both promiscuity and abstinence are unnatural. The center point of human sexuality is procreation. Homosexuality, prostitution, concubinage, adultery, and coitus with pregnant women are alien, Clement asserts, to the central purpose of generating legitimate children; these deviations should therefore be avoided. Aim for wisdom!

The remarkable *Strōmateis* holds that divine wisdom is received through faith into a cleansed receptacle where it can unfold as a seed with potential to grow from the receptive, initiatory posture of faith into that scientific certainty (*gnōsis*) familiar to the divine angels. One should act in accordance with wisdom, believing, trusting that God knows best. Experience ultimately proves the value of the initial embrace of faith, and faith practiced in following wisdom may thereby mature into knowledge. Thus, once one recognizes marriage as something created in accordance with God's wisdom, it will become apparent why it is wrong for Gnostics to be opposed to marriage (Clement is apparently addressing here an Encratite strain of heresy). Performed within the confines of marriage for the purpose of procreation, sex is a positive good, not simply a tolerable, or in some way necessary, evil. The only men who should be celibate are those genuinely uninterested in women from a sexual point of view, and such abstention must be dedicated to the Lord. (The basis of this view did not go down well with later Catholic assumptions about the priesthood.) Clement understood the Eden story in Genesis to indicate that Adam and Eve were banished from paradise because they copulated (i.e., had knowledge, knowing they were naked) prematurely. They jumped the gun. They abandoned faith in their Creator and listened instead to the voice of temptation: false wisdom promising knowledge.

Clement disapproved of speculating about the Logos, as Gnostics did constantly, apparently on the "seek and ye shall find" principle. God as Logos has revelatory, not analyzable, meaning. The revelation is to be meditated upon, not dissected, for reason cannot comprehend the true mysteries of God. "Clever-clever" knowledge bypasses wisdom. Unlike Gnostic views of the Demiurge, God had no beginning and was always and is always and forever the universal First Principle without whom we should not be.

TERTULLIAN

Quintus Septimus Florens Tertullianus was a very different kind of man to Clement of Alexandria. A lawyer hailing from Carthage on the coast of North Africa, Tertullian did not resist applying legal principles to his view of Gnostics and all who, in his judgment, too freely speculated on the contents of the scriptures. Tertullian disliked philosophy, just as some children dislike porridge, and demanded a straight revelation of religion that, once embraced, ceased all need for further seeking and finding. After all, he maintained, if you have sought and found, what value can you ascribe to what you have found if you go on seeking? You have obviously missed something! Or, worse, you have not valued what you formerly found. Those who deviate from the truth, according to Tertullian—and that category included non-Christian Jews—should be legally prevented from touching the goods they have perverted. Heretics had no right of access to the scriptures. They were unfit for presence at any trial of their works, since they had effectively infringed a divine "copyright." This is a typical example of Tertullian's terse logic.

Tertullian would defend the charismatic evangelism of the Montanist New Prophecy, which had begun in Phrygia, against all who declared its adherents misled by wicked spirits. The founder, Montanus, together with his assistants Prisca (or Priscilla) and Maximilla, embraced the spontaneous, forward-looking, enthusiastic inspiration of what they took to be the Holy Spirit, while their grip on reality was secured by disciplined, self-denying, and ascetic morals. Their tradition of New Jerusalem prophecy was declared to go back to the daughters of Philip the Evangelist (an interesting ascription in light of the Gnostic *Gospel of Philip*). The combination of Holy Spirit plus apostolic tradition appealed as strongly to Tertullian as it would to a Baptist or Methodist businessman today: straightforward men with feet firmly in both worlds. It wasn't "head" stuff; it was Christianity in action. Philosophy, for Tertullian's conviction of Christianity, was old hat, and far less useful than an old hat. It could make you lose your head. Better by far to have no rationale for believing than to believe in human cleverness as a path to truth. Tertullian's famous conviction that "I believe because it is absurd" is a paraphrase from *De Carne Christi,* his anti-Docetist work on Christ's flesh: *porsus credibile est, quia ineptum est.*

Tertullian's Christianity is probably the dominant type, generally speaking, in the world today, and he is undoubtedly a hero of Catholic theology and canon law: the no-nonsense type you want at the top, if you happen to be a pope. He would make a good Methodist and Baptist apologist as well.

Tertullian's attacks on Gnostics can be found in his works *De Praescriptione Haereticorum; Adversus Gnosticos Scorpiace; Adversus Marcionem; Adversus Praxeam;* and *Adversus Hermogenem.*

HIPPOLYTUS

Another skillful opponent of Gnostics was Hippolytus of Rome. His name means "Unleasher of Horses"; he lived up to his name. Hippolytus unleashed his intellectual cavalry on anyone he saw threatening the apostolic faith, even if that included the highest church authorities.

The ninth-century patriarch of Constantinople, Photius I, regarded Hippolytus as a disciple of Irenaeus, holding to traditions expounded by the martyr Polycarp. While that may only mean that Hippolytus adhered to the tenets of Irenaeus's *Adversus Haereses,* there is no reason that Hippolytus should not have known Irenaeus, for Hippolytus was a church presbyter in Rome under Zephyrinus, who became the capital's bishop in 199, a few years before Irenaeus's death. The great theologian Origen (ca. 182–ca. 254) heard Hippolytus when he was young. Origen would go on to study under Clement of Alexandria, afterward developing a spiritual theology that would earn him condemnation by some orthodox authorities a century after his death.

Accusing the bishops of Rome of soft-pedaling ethical requirements to be imposed on pagan converts, Hippolytus fell out with them after

217 CE. Conservatively upholding apostolic tradition over political "realities," Hippolytus pressured church leaders, making him a natural hero for those in the Catholic Church today who oppose liberalization of doctrine. By the middle of the third century, it was believed that Hippolytus had paid the martyr's price for the faith during the brief, unstable reign of Emperor Maximinus Thrax (d. 238).

In 1851, copies of books 4 to 10 of Hippolytus's *Refutation of All Heresies,* or *Refutatio,* were discovered under the title *Philosophumena* at Mount Athos's Greek Orthodox monastery. Books 2 and 3 remain lost, while book 1 has long served the needs of the interminable antiheresy effort. Other references to Gnostic heresies by Hippolytus can be found in his *Epistle to Diognetus* and from his work *Syntagma,* of which we know only those fragments Bishop Epiphanius of Salamis employed in his antiheretical *Panarion.*

It is worth noting that Hippolytus wrote of the feminine Sophia in a commentary on the Song of Songs (Songs of Solomon), the text he regarded as an allegorical exaltation of the preexisting love sanctified between Israel, Christ, and the Christian church.

EPIPHANIUS

Usually regarded as the most unscrupulous of heresiologists, Epiphanius of Salamis (ca. 310/320–ca. 405 CE) pile-drove his anti-heretical message into the *Panarion,* composed between about 374 and 377: a very late arrival on the antiheresy scene. *Panarion* is Greek for "medicine chest," being based on the conceit that every heresy owned a distinct venom that Epiphanius's all-purpose compendium could combat and eradicate. Epiphanius went so far as denoting fifty specific animals to cover each heretical strain; they all had their peculiar bite. Ebionites (Jewish Christians who did not accept that Jesus was born of God) were likened to the many-headed hydra. Gnostic heresy, predictably, was likened to the fangless nip of a serpent; its grip need not prove fatal. This detail alone gives us something of the flavor and attitude of Epiphanius's approach. He held his own humor in high regard, was superior, intolerant, and up for a fight.

Epiphanius was born at Eleutheropolis ("Free-city") in Palestine (now Beit Guvrin, Israel). Emerging within a decade of the Emperor Constantine's Edict of Milan (313), he could take for granted that new era for Christianity initiated when the emperor himself granted tolerance for Christians; those who had kept a low profile could come boldly into the open. The question now was which *kind* of Christianity deserved tolerance and which did not. The issue came to a head at the Council of Nicaea in 325, where, amid ugly scenes, the church was split between those crediting the beliefs of Arius, presbyter at Alexandria, and those of the bishop of Alexandria, ably promoted by his assistant, Athanasius, who would succeed to the bishopric himself three years later. The council met under the authority of the emperor. The Arian faction, disposed to numerous emphatic caveats to Jesus's divinity, was defeated at the council. Jesus was officially, and for all who wished to avoid excommunication, "of one substance with the Father." The Nicene Creed followed; it applied to the whole church.

Epiphanius seems to have been caught up in the enthusiasm for sorting out heretics from the true faith. Taking advantage of the era's new liberties, Epiphanius went as a young monk to Egypt (a rather experimental, novel way of life for the period). In Egypt, he came across a number of Valentinian groups, as well as other microsocieties practicing what from his account appear to have been rites of an extreme, sexual, even embryocidal nature. Returning to Palestine, Epiphanius founded his own monastery at Ad some time between the 330s and the 360s. He was appointed bishop of Salamis, Cyprus, between 365 and 367 CE. The latter date is particularly significant, as that is the date favored by scholarship for the placement of the Nag Hammadi codices in a jar at the foot of the Jabal al-Tarif near al-Qasr in Upper Egypt. The year 367 was when Bishop Athanasius's Thirty-Seventh Festal Letter specifically ordered the destruction of heretical books Athanasius knew from experience to be in circulation in the new Egyptian monasteries. The letter gave the list of the church's approved canon of apostolic and Old Testament works. Needless to say, there was no sign there of the *Gospel of Thomas,* the *Gospel of Truth,* the *Gospel of Philip,* or any of the other forty-nine books buried near the Pachomian monastery at Faw Qibli.

Epiphanius served as bishop of Salamis for some forty years. He traveled extensively, combated unorthodox beliefs, and exercised a painstaking, hands-on approach to his administration. In one famous story, which he told with pride, he found a Palestinian church, inside which hung an expensive curtain decorated with an image of Jesus. The bishop instantly tore it down. Taking his lead from the second commandment, Epiphanius would brook no images of the Lord in the house of the Holy One. When a member of the church complained about the cost of replacement, Epiphanius ordered at his own expense the finest-quality curtain he could obtain and had it delivered to the church. This tells us something about the man's general attitude.

In 399, Epiphanius got himself into a conflict with John II, bishop of Jerusalem. While Epiphanius condemned Origen for unorthodox teachings, John supported Origen's work. Initially supported by Theophilus, bishop of Alexandria, the latter bishop changed his mind in response to Epiphanius's fervent, no-fudging onslaught and Theophilus began persecuting Origenist monks in Egypt. Origen, it was held, had been too Alexandrian, too tolerant of heterodox beliefs by far. His surviving writings were therefore a threat to the church, for while much or even the greater portion might be commendable, that such truth should carry poison within it made the whole package even more dangerous, for one might absorb heresy without realizing it and accept it by association with divine truth.

Being dead did not exempt one from condemnation. The church had entered a new era of forensic, doctrinal rigor and vigorous opposition to all that deviated from it. Men like Epiphanius led the way on the basis perhaps that what saints like Irenaeus had laid down nearly two centuries earlier could now be rigidly enforced with imperial approval. Epiphanius himself was not, on the whole, too bothered to extract precise details of heretical beliefs and practices from an actual source. Ever zealous, he admitted that much of what he knew about Origen was hearsay, which, as my late history teacher used to remind me, is not heresy. Likewise, in Epiphanius's treatment of Gnostic groups, any antiheretical source would do (he relied heavily on Irenaeus, the now lost Syntagma of Hippolytus, and the lost antiheretical work of Justin Martyr [ca. 150 CE]). Epiphanius's task, as he saw it, was not to understand the heresy but to extirpate its poison by all means necessary; like a doctor dealing with gangrene, there was no need to study the phenomenon when duty required the quickest means of severing the infected limb and casting it out.

THREE

How to Be a
Superman

The First Gnostic

[. . .] their more secret rites, of which it is said that he
who first hears them will be astonished and according to
a written expression current among them will be made to
marvel, are truly full of marvel and frenzy and madness,
for they are such that not only can they not be committed
to writing but, because of their obscenity and unspeakable
conduct, cannot be mentioned by the lips of decent men.
For, whatever might be conceived as more foul than all
baseness, all this the utter abomination of the heresy of
these men has outdone who make sport of wretched
women truly weighed down with every kind of evil.

These shock-horror words were employed by the Origenist Eusebius
(ca. 184–ca. 253), bishop of Caesarea (after 313), to describe the
followers of Simon Magus and his consort Helen.[1] Taking his information from Justin Martyr's first *Apology* to Emperor Antoninus Pius (ca.
147–ca. 161), and from the later Irenaeus, Eusebius, writing between
the late 290s and 324 CE, accepts the church tradition that Simon

60

Magus was "the first author of all heresy," by which Eusebius means Simon was the first to challenge the apostles with doctrines, which, Eusebius believes, formed the basis for subsequent Gnostic-type beliefs and practices.

Justin Martyr furnished the information that Simon the magician was born in Gittho, a village of Samaria (near modern Nablus, identified with Kuryet Jit) and that he was active in Samaria during Claudius's reign (40s and 50s CE). His followers worshipped him as the "first God" and as "the Great Power of God." He was also known as "the standing one," a word with apocalyptic, John the Baptist–related meaning (see my book *The Mysteries of John the Baptist*). According to the very late Jewish-Christian propagandist work, the anti-Pauline *Pseudo-Clementine Romance* (ca. 325 CE), Simon was a colleague of John the Baptist, and had Simon not been in Alexandria when John was executed (ca. 36 CE), he would have succeeded John.

An intriguing story told by Josephus[2] of a Samaritan hothead who whipped up the people to gather for a procession from Tirathaba up to the Samaritans' holy mountain and temple at Mount Gerizim (close to Nablus) in Samaria in 36 or 37 CE, sounds a lot like the Simon who, according to patristic writers, was worshipped by huge numbers in Samaria and whose magical operations seriously troubled the apostles. Samaritans did not recognize Jerusalem as the site of God's temple. In fact, this unnamed Samaritan who excited a large assembly of people into believing that the sacred vessels of Moses were secreted in Mount Gerizim (as Josephus relates) was the indirect cause of a major atrocity at Tirathaba when the people gathered in anticipation of a revelation at Mount Gerizim. The Tirathaba gathering coincided with Syrian governor Vitellius's preparations for a march south through Samaria against Nabataea. Fearing a Samaritan insurrection could frustrate Vitellius's plans, Prefect of Judaea Pontius Pilate dispatched cavalry to Tirathaba, ordering the strongest of those captured to be killed. Luke 13:1–5's reference to a Roman slaughter of "Galileans," may reflect the atrocity, for the Roman military regarded the word "Galilean" as synonymous with "troublemaker"; it could have referred both to Samaritan nationalists or zealots from Galilee. In fact it was the Samaritan senate's complaint to Vitellius over Pilate's conduct that led to Pilate's being directed to Rome to answer for himself in 37 CE, a process apparently stalled by the Emperor Tiberius's death and Caligula's accession. These events, I argue in my book *The Mysteries of John the Baptist,* conditioned the trial and crucifixion of Jesus, which I confidently date to March of that year.

There is certainly enough information about Simon (who shared his name with the pillar of the church better known as Peter) to enable us to treat the account of Simon in Acts as simply another piece of the mysterious jigsaw puzzle in which the historical existence of Simon Magus is scattered.

The links that Acts makes between Simon and the baptizing activities of Philip are intriguing in this respect. According to Acts, Simon received the water-baptism of Philip but proved to be more interested, the story goes, in the reception of the Holy Spirit from the hands of Peter. If Simon Magus was a colleague of John the Baptist, then he had no need of Philip's ministrations. Perhaps it was Apostle Philip who was, or had been, involved with John's or Simon's entourage, or both.

It seems likely that church tradition at the time of the composition of Acts required a narrative showing Simon as a condemned breakaway from Jesus's salvation, and not an independent religious genius. We know there are serious problems in trying to understand the primitive church's relations with John's baptism and followers, glossed over in Acts. We may also note that the figure of Apollos in Acts (18:24–25), and from Paul's letters (*viz.* I Corinthians 1:12), who knows and preaches only John's baptism—deficient according to Paul—came from Alexandria. Paul claims to have come to an accommodation with him, but he and Apollos went their separate ways, anyway. If only we had a time machine to see how all of this really fit together on the ground at the time! I'm sure it was very different from the traditionally entertained sequence of events.

A notable and possibly telling absence from the Acts account of Simon trying to buy the magic of the Holy Spirit is any note of the presence of Simon's feminine consort. All other accounts of Simon are consistent in naming her as Helen or Helena, and all accounts make it clear that this woman was not only his constant traveling companion but was a central figure and symbol of his personal cult. Intriguingly, the Greek *Helenē* means "torch"; she is a source of illumination. Simon apparently made much of the mythology surrounding her alleged incarnation as Helen of Troy, daughter of Zeus and Leda, who was kidnapped into earthly incarceration by Paris (a parallel with archontic conceit). The name encapsulated a complete Gnostic symbol.

Simonians worshipped images of Simon and Helen at their assemblies, offering sacrifices and libations before them: a scandalous idea to the orthodox and one universally regarded by heresiologists as typically, blasphemously Gnostic. Carpocratians were also accused of worshipping pictures of their spiritual and philosophical heroes, including Jesus. Pictures of Jesus are now, of course, commonplace in churches, places of entertainment, and bedrooms.

We have the at-first-sight rather colorful story of Simon discovering Helen in a brothel in Tyre, Phoenicia, and realizing that this ignominiously oppressed whore was his lost Idea or First Thought from primal times before he, Simon, as first God, got wrapped up in the creation of the cosmos and its demonic rulers: rulers who progressively raped and abused Helen through a series of vicious incarnations. Simon's followers, who Eusebius asks us to believe, persisted—rather remarkably—into the fourth century, held the two as an eternal syzygy, promising liberation from the powers of the world. Helen was perhaps the original "tart with a heart."

One can hardly escape the feeling that this story of Simon and his redeemed prostitute has some historical truth behind it, for, in it, do we not get a glimpse of the remarkable, alienated, naughty humor of this curious Samaritan egotist whom church history regarded as a victim of his own stupendous pride?

Believing he could fly, goes the apocryphal story of wide patristic currency, Peter challenged Simon to a duel in Rome: a duel of wills. Simon did, according to the Acts of Peter and other apocryphal accounts, fly by magic, but Peter implored the Lord to quash the demons sustaining Simon's flight. Simon died, apparently, from wounds so inflicted, and was, according to Justin Martyr, honored in Rome with a statue and inscription. This alleged Simonian inscription was discovered on an island in the Tiber in 1574, its dedication addressed to the god Sancus, not Simon; either Justin Martyr's Latin was not very good or he received the tale as hearsay! The story of Simon's fatal flight was retold in Paul Newman's first starring vehicle, *The Silver Chalice* (1954), where in a nuanced and villainous role, the splendidly sinister Jack Palance played Simon. Paul Newman regretted the film, but it is a brave outpost of maverick creativity in a timid early-1950s Hollywood that just doesn't quite come off, being a trifle too artistic (Symbolist tropes dominate), experimental, and otherworldly for its own good: a bit like Simon Magus perhaps. In 1994–1995, Columba Powell and I wrote a comedic time-travel movie script with Simon Magus as the main protagonist, searching for Helen in the 1920s movie industry, with a cunning plan to go back to the first century and film the Resurrection! Yet to appear, *The Gatecrashers* (as we called the script) at least testifies that contrary to Simon's patristic opponents, he is still the standing one and has not yet lain down and disappeared for the church's convenience.

I hope readers will forgive the digression, but it gives us a flavor of the remarkable individual or, if you prefer, crazy son of a bitch who all the heresiologists are content to see as the father of the "gnosis falsely so-called." If they were right about this—a supposition very far from certain—Simon Magus would have to be a larger-than-life character, and it is distressing, in a way, that it is practically impossible to get beyond the image of him painted (but not worshipped) by his enemies, the "straight-teachers" or orthodox, who have loathed and reviled him and everything he stood or stands for to this very day.

SEX AND SIMON

Besides Acts, Justin Martyr's was the first account of Simon, coming less than a century after Simon's adventurous heyday. What I think cries out from Justin's, admittedly hostile, account is that from the very start, we cannot avoid the fact that sex has a lot to do with Simon's image in the minds of heresiologists, and what's more, sex has a lot to do with Simon himself and his self-regarding proclamations. Was he providing an ironic, superior, knowing comment on the claims of a certain messiah active in Phoenicia as well as Galilee and Judea? Was Simon's the kind of creative mind that could have written a *Life of Brian,* to show the fallacies eagerly entertained by the "sheep" that thoughtlessly follow signs and wonders? For Simon knew all about signs and wonders: they were his stock-in-trade. Like Turner (as played by Mick Jagger) in Nick Roeg and Donald Cammell's fabulous 1969 movie *Performance,* Simon knew a thing or two about *performing.* He could do more than juggle, my friend. He could play the crowds. As Turner says in that infinitely fascinating spectacle: The performance that counts, the one that really "makes it" . . . *is the one that achieves madness!*

What are we to make of a man who picks up a whore in a brothel, a despised person, and makes of her his queen of heaven? Is he a romantic? Helen is a whore. Simon befriends her, makes her his equal. What a duo they must have been! But were they acting? Was it all a pose, like Aleister Crowley and his "Scarlet Women," or was it, like Crowley again, a pose, but something profound as well? For the time being, we must content ourselves with the reports of the heresiologists. That's a pity, I know, but this isn't a film, it's an investigation, let us not forget, into Gnostic sex.

The theme of jealous angels "coming on" as God, appears in the earliest stratum of Simonian discourse, but we cannot be sure how much of this was backdated to the mid-first century by second-century "Gnosticized" Simonians. It is possible that Simon's alleged followers in the second and fourth centuries were already Gnostics who fastened their outlook onto the legends of Simon: stories about him made him a very eligible candidate for Gnostic mythologizing. However, it is also possible that Simon self-mythologized and interpreted his own experience through an extravagantly synthetic, and original, personal mythos to impress impressionable audiences. According to opponents, he was quite prepared to assume another's identity. Thus, the story goes, he claimed he had appeared as the Son among Jews, as the Father in Samaria, and as the Holy Spirit among other nations. His fame during his own lifetime, however, seems to have been built less on theological audacities than on the ability to deceive the eye by "miracles"; how much of his magic was pure trickery, how much occult, and how much enlightened manipulation of public ignorance, we cannot now know. Whatever he did, he was very good at it, and it was clearly threatening to the primitive church.

The connection between Simon's First Thought—almost certainly a product of Alexandrian Sophia speculation—and the Helen compelled to operate in a Tyrian brothel is highly resonant, when we consider the second-century Gnostic presentation of Wisdom as both virgin and whore: she who gives herself freely but remains ever pure, she who has "mucked in" with the world, deeply involved in its evolution, while remaining radiantly, and resolutely, divine, literally untouched by progress; she whom the world cannot denigrate. I can imagine a clever, perhaps too clever, man using such ideas to glorify his activities, selling the yarn to his followers; unless, of course, he genuinely believed Helen was in fact the Wisdom abused through time, subject to reincarnations by wicked angels. We have an echo of such ideas perhaps in the usually sentimentalized traditions regarding Jesus's "hanging out" (as we might say today) with prostitutes, coming to the rescue of a woman taken in flagrante, and being accessible to, and healing, the woman with the issue of blood (in Jewish terms, an "unclean" person): all stories, which Gnostic commentators took as allegories, illustrating and authorizing their systems. And, of course, in the third-century Gnostic *Gospel of Philip,* Mary Magdalene has become the symbol of Wisdom herself, and the personal consort—powerfully reminiscent of the Tyrian Helen—of the Savior who often "kissed" her (that is, imparted his spirit to her). This is all intriguing and we shall return to this echo-laden myth, but we have not as yet found out whether Simon taught any distinctive sexual practice to be passed on to others of his, or his pretended, persuasion.

What saith Irenaeus?

Now this Simon of Samaria, from whom all sorts of heresies derive their origin, formed his sect out of the following materials: Having redeemed from slavery at Tyre, a city of Phoenicia, a certain woman named Helena, he was in the habit of carrying her about with him, declaring that this woman was the first conception of his mind, the mother of all, by whom, in the beginning, he conceived in his mind [the thought] of forming angels and archangels. For this Ennoea [First Thought] leaping forth from him, and comprehending the will of her father, descended to the lower regions [of space], and generated angels and powers, by whom also he declared this word was formed. But after she had produced them, she was detained by them through motives of jealousy, because they were unwilling to be looked upon as the progeny of any other being. As to himself, they had no knowledge of him whatever; but his Ennoea was detained by those powers and angels who had been produced by her. She suffered all kinds of contumely [insulting language and treatment] from them, so that she could not return upwards to her father, but was even shut up in a human body, and for ages passed in succession from one female body to another, as from vessel to vessel. She was, for example, in that Helen on whose account the Trojan War was undertaken; for whose sake also Stesichorus was struck blind, because he had cursed her in his verses, but afterwards, repenting and writing what are called palinodes, in which he sang her praise, he was restored to sight. Thus she, passing from body to body, and suffering insults in every one of them, at last became a common prostitute; and she it was that was meant by the lost sheep. (*Adversus Haereses,* I.23, 2)

Well, there is no sign here of unusual sexual practices; quite the opposite in fact. Poor Helena is abused time and time again through all time by the very powers she has created.

Two things are worth noting here. First, Irenaeus uses the expression "leaping forth from him." This suggestion of Sophia's vigorous precociousness is developed in other Gnostic systems into a full-blown, sexually driven extroversion on Sophia's part that, as we have indicated, tears a wound in the harmony of the Pleroma. Here, however, the creation of the angelic hierarchy is presented as Sophia's correct comprehension of the Father's will—not in defiance of it as in the Valentinian speculation.

Sophia is stuck in her lower creation on account of jealousy. The angels, desirous of possessing her, while neutralizing her power, and knowing not their ultimate origin, cannot cope with the idea of a superior being. No one, to my knowledge, has ever suggested that behind this myth might also lurk the covert message that the pagan gods of Rome and Greece are the jealous and sexually cruel oppressors of the monotheism of the Samaritans, with which Simon appears to identify, though apparently in a staggeringly arrogant manner. I also would suggest that we see here at work the same kind of speculation about the spiritual powers that be that we find in its purely Jewish form in the apocryphal *Book of Enoch,* the hottest esoteric work of the first century (the lost text of which, by the way, was brought from Ethiopia to London by Scottish explorer James Bruce in 1774, along with the Gnostic *Books of Jeu*).

It seems perfectly plausible to imagine that the classic Gnostic archons (rulers), the grim angels who control material existence across the spectrum of developed Gnostic mythology, were a development on the picture presented in *Enoch* that I show in my books, *The Missing Family of Jesus* and *The Mysteries of John the Baptist,* to explain the authentic antidemonic ministry, or operation of Jesus and the Natsarim (Watchers, Keepers, or Guardians).

In the earliest part of the *Book of Enoch,* which we know to have been in circulation by 37 CE, Enoch is called to publish from Dan (Caesarea Philippi) the divine intention of permanently putting in bonds the wicked, fallen Watchers, who, according to Genesis 6, had fled heaven, so enamored were they of the beauty of human women, and through whose lust, the *Nephilim,* or "sons of God" begat a race of giants. The *Book of Enoch* recounts the corruption of God's creation to these beings, while deliverance from them constituted an apocalyptic scenario of cosmic importance. Significantly, these fallen Watchers were identified as the gods of the Gentile world; such a subversive thought can only have given confidence to Jews and Samaritans oppressed by the ruthless forces of the Roman Empire.

St. Paul's *ta stoicheia tou kosmou* ("elementary principles of the universe") in Galatians 4:3, 9 and Colossians 2:8 appears to have been equated in Ephesians 6:12 (long held erroneously to be Paul's exclusive work) with the principalities and powers that are the enemies of Christ. The epistle of Judas (Jude v. 14, probably written by Jesus's brother during the persecutions of Herod Agrippa in the 40s CE) correctly attributes the prophecy against the wicked Watchers to Enoch. If the historical Simon Magus did claim his Helena to have been since the beginning of time assaulted by angels, the Enochian prophetic picture appears to have been familiar to him. Besides, the basic idea is already to be found in Genesis 6, familiar to Samaritans. Helena was only the first to be subjected to sexual enslavement by the wicked powers, jealous of her spectacular sexual nature and beauty of mind, and keen to drag it down to their filthy, egotistical level.

It should be noted that such an inference would rather suggest that Simon was a kind of generous proto-feminist with sympathy for those subjected to corruption and sexual oppression in the real world. His redemption then is a magician's transformation: he denies the reality of the world as itself a trick, a hallucination, and exposes its architects.

He can practice free love because he has freed his love from the grip of the world's corrupters. As a magician of the period, he would certainly have been familiar with Enoch's ascription of blame for the world's condition to Azazel, the leader of the Enochian, fallen Watchers; it was a magician's first duty to acquaint himself with the ruling demons of the world and subject them to his power. If Simon had seriously undertaken this path, then he had reason to see himself as being above the world and as a god in human form. We should recognize the peculiar interest magicians have always taken in religion, as providing theoretical, epistemological content for practical application. If Enoch declared the wicked Watchers bound by the Father of Light's command to Earth, then a magician could, in theory, control them, as long as his consciousness was sufficiently exalted; and this exaltation of consciousness to union with the One beyond creation (the Father) appears to be the root supporting the claims Simon's followers (note!) made for their master.

Now, it does not take quite the amazing leap we might have thought it did to progress (if that is the right word) from the thought that the world was corrupted by evil angels who had been involved in its first creation, to asking whether these evil beings had also corrupted the books sacred to Jews; that is to say, that words attributed to God in the scriptures were the surreptitious, deceiving work of lower powers or a single dominant but lower power, so that aspects of the Jewish God as expressed in the scriptures—jealous, angry, intolerant, conquering, violent, capricious—collectively constituted an inferior, enslaving deity.

It must be remembered that Simon was a Samaritan, and Judean religious authorities reviled Samaritans. Samaritans were accused of holding to a false version of Mosaic law, of being essentially foreign (allegedly having been transplanted by Assyrian powers to what had been Israel from Cutha in what is now Iraq, and from elsewhere), for falsely believing Mount Gerizim was where God ordered his name to be established, and of having tolerated and practiced paganism. When Luke's Jesus tells the parable indicating the Samaritan was a superior neighbor to the afflicted than the religious authorities of Judea, he would have utterly astounded most of his listeners, though Samaritans would have been chuffed.

Since we have testimony that Simon favored Mount Gerizim over Jerusalem's Temple Mount, in conformity with the Samaritan understanding of themselves as Guardians, Keepers, and Watchers of the preexilic law (they had their own preexilic version of the Pentateuch), and that Simon may have been the leader referred to by Josephus who called for a public march to Gerizim to find the authentic, secreted Mosaic sacred vessels (including the Ark?), it would seem a considerably advantageous thought to realize Simon Magus had a stake in showing inadequacies in the precious Judean sacred manuscript tradition, significant aspects of which denigrated and excluded Samaritans.

This then is one possible origin for what became much of the Gnostic Demiurge myth whereby a deficient deity established himself with threats as the ultimate God, whose weapon was the rod of the law, but who was not the father of Jesus, the angel come to Earth as a man. This understanding helps us also to see in a flash why the issue of sex reappears consistently in a Gnostic and anti-Gnostic context. Simon's intuition may have revealed to him that the authentic sexual impulse is the impulse of divine creation—the First Thought—a magical power that has become enslaved and perverted by men terrified of false gods.

Sex then is the essential battleground between heresy and orthodoxy, in whose historic denigration, orthodoxy saw itself triumphant as if over Azazel, the great Tempter, himself!

If it was sex that brought the wicked Watchers down from heaven, then could not sex redeemed take the good Watchers back to their eternal home?

Not if your name was Irenaeus! Despite himself, however, in reporting the beliefs of Simonians, Irenaeus's following passage precisely confirms the interpretation of Simon's magic I have offered above. Subtract the negative charge that infuses the statement, and it becomes a straightforward account of the metaphysical underpinning for freed love, and, if I may say so, cosmic sex—no wonder Simon had his devotees!

For this purpose, then, he [Simon] had come that he might win her first, and free her from slavery, while he conferred salvation upon men, by making himself known to them. For since the angels ruled the world badly because each one of them coveted the principal power for himself, he had come to amend matters, and had descended, transfigured, and assimilated to powers and principalities and angels, so that he might appear among men to be a man, while yet he was not a man; and that thus he was thought to have suffered in Judaea, when he had not suffered [a significant Gnostic position regarding the crucifixion]. Moreover, the prophets uttered their predictions under the inspiration of those angels who formed the world [the Jewish scriptures were flawed]; for which reason those who place their trust in him and Helena no longer regarded them, but, as being free, live as they please; for men are saved through his grace, and not on account of their own righteous actions [the law does not justify—a Pauline doctrine!]. For such deeds are not righteous in the nature of things, but by mere accident, just as those angels who made the world, have thought fit to constitute them, seeking, by means of such precepts, to bring men into bondage. On this account, he pledged himself that the world should be dissolved, and that those who are his should be freed from the rule of them who made the world. (*Adversus Haereses*, I.23, 4)

If my interpretation is on the right lines, we can see at once what gives the Gnostic essence its most peculiar characteristic, which so enraged orthodox minds. This was a liberationist religion conceived by a magician. Gnosis is in essence a magical religion; not content with metaphysical theory, it engages, in Simon's instance, with metaphysical practice. It becomes a vehicle for the will, and the will to power: enabling man to rise and work his wonders, and leads to the tumultuous statement of the Hermetic *Asklēpios:* "A great miracle, O Asklepios, is man!"

No! says Irenaeus, leading the orthodox opposition choir; on the contrary: man is a great sinner! And none greater, it would appear, than Simon Magus!

Irenaeus was never likely to see how the tale of Simon's offering to buy the trick of passing on the Holy Spirit by laying on of hands makes perfect sense to a magical ironist and parody-messiah, eager to know what his rival (?) Jesus had let his followers in on. (In this context, it is interesting to note in Gnostic literature how Jesus passes on his holy spirit, not through hands—the Pauline apostolic rite—but by kissing; that is, passing the breath of life from mouth to mouth.) Such a tradition is, of course, wide open to debasement of its high intention, and the tone of Irenaeus's last word on Simon Magus makes it clear that Irenaeus thought such debasement had always been the case, rather than the equal possibility of its having been a degeneration over the five generations of followers between Simon's heyday and Irenaeus's time:

> Thus, then, the mystic priests belonging to this sect both lead profligate lives and practise magical arts, each one to the extent of his ability. They use exorcisms and incantations. Love-potions, too, and charms, as well as those beings who are called Paredri [familiars] and Oniropompi [dream-senders], and whatever other curious arts can be had recourse to, are eagerly pressed into their service. They also have an image of Simon fashioned after the likeness of Jupiter, and another of Helena in the shape of Minerva; and these they worship. To sum up, they have a name derived from Simon, the author of these most impious doctrines, being called Simonians; and from them "knowledge, falsely so-called" received its beginning, as one may learn even from their own assertions.

Notable here is the sexual equality granted Simon and Helena and the Simonians' own belief that the gnosis originated with them. The implication of "profligate lives" means surely that they practiced free love, as the righteous would see it, whether in or entirely outside marriage is not indicated. Sexual love was apparently very important to the mystic priests. Was it a part of their ritual? Using incantations was a theurgic means of calling on higher spiritual powers to purify ritual acts. That they practiced exorcisms, as did the apostles, also suggests a picture of Simonian priests (and priestesses?) involved in a ministry of liberating souls from lower powers, that is, from cosmic angels or possessive demons. That they did not conform to the standards of St. Paul is clear. Paul, and we may suppose Irenaeus too, regarded women as secondary and potentially dangerous and sex as something of a problem, necessitating strict marriage in order to lessen its immoral impact on the soul, for flesh and blood could not inherit eternal life. Simonians, like other Gnostics, seem to have agreed in part with this view, but they asserted also that flesh and blood infused with spiritual intelligence, united in high intention, can assist in raising the mind to mystical, divine levels, and that to transform sex from the wicked angels' imprisoning cycle of mere lust and reproduction constituted the redemption of sex and the paradoxical sanctification of sin through love. Was it not Jesus who said, "Be ye therefore as wise as serpents, and as harmless as doves" (Matthew 10:16) and "The light of the body is the eye: if therefore thine eye be single, thy whole body is full of light" (Matthew 6:22)?

SIMON SAYS—ACCORDING TO HIPPOLYTUS

Hippolytus's treatment of Simon Magus is very different from that of Irenaeus. In fact, he devotes fourteen meaty chapters (2–15) of book VI of his *Refutation of All Heresies* to expounding on the Samaritan magician's philosophy. However, he establishes the idea that Simon's doctrines now travel under a change of name, so he may be describing a variety of groups who share something in common with the tradition of Simon: the Carpocratians, for example. He recognizes that Simon's legacy is basically one of magic and cites a magician called Thrasymedes as a kind of progenitor, or possibly successor (book IV of Hippolytus's *Elenchos,* containing a section on Thrasymedes, has not survived). Anyway, Hippolytus's main thrust is that the philosophy of Simon is a pinch from Pythagoreanism and pre-Socratic philosophers such as Heraclitus. However, the practice of Simonian groups he immediately condemns as orgiastic; they inspire God's anger.

Simon attempted to deify himself, but was a "mere cheat, and full of folly." To grasp that folly, Hippolytus cites the case of the Libyan Apsethus who tried to become a god. Having failed to convince his compatriots of his divine nature, he taught a parrot to say, "Apsethus is a god," which the parrot spread abroad until other birds throughout North Africa parroted the phrase. All nature then seemed to testify to Apsethus's divinity—but it was a trick, and so Hippolytus takes Simon's following as just such a trick and a gormless parroting of something without substance. His followers are "parrots." That's for starters!

Hippolytus then attributes to Simon a speculative text of some interest, titled: *This is the treatise of a revelation of [the] voice and name [recognizable] by means of intellectual apprehension of the Great Indefinite Power. Wherefore it will be sealed, [and] kept secret, [and] hid, [and] will repose in the habitation, at the foundation of which lies the root of all things.* The element of fire is not simple; it has, asserts Simon, a double nature (this Hippolytus attributes to Aristotle's distinction between "intelligible" and "sensible" natures). Behind the visible creation is a hidden, secret fire, protean or indefinite—in the sense also of undefined, limitless, and undefinable. It is likened to a tree. This correspondence of the fire and the tree will become more resonant as we pursue our secret sexual gnosis in due course.

> [. . .] the super-celestial [fire], is a treasure, as it were a large tree, just such a one as in a dream was seen by Nabuchodonosor [Nebuchadnezzar], out of which all flesh is nourished. And the manifest portion of the fire he regards as the stem, the branches, the leaves, [and] the external rind which overlaps them. All these [appendages], he says, of the Great Tree being kindled, are made to disappear by reason of the blaze of the all-devouring fire. The fruit, however, of the tree, when it is fully grown, and has received

its own form, is deposited in a granary, not (flung) into the fire. For, he says, the fruit has been produced for the purpose of being laid in the storehouse, whereas the chaff that it may be delivered over to the fire. [Now the chaff] is stem, [and is] generated not for its own sake, but for that of the fruit. (*Refutatio*, VI, 4)

Hippolytus does not have much to say about what seems to me to be a fairly straightforward myth of sexual alchemy, allegorizing John the Baptist's speech in Matthew 3:7–12, where John announces that every tree that bears not fruit will be burned in the harvest fire. John goes on to explain a coming baptism of fire, later claimed by Paul to be his hand-baptism as opposed to John's and Apollos of Alexandria's "mere" baptism of water. This harvesting or judgment fire is the root of the Simonian fire above: the fire that, says Simon in a Kabbalah-style observation, illuminated Moses's burning bush. When the body or rind is burned away by its all-devouring fire, what remains is the fruit of spirit, the fire invisible to the uninitiated, but existing within and sustaining all things. The lusts of the flesh are *consumed* by the fire in the supreme rite, revealing the essence of the Great Tree wherein God speaks to the holy. That an actual spiritual-sexual rite is being alluded to by allegorical means becomes clearer when we read what Hippolytus next has to say about Simon's justification, a quotation from scripture:

And this, he [Simon] says, is what has been written in Scripture: "For the vineyard of the Lord of Sabaoth is the house of Israel, and the man of Judah is His beloved plant." [Isaiah 5:7 paraphrase] If, however, the man of Judah the beloved plant, it has been proved, he says, that there is not any other tree but that man. But concerning the secretion and dissolution of this [tree], Scripture, he says, has spoken sufficiently. And as regards instruction for those who have been fashioned after the image [of him], that statement is enough which is made [in Scripture], that "all flesh is grass, and all the glory of flesh, as it were, a flower of grass. The grass withereth, and its flower falleth; but the word of the Lord abideth forever." The word of the Lord, he says, is that word which is produced in the mouth, and a Logos, but nowhere else exists there a place of generation. (*Refutatio*, VI, 5)

The last cryptic sentence of the quotation above refers, we can be fairly sure, to the vagina of the priestess, understood as the mystic yoni: the place of generation where the Logos, that is the Word, becomes flesh and vice versa. The body dissolves in the fire of supernal orgasm, bringing forth the pure fire secreted *within* the fire: God. That the plant is expressed in the phallus is clear enough. The secret is contained in the words "the secretion and dissolution of this [tree]." At the height of passionate fire, the plant withers, but its engendered virtue "liveth forever," that is, the seed partakes of the substance of eternity: the new seed also has within it the hidden fire. This is a formula for the magical energizing of sexual fluids. Now perhaps we can understand better the famous injunction in the Gnostic *Gospel of Thomas* that *If you do not bring forth what is within you, what is within you will destroy you*: spiritual orgasm is salvation; suppression of the seed is death. That plant that does not bring forth fruit unto the Lord will be swallowed up in its external fire. One can only wonder if John the Baptist, historically, had any inkling of such allegorical conceptions. According to Simonian tradition, he did, for John was the herald of the harvest, the master of ceremonies at the Hermetic conflagration!

Hippolytus doesn't "get" any of this at all. He seems to think he's reading a treatise on philosophy like Heraclitus's speculations on the origin of the universe (created from primal Fire). Hippolytus next throws in Empedocles as the source for the speculation contained in another work attributed to Simon: the *Apophasis Megalē*, or "Great Announcement."

Hippolytus outlines a confused account of the existence of six roots—the tree theme again—made from the fire in pairs, these root-pairs being Mind and Intelligence, Voice and Name, Ratiocination and

Reflection: all aspects of consciousness, which, when activated together, creating awareness, generate progeny: the Logos or Son "without whom was nothing made" (John 1.3). The child of the magic rite is its willed intention made manifest.

Within the six roots, the indefinite power exists in potential, but not in actuality. The magic is necessary to turn potential into realization. The indefinite power is identified with Simon's followers' soubriquet for their erect master: "He who stood, stands and will stand." What he can stand is the fire, the purging, the judgment, or testing that comes to all created things: the fire within. Interestingly, the Mandaeans believe their great prophet, John the Baptist, could not be burned by fire; Simonians claimed precisely the same for their master.

The scriptural source for the standing motif appears to be Malachi 3:1–2, where Malachi (the "messenger") declares the coming of God's messenger who will purge the sons of Levi: "But who may abide the day of his coming? And who shall stand when he [the messenger] appeareth?" The quotation is key to Mark's gospel's introduction to the message of John the Baptist. *Who can "stand" when the messenger appeareth?*

Interestingly, the Simonian text then suggests that this name can apply to all people who realize in themselves the potential of the six roots. If, however, the indefinite power of the six roots remains only in potential, the six roots then fail to produce an image, and the man vanishes. This vanishing is compared to loss of intellectual ability in senility. The six roots offer the capacity to take on an art, whereby "a light of existent things" is produced, but if the capacity does not take unto itself an art, "unskillfulness and ignorance" result, and as with the power becoming nonexistent from nonexpression, the capacity dies with the expiring man. In this case, the man has not stood and therefore will not stand. This is a fine reworking of the spiritual message of the parable of the sower and, on a more prosaic, banal level, the "use it or lose it" ethic. Hippolytus doesn't grasp the humor of it at all.

The hidden fire needs to seize its means of expression, and therefore, one can see what Hippolytus apparently cannot, that this Simonian tradition was advocating a form of sexual magic as the means of realizing the potential inner man, awakening abilities dormant in the soul and firing up the great hidden being of man to his proper dimensions: *become the genius, or die!* This dovetails with Jesus's saying that "For whoever has, to him more shall be given; and whoever does not have, even what he has shall be taken away from him," and indeed explains what otherwise might seem like a merely vindictive warning (Mark 4:25; *cf.* Matthew 25:29).

Sexual imagery is even more explicit in the further adumbration of the Simonian system. Of the seven powers (the six root-pairs, plus the "indefinite power"), the first pair, Mind and Intelligence, are called Heaven and Earth, where *Heaven* is masculine, looking down from above on his partner, the *Earth,* who receives from above the "rational fruits, akin to the Earth." It seems the "missionary position" has Gnostic significance. (We may also think of Isis, born of the coitus of Geb—the Earth—and Nuit—the starry heavens above.)

The Logos, says the Great Announcement, is always looking to what Mind and Intelligence generate from the intercourse of heaven and Earth, and as the seventh power (he who stands), exclaims: "Hear, O Heaven, and give ear, O Earth, because the Lord has spoken. I have brought forth children, and exalted them; and these have rejected me."

Voice and *Name* correspond to Sun and Moon, while *Ratiocination* and *Reflection* correspond to Air and Water, all significant principles in Egyptian alchemy. These are linked to the Simonian allegorical treatment of the six days of creation in Genesis, considered as Moses's composition; with the creation presented as a kind of alchemical operation.

Thus, there were three days before sun and moon appeared, the three days standing for Mind and Intelligence (Heaven and Earth) plus the seventh power (which we might call the indefinable ever-existent). According to the Simonian text, this seventh power is that referred to by Moses in Genesis 1:2 thus: "And the spirit of God was wafted over the water." We can see that the Simonians have linked the magical sexual generation to the primal creation of the heavens and the Earth. That too involved the actualization of the indefinite power or spirit of God functioning as: "an image from an incorruptible form that alone reduces all things to order."

This "image" is very close to the *logos* of Stoicism, that philosophy founded by Cypriot Zeno of Citium in the second century BCE: *logos* being the intelligible formative and distinguishing principle in all things. The Jewish philosopher Philo of Alexandria (ca. 20 BCE–50 CE), Simon's older contemporary, identified the Stoic logos with Sophia (Greek for the Hebrew Hokhmah = Wisdom).

Genesis 1:26 has God (*Elohim* = Gods) saying: "Let *us* create man in *our* image." The first-person plural us was taken in first and second century Alexandria to suggest the Logos-Sophia's being coinstrumental in man's creation, and according to Philo (*de Opficio Mundi* 74–75), it was in fact the shared nature of the work that accounted for man's imperfection! Man was "good" but not absolutely perfect or, in Simonian terms, not fully actualized; he did not have the gnosis automatically.

The Simonian text now links powerfully the creation of man with the warning of judgment-fire that permanently condemns the potential but not actualized world:

[...] the Deity, he says, proceeded to form man, taking clay from the earth. And He formed him not uncompounded, but twofold, according to [His own] image and likeness. Now the image is the Spirit that is wafted over the water; and whosoever is not fashioned into a figure of this will perish with the world, inasmuch as he continues only potentially, and does exist actually. This, he says, is what has been spoken, "that we should not be condemned with the world." If one, however, be made into the figure of (the Spirit), and be generated from an indivisible point, as it has been written in the Announcement, [such a one, albeit] small, will become great. But what is great will continue unto infinite and unalterable duration, as being that which no longer is subject to the conditions of a generated entity. (*Refutatio*, VI, 9)

The Great Announcement next asks where God formed man. *Answer:* in paradise. The Simonian text jumps to interpret *paradise* as referring to the womb, offering the following text as suggestive proof: "I am He who forms thee in thy mother's womb" (Isaiah 44:24; *cf.* Psalm 139:13; Jeremiah 1:5). Well wide of the mark, Hippolytus's concern is that this interpretation not only forces the text, but that it is not a properly exact quotation either! Clever Hippolytus continually misses the point that the text is offering spiritual allegories for rituals of sacramentalized sex, possibly to the end of producing children made in the image of the seventh power: such children being either actual and sensible or, more likely perhaps, willed intentions born into the world of cause and effect from male and female intercourse to accomplish the magician's (the awakened man's) will.

The will is accomplished through the child's acting upon the universal potential fire with actualizing, superior occult fire. This is, that fire stolen by the lower angels from heaven and abused by the ignorant in this world, as Helena was abused, while never being truly possessed, until her father and consort returned to her. This is the Simonian conception of Holy Spirit. Until one understands the occult meaning of this mythos, the signs on the gates of the Gnostic garden will forever be misunderstood, as indeed they appear to have been by most scholars in the field, with some few notable exceptions, as we shall see.

Chapter 10 of book VI of the *Refutatio* is a little more difficult, especially on account of the manner in which Hippolytus has expressed his Simonian source, but it is not too hard to see behind his garbling a coded account of the magical value of spiritually directed sex and sexual fluids.

The Simonian text takes the rivers that flow from Eden (the womb) as signifying the four senses pertaining to the child in the womb: sight, taste, smell, and touch. Four of the five Mosaic books are said to refer to these senses. Genesis pertains to *vision,* for vision is necessary to acquire first knowledge of the universe. Exodus pertains to taste. To go beyond vision of the universe, which even the Gentiles have, it is necessary to be liberated, signified by crossing the Red Sea, which the text indicates as blood. To tread that liquid path leads to knowledge, but is nonetheless a path that first entails entering the wilderness, tasted through bitter water reflecting the bitterness of the human existential lot, without knowledge, that is. However, Moses sweetens the bitter water by means of the Logos (Moses strikes the rock with his magic rod in the wilderness generating trickling nourishment for the thirsty; Exodus 17:5–7), whereafter this knowledge (gnosis) is expressed by Homer: "Dark at the root, like milk, the flower, Gods call it 'Moly,' and hard for mortal men to dig, but power divine is boundless."

The Exodus is an escape from the values of this world, the world of dark powers. The symbolism seems fairly plain to this author: escape requires a transgressive leap. First, the menstrual blood should be drunk as a reminder of what has been left behind: the fruitless existence. The passing of sacramentalized semen to the otherwise infertile womb generates, through mixture with vaginal fluids, a milk that is the flower of the primal, divine generation whose boundless power divine constitutes the elixir of the sect. It is as ironic as it is remarkable that Hippolytus has inadvertently passed on to the profane the secrets of sexual magic without ever realizing it!

That the elixir was for consumption is indicated in the reference to "moly," a magical herb. In book 10 of Homer's *Odyssey,* Hermes offers it to Odysseus as an antidote to Circe's magic: the bewitchment of the world as Simonians would see it. Believed to have grown from the blood of the Gigante killed on the Isle of Kirke, the plant has a white flower. Helios (the Sun) was Kirke's ally in defeating the Gigante. The plant's name was believed to come from the hardness (Greek: *malos*) of the combat: the fruit of the bitter phase in Simonian understanding. These details further suggest the vigorous sacrificial sexual connotations significant to Simonians, as do Homer's words describing it: "The root was black, while the flower was as white as milk; the gods call it Moly, Dangerous for a mortal man to pluck from the soil, but not for the deathless gods. All lies within their power."

These "deathless gods" then are the Simonians who have actualized their potential fire. Awakening to this power is the subject of the Great Announcement and the reason, according to the Simonians, for Simon's Samaritan title as the Great Power of God. That great power exists *in potentia* in every man and woman. Humanity will escape the bonds of Earth!

Simonian interpretations of the nature of the books of Leviticus, Numbers, and Deuteronomy (also attributed to Moses) follow the sexually symbolic lines of Genesis and Exodus. Thus, since Leviticus deals with sacrifices—giving of self in orgasm—it corresponds to the child's sense of smell. The book of Numbers obscurely correlates with the sense of taste to numerical arrangement, "where the discourse is operative." Since Deuteronomy is a summary of the preceding four pentateuchal books in terms of law, Simonians regard it as corresponding to the sense of touch: "testing what is rough or warm or clammy."

What exists in humankind that is of God (unbegotten), being only potential, not actual, requires then external instruction, which received, can make the bitter sweet and turn swords into plowshares. Quoting John the Baptist: "Every tree, he says, which does not produce good fruit, is hewn down and cast into the fire" (Matthew 3:10). Correct sexual knowledge ensures the production of the "good fruit," and the generation of those that "can stand and will stand": generations other Gnostics will call the generation of Seth, for Seth was Adam's child perfected, after the disaster of Cain and Abel.

We have then in the Simonian Great Announcement that which has been rendered obscure in the Valentinian and Sethian traditions, both by heresiologists and contemporary scholarship apt to see spiritual philosophy and primitive psychology about knowing oneself, where in fact sexual symbolism and actualized spiritual magic is the intention:

Wherefore the desire after mutable generation is denominated to be inflamed. For when the fire is one, it admits of two conversions. For, he [Simon] says, blood in the man being both warm and yellow, is converted as a figured flame into seed; but in the woman this same blood is converted into milk. And the conversion of the male becomes generation, but the conversion of the female nourishment for the foetus. This, he says, is "the flaming sword, which turned to guard the way of the tree of life." For the blood is converted into seed and milk, and this power becomes mother and father—father of those things that are in process of generation, and the augmentation of those things that are being nourished; [and this power is] without further want, [and] self-sufficient. And, he says, the tree of life is guarded, as we have stated, by the brandished flaming sword. And it is the seventh power, that which [is produced] from itself, [and] which contains all [powers, and] which reposes in the six powers. For if the flaming sword be not brandished, that good tree will be destroyed and perish. If, however, these be converted into seed and milk, the principle that resides in these potentially, and is in possession of a proper position, in which is evolved a principle of souls, [such a principle] beginning, as it were, from a very small spark, will be altogether magnified, and will increase and become a power indefinite [and] unalterable, [equal and similar] to an unalterable age, which no longer passes into the indefinite age. (*Refutatio,* VI, 12)

One aim of Simonian practices appears then to have been the generation of "supermen" and, we may assume, "superwomen," or rather the androgynous super-being. Such would certainly account for the arrogance heresiologists persistently detect among the heretics, somewhat reminiscent of the image of the spoiled child.

Hippolytus quotes from Simon's *Revelation* to the effect that the primal power is hermaphroditic, though in reality one, as the pair Power and Intelligence is really one. However, in the world of duality, at a remove from the primal source, what is one appears as two.

The dynamic of an Earth that is feminine, intelligent, and that receives power from above is a creative dynamic, a living tree. We see here in the second century the essential binary dynamic of Jacob Böhme's seventeenth-century theosophical system and the historical dialectic of Hegel in essence. Manifestation of the one requires duality: each opposite longing for the other, so to speak. Therefore, to approach sexual congress in full knowledge of the hermaphroditic nature of the power that "stood, stands, and will stand" is to participate actively in the cosmic process, expressing it sacramentally, at the same time as we rise in knowledge above it.

Students of esotericism will observe the correspondence between the Simonian fire and the nineteenth-century concept of the fluidic "astral light" of Eliphas Lévi (1810–1875) on which the will of the magician may be impressed, a magical conception derived in part from Franz Anton Mesmer (1734–1815) and his "animal magnetism": the supposed invisible medium through which magical acts of healing may be accomplished. Simon's divine fire is an occult energy. Had a historical Simon observed an apostle transferring Holy Spirit by hand, he would have seen the activity in this light as a matter of course, as an occult ability whose secret could be purchased and mastered.

The Simon of the *Revelation* is a theosopher, after all. The sexual doctrines manifest the philosophy: "This, [therefore] is Mind [subsisting] in Intelligence; and these are separable one from the other, [though both taken together] are one, [and] are discovered in a state of duality" (*Refutatio,* VI, 13). When we think in terms of our created selves, we are in a state of duality. When through activation of the potential in the fire we may see that the duality is in fact one, for the mystic has joined the one, being now one with the hidden fire that is God. This monadic-hermaphroditic identity is apparently transpersonal, and on this basis, the otherwise ludicrous claim of Simon to have been also the one who suffered in Judea—and of Helen to have been Helen of Troy— makes metaphysical sense to the initiated, or as John Lennon perhaps expressed something of the kind in his transpersonalized work, "I Am the Walrus," based on LSD-induced visions in 1967: "I am he as you are he as you are me and we are all together."

Hippolytus recounts Simonian arguments for the meaning of Helen in chapter 14 of the *Refutatio*. They are far from uninteresting. Manifesting divine intelligence above the norm of the lower world, Helen of Troy caused a war by virtue of the opposite sides desiring to possess what was above them. The poet Stesichorus loses his eyesight when he denigrates "the Lady" in his verses, but recovers his vision when he sings her praises! This is a fine allegory of what it is a poet should see to be a poet, though it is wasted on Hippolytus, who thinks he's dealing with banal claims of historical accuracy. Simon seems to be aware of a metahistorical viewpoint that would return with William Blake and Louis-Claude de St. Martin and his associates and Martinist followers in the eighteenth century and beyond. There is nothing new under the sun!

Hippolytus calls Simon a "filthy fellow," who, rather than having redeemed the girl from bondage, having glimpsed her on the roof of the Tyrian brothel, was simply so enamoured he bought her and "enjoyed her person." His stories were, according to Hippolytus, concocted to cover his shame regarding his obsession with her. It is a pity that we do not have Helen's own testimony.

Hippolytus now ascribes Simonian practices to an imitation of Simon's lust. They "irrationally allege the necessity of promiscuous intercourse," and say: "All earth is earth, and there is no difference where anyone sows, provided he does sow." They congratulate one another, says Hippolytus, on their "indiscriminate intercourse," using expressions like *holy of holies* (presumably for the womb) and *sanctify one another,* all of which surely proves that they were practicing sacramental sex.

They claim Simon's redemption of Helen is the archetype for all human redemption from the powers of the lower realm. Rather like Jean-Luc Godard's use of the image and metaphor of prostitution in his films, Simon apparently had concluded that the world was one great brothel where flesh and innocence are defiled, bought, and sold, profited from and disposed of.

Chapter 14 of the *Refutatio* makes clear what I have suggested earlier, namely, the transpersonalizing nature of the Simonian redemption myth. For here we see how the Simonian gnosis can be, and in fact is, transferred practically entire—no pun intended—to the Christian kerygma to generate the numerous peculiarities of Christian gnosis that so enraged the heresiologists:

"And [Jesus], by having redeemed Helen in this way," [Simon says] "has afforded salvation to men through his own peculiar intelligence. For inasmuch as the angels, by reason of their lust for pre-eminence, improperly managed the world, [Jesus Christ] being transformed, and being assimilated to the rulers and powers and angels, came for the restoration [of things]. And so [it was that Jesus] appeared as man, when in reality he was not a man. And [so it was] that likewise he suffered—though not actually undergoing suffering, but appearing to the Jews to do so—in Judea as 'Son,' and in Samaria as 'Father,' and among the rest of the Gentiles as 'Holy Spirit.'" And [Simon alleges] that Jesus tolerated being styled by whichever name [of the three just mentioned] men might wish to call him [amusing early support for the concept of the trinity!]. "And that the prophets, deriving their inspiration from the world-making angels, uttered predictions" [concerning him]. Wherefore, [Simon said,] that towards these [prophets] those felt no concern up to the present, who believe on Simon and Helen, and that they do whatsoever they please, as persons free; for they allege that they are saved by grace. For that there is no reason for punishment, even though one shall act wickedly; for such a one is not wicked by nature, but by enactment. "For the angels who created the world made," he says, "whatever enactments they pleased," thinking by such [legislative] words to enslave those who listened to them. But, again, they speak of a dissolution of the world, for the redemption of his own particular adherents.

Hippolytus is in no doubt that the whole cult is a massive pretense, for they are driven by self-centered lust and are covering it up with a lot of philosophical claptrap, and are deceiving themselves if they think they are redeemed and free of the laws of the world to do as they wish with whomsoever they please.

According to Hippolytus's last word on the sorcerer, Simon's end came in opposition to Peter, when, making his last boast, Simon in Rome asked his disciples to bury him in the earth, wherefrom after three days he would emerge triumphant. But, according to Hippolytus, he did not emerge "for he was not the Christ." It is somewhat difficult to imagine he would have had a significant following had such an event occurred as reported. What happened to the story of Simon's last flight?

Hippolytus concludes by saying that Valentinus received from Simonian discourse "the starting-point for his own doctrine," indicating that Valentinus's more complex aeon theory was an obvious extension of Simon's six-root speculation, summed up by the heresiologist as a "tissue of legends." Hippolytus may have thought he had refuted Simonian views thoroughly, but they refused to lie down.

EPIPHANIUS ON SIMON

Over a century and a half after Hippolytus, Epiphanius felt it incumbent upon himself to attack Simon Magus and his followers' "pornography" (*Panarion*, I, part 5, section 23). Encratite in outlook, Epiphanius refers to intercourse as "the obscene act." Epiphanius has little substantial to add to the accounts of Justin Martyr, Irenaeus, and Hippolytus, though in Book I, part 21, section 2, 2:4, he introduces into the Simonian myth's dramatis personae the titles Prunicus and Barbelo (or Barbero). Prunicus is associated by Epiphanius with the Holy Spirit and thus with Helen. Epiphanius says other sects call Prunicus Barbelo.

However, in implying that Barbelo is another name for Helen, he may be mistaken, for in other, mostly Sethian, Gnostic texts, while Barbelo is also identified with the Father's First Thought (Ennoea), she does not descend to experience travails, as do Helen and Sophia in Simonian and Valentinian myths, respectively.

> Simon told a fairy tale about this, and said that the power kept transforming her appearance on her way down from on high, and that the poets had spoken of this in allegories. For these angels went to war over the power from on high—they call her Prunicus, but she is called Barbero or Barbelo by other sects—because *she displayed her beauty and drove them wild,* and was sent for this purpose, to despoil the archons who had made this world. She has suffered no harm, but she brought them to the point of slaughtering each other from the lust for her that she aroused in them. (*Panarion,* I, part 21, section 2, 2:5, my italics)

Precisely what the curious title *Prunicus* means we shall investigate in chapter 10, though Epiphanius has no hesitation in taking the honorific to mean "lascivious one," and having found it in connection with Helen the whore, as displayed by her tramp, finds all he needs to confirm that ascription.

Epiphanius offers the idea that Helen/Prunicus has to suffer the intercourse of the "archons who made the world" through many baleful incarnations so that in encouraging them to kill or be killed through their jealousy of her—Epiphanius sees no problem with the idea of angels slaughtering one another—the archons would suffer diminution by loss of blood. "Then, by gathering the power again, she would be able to ascend to heaven once more" (*Panarion,* 1, part 21, section 2, 2:6). While this would contradict the idea that Simon came to save her, the emphasis seems to be on a doctrine that Epiphanius is garbling, either deliberately or through ignorance of it. What is in the blood of the archons that could deliver her? Well, if we look at Sethian and Valentinian Gnostic variants, we shall find it commonly held that the archons inherited seed of pneuma (spirit) from their original source, though deficient in quantity or through admixture, and that this has been passed on in the process of human evolution under archontic control. However, in the context of Gnostic groups referred to by Epiphanius elsewhere, especially the Borborites as he calls them, or "filthy people," we may imagine that this blood of the archons is linked to the potential seed, that is, sperm in believers that requires gathering up like the lost sheep; for we may recall that among the earliest titles for Helen was that of the lost sheep whom Simon came to gather up as a type for the redemption of all in the grip of the archons. Thus the Simonian discourse on gathering the "blood of the archons" is probably informed by radical interpretation of the critical phrase "without the shedding of blood [read semen] there is no remission" (Hebrews 9:22; *cf.* Leviticus 17:11) where shedding of blood effects atonement: "For the life of the creature is in the blood, and I have given it to you to make atonement for yourselves on the altar; it is the blood that makes atonement for one's life." Sexual magic effected spiritual atonement: the "healing of the passions of matter."

Our interpretation of Hippolytus's refutations of Simonian doctrine in the Great Announcement attributed to him by devotees is confirmed precisely, though wholly negatively as we should expect, by Epiphanius:

> He instituted mysteries consisting of dirt and, to put it politely, the fluids that flow from bodies—men's through the seminal emission and women's through the regular menses, which are gathered as mysteries by a most indecent method of collection.
>
> And he said that these are mysteries of life and the fullest knowledge. But for anyone to whom God has given understanding, knowledge is above all a matter of regarding these things as abomination instead, and death rather than life. (*Panarion,* I, part 21, section 2, 4:1, 4:2)

Scholarship is not united on the question of whether Simon Magus was the first Gnostic. It does seem like a convenient assertion from the orthodox point of view, for Simon was condemned by Peter from the start, according to Acts (8:9–24), and as Epiphanius protests: How could Peter condemn anything unless it was not good? How, asks Epiphanius, could the world not belong to a good God, when "all the good have been chosen from it"? How can the law and the words of the prophets be perverted utterances of archons when they testify about Christ and forbid wrongdoing?

Epiphanius is in no doubt that all the essential ideas to be found among all the Gnostic-type heretical groups are found in Simon's first, including the central and most damning one:

> This world has been defectively constructed by wicked principalities and authorities, he [Simon] says. But he teaches that there is a decay and destruction of flesh, and a purification only of souls—and of these [only] if they are established in their initiation through his erroneous "knowledge." And thus the imposture of the so-called Gnostics begins. (*Panarion,* I, part 21, section 2, 4:4)

However, Epiphanius is looking back with hindsight. We cannot be certain that Simonian ideas themselves did not emerge as a Gnosticizing of a core tradition around Simon concerning magic, Helen, and a possibly radical initiatory doctrine. Irenaeus, of course, knows Simon as the first heretical deceiver of Jesus's early followers, but he knows it from limited sources (Acts and Justin Martyr) and seems unaware of the complexities familiar to Hippolytus some forty or so years later. Furthermore, Simon plays no part in any text of the Nag Hammadi corpus, save a brief reference to Simonians in the Encratite *Testimony of Truth* (dated ca. 190–300 CE), which is critical of Simonians, though nonetheless gives us the snippet that while permitted pleasures, they married and had children, evincing carnal procreation the text regards as a reign of horror whose hold over the true Gnostic has passed (Nag Hammadi Library, *Testimony of Truth,* IX, 3, 58).

However, it remains attractive to see the other Gnostic groups sprouting forth from a Simonian source, because the logic of mythological development favors the simpler presentation first, after which come the deviations, disagreements, caveats, and additions, depending on the genius or folly of the heresiarch concerned. Something attracted the author or authors of the *Great Announcement* and Simon's *Revelation* to the mixed stories circulating about the Samaritan magus, unless we take the texts at their word and see Simon not as a myth-starter and more of a myth-initiator and philosophical expounder.

We should not be entirely surprised if subsequent anti-orthodox figures deliberately obscured the "beastly filth" (Epiphanius's phrase) of Simon as the real source of their speculations; such would be typical of occult history: when the once-radical aims at respectability, he cleans up his past and obscures the genius or geniuses who took the real risks. If Simon's reputation had become unenviable, or the behavior of his followers was held to be embarrassing, then would-be founders of Gnostic schools would doubtless favor textual material believed to have apostolic authority, especially if apocryphal and easily subject to retelling and reinterpretation. Gnostics counted it a virtue to create their own spiritual works, prizing the living Jesus over episcopal text control, as Elaine Pagels has repeated many times.

For Epiphanius, as for Irenaeus, Simon is the one who dreamt up the story of angels making the Earth, before they turned completely insane with lust for Helen—itself a kind of midrash on Genesis 6:1–7, where God regrets his creation after the sons of God lusted after human women—but that in Simonian tradition, what they lusted over was truly above them, but they could not see it. Is there not here just a hint of Jesus's traditionally tolerant attitude to those condemned by the righteous as prostitutes?

It is difficult not to wonder if the authentic Simon regarded all hypocrites as evil Watchers (in the Enochian mold) and was particularly mindful of the Herodian priesthood dominating Jerusalem with its alien cult, and that Simon, understanding the magical power of imagination, was simply telling the truth when he said he created the world in which Helen was saved from the grip of the wicked. For his mythos, with which he held his followers spellbound, was in truth his creation, and if he had redeemed Helen, could not his followers become free of the imagined power structure of others too? Could they not redraw the world?

This is speculation, of course, but there seems to be a kernel of authenticity in the jokes that Epiphanius repeats, attributed to Simon:

> And again, of the lawful wedlock which Simon himself shamefully corrupts to make provision for his own lust, he says elsewhere, "Those whom God hath joined together, let not man put asunder." (*Panarion*, I, part 21, section 2, 5:8)

This is not only an apt description of the spiritual nature of a conjugal union, whether inside or outside marriage, dedicated to realizing the hidden God, but serves as the kind of riposte an intelligent, witty man might offer a Pharisee who condemned as unclean a man who dwelled with an unmarried whore and who dared call himself free.

But it was perhaps the sex that condemned Simon, above all. There remains within the earliest traditions concerning him a horror of mixing sex with the Holy Spirit. This horror remains to this day, and to feel it and think it is to join one's mind to that of Epiphanius who condemned Simon's alleged doctrines as "charlatan's drivel" and who regarded even lawful Christian marriage as beneath the standard required within the kingdom of heaven:

> And many other arguments can be found in opposition to the charlatan's drivel. How can unnatural acts be life-giving, unless perhaps it is the will of demons, when the Lord himself in the Gospel speaks in reply to those who told him, "If the case of the man and wife be so, it is not good to marry?" And he said to them, "All men cannot receive this, for there be eunuchs which have made themselves eunuchs for the kingdom of heaven's sake" [Matthew 19:10–12]— and proved that true abstention from marriage is the gift of the kingdom of heaven. (*Panarion*, I, part 21, section 2, 5:7)

In Epiphanius's many healings of the poison of Simon, he never mentions one obvious contradiction in the Simonian doctrine as he spits it out. If the angels have created such a deficient world, how is it that sacramental sex has the capacity to awaken the potential, undefinable God-Logos-Fire? Simon, unlike Epiphanius and, as far as we can tell, a significant amount of the literary gnosis available to Pachomian monasteries, does not reject the body altogether, in this life. It was Paul who declared that flesh and blood could not inherit eternal life, yet Epiphanius condemns Simon for believing the same thing with respect to not believing in the body's resurrection. Epiphanius is an Encratite, rejecting the body and looking down on procreation. What is the practical difference between believing the creation is God's, but that the body is corrupt, and believing the creation is deficient, but that the body can contribute to the spirit's redemption?

It was probably converted German Catholic theologian Erik Peterson (1890–1960) who pioneered the view that Encratism could be distinguished from Gnosticism (see the brilliant analysis of Gilles Quispel's *A Study of Encratism*). Before Peterson, it was common to share Isaac Newton's assumption that body hatred (and especially female body hatred) coincided precisely with the creation-rejection of Gnostics, even though it left the question of how Encratite-oriented bishops like Epiphanius could hate Gnostics so much in the fourth century, berating them violently for not hating the flesh and renouncing procreation and its means.

We know Irenaeus condemned the Encratites circa 180 for their rejection of meat, wine, and marriage, but we get more information about them from the third book of Clement of Alexandria's *Strōmateis* (ca. 200 CE). Encratite origins appear to be Jewish-Christian, located principally in modern-day Syria (northern Mesopotamia) and Alexandria. The immanent messianic kingdom precluded marriage. Jesus should be followed and imitated; he was poor and did not marry. The eating of the forbidden fruit of copulation had resulted in death (*post coitum triste*); this was the fruit that contained bitterness. This idea may have been important to the Simonian bitter water of the womb's spiritually infertile "wilderness" discussed earlier; Simonian Gnostics had to overcome the Fall's effect, whereby sex had become fatal and escape from bondage was only achieved by correct understanding of the four rivers that flowed from Eden.

Encratite priorities are visible in the *Gospel of Thomas* (a sayings collection probably compiled in Edessa, ca. 140) and the *Gospel of the Egyptians* (Jewish Christian and assuredly Encratite) and very strongly in the Nag Hammadi *Book of Thomas the Contender*, thought by professor of religion John D. Turner to have been composed in Syrian Edessa's Thomas-venerating Encratite culture in the mid-third century.

In the *Gospel of the Egyptians,* thanatos (death) is the consequence of eros (sexual love). In Encratism, the redeemed must trample on the "garment of shame" (the body); there can be no more male or female: sexual identity is no identity. No more children; no more death. Cease lusting; cease suffering. Desire creates illusion (the world). How different is the Simonian tradition of venerating the images of the Lord (Simon) and the Lady (Helena) equally, from line 114 of the Gnostic *Gospel of Thomas,* where to enter the kingdom of heaven the female must become male! When Simon redeems his lost First Thought, he does not reject her femininity.

Encratism was not indigenous to Gnosticism, but it clearly became involved with it, leading to great confusion when trying to assess Gnostic philosophy as a whole. My own view, which I state here for the first time, is that Gnostic thought underwent considerable change in the third and fourth centuries when the Encratite position found ingress to congenial Gnostic settings that had already rejected the fleshly Jesus and the physical resurrection. The libido, if you like, departed much of the movement, perhaps leaving Valentinians struggling to make sense of their traditional openness to spiritually transforming romantic love, a struggle arguably evinced in the *Gospel of Philip*. Radical Sethians and Simonians, once central, perhaps now moved to the fringes, were isolated by their refusal to abandon the pleasure principle and out of tune with the changing times. It may be that the antilibertine polemic of the heresiologists had taken root and generated a reactive realignment with the desire for a historically more authentic, and perhaps even intellectually fashionable, movement in the wake of protracted political uncertainty.

If there is one good argument for holding the Simonian tradition as the first genuinely Gnostic reinterpretation of the logic of salvation, it may just lie here, in the suggestion of a tacit resistance to a growing Encratism that would not only swallow the Catholic Church virtually whole by the end of the fourth century, but would transform much of the third- and fourth-century literature of the gnosis as well, if the surviving works of the Nag Hammadi Library are anything to go by.

Simon, being a magician, not a theologian, did not take the world as read; he seems to have believed in the positive approach to transforming the existential realities through the power of imagination to act upon the sleeping, unseen potential within the human being. He changed his reality, creating his own universe, and told the detritus where it could stick itself. Arguably, by contrast, third-century gnosis, shorn of magic, stands as spiritual psychology, which may explain the appeal of Valentinianism today to Christians floundering with modernism and reacting against the ancient assumption that Christianity is fundamentally ascetic, that world rejection characterizes the Christian saint. For in Valentinian gnosis, world rejection is essentially a spiritual, not a physical, labor as with the orthodox Encratistic tradition, which for much of the post-World War II world spells nothing but an unwelcome, colorless agony of soul and a protracted embrace of suffering. The *Gospel of Philip* gives us the post-1960s spiritual message: "He [Christ] came crucifying the world." The essential job has been done; one does not have to crucify oneself. The cross becomes conceptual, wiped clean of blood. Nobody who accepts cremation truly believes in the resurrection of the *body*.

FOUR

AFTER SIMON, THE DELUGE

Of the Gnostics, so much has been cursorily, as it were, written. We proceed now to the sequel, and must again contemplate faith; for there are some who draw the distinction that faith has reference to the Son, and knowledge (gnosis) to the Spirit. But it has escaped their notice that, in order to believe truly in the Son, we must believe that he is the Son, and that he came, and how, and for what, and respecting his passion; and we must know who is the Son of God. Now neither is knowledge without faith, nor faith without knowledge. Nor is the Father without the Son; for the Son is with the Father. And the Son is the true teacher respecting the Father; and that we may believe in the Son, we must know the Father, with whom also is the Son. Again, in order that we may know the Father, we must believe in the Son, that it is the Son of God who teaches; for from faith to knowledge of the Son is the Father. And the knowledge of the Son and the Father, which is according to the Gnostic rule—that which in reality is Gnostic—is the attainment and comprehension of the truth by the truth.

Now the sacrifice which is acceptable to God is unswerving abstraction from the body and its passions. This is the really true piety. (Clement of Alexandria, *Strōmateis,* V, 1; 11, ca. 200 CE)

That Simon Magus may personally have set the radical Gnostic ball rolling with his self-made interpretations of Jewish scripture seems to be confirmed by the names and whereabouts of heresiarchs linked by opponents to Simon's legacy. There is a time gap, however. Church tradition places Simon's death in Rome during Nero's reign of 54–68 CE, while his appearance in heresiological writings does not occur until the period 149–160 CE. Scholarship has also shown that numerous key twists of Christian practice later associated with Gnostics were present, at least in Pauline churches, from the 50s onward. Such twists, however, do not seem to have been worked into thoroughgoing all-in systems until the lifetime of Justin Martyr (ca. 100–165 CE), himself a native of Samaria with good knowledge of the region and its characters.

According to Justin's *Apology* to Emperor Antoninus Pius, among the first heresiarchs to impact on his territory was Menander, a Samaritan, like Simon, and said to be his pupil.[1] Menander was successful in Antioch in the early second century persuading followers that they would not die. (See the opening lines of the *Gospel of Thomas:* "These are the secret words which the living Jesus spoke, and Didymus Judas Thomas wrote them down. And he said: 'He who shall find the interpretation of the words shall not taste of death.'") Menander's promise does sound rather Simonian in its audacity. Hippolytus countered Menander's "realized resurrection"—spiritual awakening to eternal life before death—with the remark that death was simply a "debt of nature."

Irenaeus distinguished Menander from his predecessor Simon, in that Menander held the chief power to be unknown to all; the world was not made at Simon's behest, but, as Simon himself taught, was fashioned by angels, themselves the work of the Ennoea of the supreme power: God's First Thought, Wisdom.[2] We see at once in Menander the rift with nature also evident in the famous heresy of Menander's contemporary, Marcion of Sinope (ca. 85–ca. 180), who according to Justin Martyr held that the Father of Jesus had no contact with the world, the world's maker being a fairly savage deity responsible for the Old Testament's violent threats and cursings.

It is this rift with nature that gives Gnostic-type groups two possible paths in assessing the lusts of the flesh, even though the two radically divergent paths are deduced from the same premises. First, flesh is part of the deficient creation, so involvement with it drags the spirit down to Earth, into the realm of death and spiritual sleep. Thus, the lusts of the flesh must be subdued: a conclusion shared by Palestinian and Syrian Encratites who went so far as to abjure marriage altogether, *fearing* (most un-Carpocratian!) contamination with impurities.

Second, the spiritual person or pneumatic is above nature, having escaped the tragic born-to-die cycle, and so long as he or she knows and maintains awareness of this superior state, the lusts and needs of the flesh cannot harm the essential being, for the flesh is weak and the spirit ever willing. The Gnostic is above them all. Thus marriage becomes incidental, a matter of spiritual indifference, or, to use Hippolytus's phrase, "a debt of nature" for the provision of heirs or, note, the right kind of heirs: inheritors of spiritual seed. The Simonian tradition seems to have been: "make the most of it." If sex exists, and we're passing through, let's use sex to its highest potential; that way we, forever *contra mundum,* can at least banjax the powers of the world!

Irenaeus expresses the indifferent attitude very well in chapter 6 of his *Adversus Haereses,* where, describing the followers of the Gnostic Ptolemy, he sums up a prevalent conceit of Gnostic groups in his period: "For even as gold, when submersed in filth, loses not on that account its beauty, but retains its own native qualities; the filth having no power to injure the gold, so they affirm that they cannot in any measure suffer hurt, or lose their spiritual substance, whatever the material actions in which they may be involved." The idea seems to be: This Earth is the Demiurge's inn—or brothel. We're not here long; it behooves us to follow some of the rules, so long as we don't forget that we know better and will be checking out soon enough with credit.

Again, I think we see the legacy of the *Book of Enoch.* It is a short, though highly significant, step to go from seeing the corruption of the world as the work of the fugitive Watchers under the leadership of Azazel, to attributing the nature and indeed origin of the present creation to those same agencies, having rebelled against their maker, or gone demented with jealousy over her: the feminine Wisdom who got beyond herself.

Menander advised his followers to get the better of the creative angels. According to Irenaeus, this they achieved by magic, taught them by the revealer, Menander himself, who passed on the gnosis as a magical attainment.[3] Menander's followers "obtain the resurrection by being baptized into him." Might this have indicated some kind of homosexual, or indeed heterosexual, rite? We may presume that, if it did, Irenaeus would have been glad to pass on the news. However, doing so might have made ordinary Christians question what it was to be baptized into Jesus. The emphasis then is probably on Menander's imposture in setting himself up in Jesus's place. Anyhow, Irenaeus does not impute specific sexual activity to Menander, being content with repeating the charge against Simon that Menander was a perfect adept at magic and taught how one may overcome the angels that made the world. Since Irenaeus says he taught followers that through his resurrection they would attain eternal youthfulness, there may well have been a magical elixir produced, not only figuratively but actually, and we are free to speculate that such an elixir may well have been the product of sexual activity, diverting the will of the angels for human reproduction with alternative, transgressive uses for sexual fluids.

If, incidentally, you find this discourse about dark angels a trifle incredible, it might help to see them in more psychological terms as "chains of the mind," subconscious powers that inhibit growth and awareness, though I dare say Professor Jonas would have regarded such a transposition as soft. These Gnostics believed firmly in the reality of these angels in the objective universe, which, anyhow, was their work.

Irenaeus asserts that it was at Antioch where Simon's doctrinal virus was passed by Menander to Saturninus (or Satornilos) and to Basilides, whence it found itself replanted in Alexandria, there to be subjected to extensive philosophical exploitation and theological development. It also seems likely that the link with magic continued as well, for we read in Tertullian's *On the Prescription of Heretics:**

> I shall not in this place omit to describe the conversation of heretics, how vain, and earthly, and frail it is, without weight, without authority, without discipline, though at the same time we shall readily allow it to be in every respect suitable to the faith they profess. The conversation of heretics is infamously notorious. They are almost continually with magicians, with jugglers, with astrologers, with philosophers. For the enchanting pleasure of curiosity must be gratified; "seek and ye shall find," is with them a precept never to be forgotten, a precept eternally to be insisted upon.[4]

Such sarcasm is leveled by every heresiologist at every heresy, heresies whose chief proponents in this period (early to mid-second century) were Cerdo, Marcion, Cerinthus, Saturnilus, and Basilides: all come in for the sarcastic treatment.

CERDO

Apparently starting as a Simonian, Cerdo was active in Syria around 138, shortly after the Bar Kokhba rebellion provoked the traumatic Jewish expulsion from Jerusalem and the general diaspora, accompanied by eradication of Jewish and Samaritan political identity. Hippolytus credits Cerdo with having shared his two-gods theory with Marcion, but then Hippolytus also says Marcion got his two-gods idea from Empedocles. Tertullian's take is that after Cerdo, "emerged a disciple of his, one Marcion by name, a native of Pontus, son of a bishop, excommunicated because of a rape committed on a certain virgin." Starting

---

*A *prescription* was a Roman legal means of denying a plaintiff a court hearing.

from the fact that, it is said, "Every good tree beareth good fruit, but an evil [tree] evil," he attempted to approve the heresy of Cerdo; so that his assertions are identical with those of the former heretic before him."[5] That is to say, the world contains evil so it must be the work of one disposed to evil. Since this idea, to the orthodox, was abominably blasphemous enough, that may account for why we hear nothing concerning sexual peculiarities related to either Cerdo or Marcion. However, it is likely that Tertullian couldn't find anything more to pin on Marcion, other than his abominable ideas and that he had had an illicit affair, an accusation doubted by many scholars who think Tertullian misunderstood, or chose to misunderstand, an earlier accusation that Marcion had defiled the virgin *church* with his heresy.

Denial that the supreme God made the world was also attributed to Cerinthus, active around 100 CE. Hippolytus attributes Cerinthus's teaching that the Old Testament God was just, but the Father of Jesus was good, to his "being disciplined in the teaching of the Egyptians."[6] This jibe may simply have meant Cerinthus had been influenced by paganism.

Justin Martyr's *Dialogue with Trypho*[7] (ca. 150–ca. 60 CE) associates Marcionites with the followers of Basilides and with Saturnilus (or Saturninus or Satornilus), whose teacher, allegedly, was Menander. Saturnilus, in his turn, allegedly taught Basilides, and Basilides would influence Valentinus, but the connections are vague and based on similarities of idea.

SATURNILUS

Saturnilus was apparently an Encratite—Irenaeus included Encratites in his list of heresies—on account of his being ascetic, eschewing marriage. Jesus was only the appearance of the divine savior who came to save the pneuma scattered among men. Man's creation came about after the angels below caught a glimpse of a heavenly being, presumably the Logos or Gnostic *anthrōpos* (divine idea or ever-existing aeon of man), and tried to make one in the likeness of what they had glimpsed and in the image of themselves. Their creation was unable to stand (a Simonian echo), so the higher deity took pity and sent down *pneuma* to the creature, which, working as a spark and dynamic breath within man, over time, evolved within him to create the upright figure able to stand the doctrine of pneuma-salvation. Clearly, the theory of human evolution from a crawling thing to erect posture is not new ("creationists" and anti-creationists should both note!), but the spiritual motivator or spark of Logos-within might alert evolutionists to a variant interpretation of the usual materialism. Even after all this innovative pneumatic evolution, however, the heresiologists believed that, for Saturnilus, the body did not count, since the spark flees heavenward when the corpse is discarded. The highest God might just as well have kept the pneuma to himself in the first place, rather than subject it to ignominious incarnation!

Now it may be that, contrary to the last chapter's suggestion, a fully Encratite type of Gnostic was indeed active in the early to mid-second century, of a Syrian-Palestinian /northwest Mesopotamian provenance. However, it is just as possible that these ideas were backdated from the late second and early third century, when Encratism was considered a priority problem for orthodox authorities, a problem sufficiently painful to inspire the anti-Encratite chapter 26 of book 4 of Clement of Alexandria's *Strōmateis,* titled "How the Perfect Man Treats the Body and the Things of the World." On the other hand, the libertine Simonian strain might have been the exception, but this is unlikely. Irenaeus, for example, mentions a sect of Nicolaitanes, followers, he says of Nicholas, one of the seven apostle-appointed deacons referred to in the Acts of the Apostles. "They lead," Irenaeus says, "lives of unrestrained indulgence," deeming adultery a thing indifferent.[8]

In book 1, chapter 28, Irenaeus refers to the Encratites directly, saying they are "springing from Saturninus and Marcion," suggesting perhaps that followers of the latter have "moved on" from older heresies with new, stricter ideas about denying marriage, insisting on vegetarianism, lest they take in "created" flesh and corrupt themselves. Encratites, Irenaeus insists, set aside "the original creation of God" (male and female) and gainsay the divine wisdom of procreation. They "indirectly" blame God for having made men and women. This suggests another take on the androgynous, or more likely, sexless, spirit. Encratites also deny that Adam (the first created) will be saved. This, however, says Irenaeus, is only the latest notion (ca. 180 CE), and he attributes it to one Tatian, originally a "hearer" (or uncommitted acolyte) of Justin, and who, after Justin's martyrdom, allegedly separated himself from the church to assume big ideas about being a teacher, inventing his own system of invisible aeons, "while like Marcion and Saturninus, he declared that marriage was nothing else than corruption and fornication."[9] Irenaeus concedes laconically that denying Adam's salvation really was original to Tatian!—its very originality rendering it ridiculous.

Immediately after implying that Gnostics might be "going Encratite," Irenaeus presents us with fresh fever:

> Others, again, following upon Basilides and Carpocrates, have introduced promiscuous intercourse and a plurality of wives and are indifferent about eating meats sacrificed to idols, maintaining that God does not greatly regard such matters. But why continue? For it is an impracticable attempt to mention all those who, in one way or another, have fallen away from the truth.

If the picture appeared confusing to Irenaeus, a man on the ground so to speak, we must be permitted some margin for error in assessing the facts of the situation over eighteen hundred years later.

Again, we cannot be sure if all the views attributed to Saturnilus by Hippolytus[10] are not those of later followers, but it is most interesting to see how, in Hippolytus's account of Saturnilus, beliefs about marriage are tied in with what is clearly a development of the ideas of the earlier and post-Jesus portions of the *Book of Enoch*. That is to say that in the earliest part of the *Book of Enoch,* written between the first century BCE and the lifetime of Jesus, God (the Father of Lights) determines to quash the earthly power of the evil angels (Watchers), led by Azazel, who have sinned and fornicated with the daughters of men, while in the later sections, the agent of the angels' apocalyptic downfall is named as the "Son of Man" (considered by scholars as a Jewish-Christian interpolation). The Enochian picture appears directly in Hippolytus's account of Saturnilus where the wicked "Watchers" have probably been translated into the Greek "Archons" or "Rulers" of zodiacal fate:

> And he says that the God of the Jews is one of the angels, and, *on account of the Father's wishing to deprive of sovereignty all the Archons* [my italics], that Christ came for the overthrow of the God of the Jews, and for the salvation of those that believe upon Him; and that these have in them the scintillation of life. For he asserted that two kinds of men had been formed by the angels—one wicked, but the other good. And, since demons from time to time assisted wicked [men, Saturnilus affirms] that the Savior came for the overthrow of worthless men and demons, but for the salvation of good men. *And he affirms that marriage and procreation are from Satan* [my italics]. The majority, however, of those who belong to this [heretic's school] abstain from animal food likewise, [and] by this affectation of asceticism [make many their dupes]. And [they maintain] that the prophecies have been uttered, partly by the world-making angels, and partly by Satan, who is also the very angel whom they suppose to act in antagonism to the cosmic [angels] and especially to the God of the Jews. These, then, are in truth the tenets of Saturnilus.

I suspect here that we have perhaps one of the best sources to account for negative views on marriage advocated by some of those promoting a redemptive gnosis from the grip of the archons. The wicked angels have defiled the relations that should pertain to spiritual beings by means of their evil seed, passed on from generation to generation. Such believers would find nothing to admire in the sex-charged Simonians, unless, of course, they accepted an interpretation of Simonian sex magic as the sacramental means for redeeming the vulnerable *logos spermatikos,* but it is impossible to believe the Encratite type could ever tolerate the thought of spermatophagous rites.

Such qualms would not have bothered some of the other Gnostic groups that had emerged by, at least, the 170s.

FIVE

THE DIRTY PEOPLE

Masochism, too, is normal to man;
for the sex-act is the Descent into Hell of the Savior.

ALEISTER CROWLEY, DIARY, 1920

In matters of doctrine, whatsoever is truly new is
certainly false.

ARCHDEACON RALPH CHURTON (1754–1831),
A DEFENSE OF THE CHURCH OF ENGLAND, OXFORD, 1795

Irenaeus believed that a group of sects he more or less lumps together, namely the Barbeliotes (or Borborians), the Cainites, the Ophites, and the Sethians, were but offshoots, like the Lernaean hydra, of the school of Valentinus.[1] This the bishop apparently deduces from similarities of language, theme, tone: from ideas evincing elaboration of aeon or emanation theory and from the attention given to the exiled Sophia and her part in the creation of the cosmos and of men and women. This must have been quite a "school," for Irenaeus already maintained that Ptolemy, Marcus, and Heracleon, each with his own sphere of influence, were also students of Valentinus. Clement of Alexandria asserts as much for Theodotus.

It is impossible for us to tell how accurate Irenaeus was being in this matter since the heretics themselves do not name their immediate influences, other than to assert privileged access to secret, unverifiable, apostolic, and messianic traditions. Thus Clement of Alexandria further informs us that while Basilides claimed a transmission of secret tradition through Glaucias, hearer of Peter, Valentinians claimed Valentinus to have been a hearer of Theudas (or Theodas), pupil of Paul, privy to the latter's otherwise unwritten mystery gnosis.[2] According to Hippolytus, the Naassenes, or serpent-worshippers, received secret matter through Mariamne—presumably Mary Magdalene—from James, the brother of the Lord.[3] This claim fits very well with titles of several extant Gnostic works (two *Apocalypses* of James, the *Pistis Sophia,* and the *Gospel of Mary,* for example).

Sethians claimed intimate access to the supernatural mind of Seth, or the Great Seth, identified also with Jesus since they claimed to be heirs of the Sethian seed, that is, spiritual descendants of the glorious, perfect man Seth whose birth consoled Adam and Eve after the horror that befell Abel through Cain's wickedness. The Sethian seed constituted a pre-Hebraic alien race of unmovable ones (reminiscent of Simonian *stood-stands-will stand* language), strangers in, but not of, the world: children of their true heavenly Mother, Barbelo.

It is, however, notable that Tertullian attributes the plethora of sects—which plethora Clement of Alexandria complained was keeping potential converts from approaching Christianity—to the influence of Greek philosophy. Thus while Tertullian calls Marcion a Stoic, Valentinus is denigrated as a pupil of Plato; Aristotle too is suspect: "Unhappy Aristotle! Who has furnished them with sophistry." Tertullian jibes with triumphalist amusement, believing the days of philosophy numbered.[4] The nature of the Socratic method is what has made for perpetual novelty of exposition, Tertullian asserted. He blames Athens and Alexandria for corrupting the simplicity of the faith, a position Clement of Alexandria would seriously wish to qualify. The suspicion remains then that the sects above named did not stem from one teaching source in their immediate contexts, but came out of a shared culture, a kind of spiritual marketplace at the Egyptian crossroads of East and West that was Alexandria, drenched in competing—but often fundamentally similar—exoteric and esoteric philosophies: Greek, Jewish, Syrian, Persian, Indian, Greco-Egyptian, and so on, illuminated by star names, in the manner of 1960s radical students brandishing paperbacks: Jean-Paul Sartre, Albert Camus, Friedrich Nietzsche, Louis Pierre Althusser, Mao Zedong, Karl Marx, Jack Kerouac, Bob Dylan, Elvis Presley.

Through the Gordian-knotted foliage, it is nonetheless possible to discern a certain dynamic of transmission. We seem to have a movement of ideas sited in the early to mid-second century in Samaria, Syria, and Upper Mesopotamia (the Edessa region toward the border with Parthia) with connections to Alexandria. Perhaps consequential upon the Romans' vastation of Judea (135 CE) and the war with Parthia (161–166 CE), when Emperor Lucius Verus sacked Edessa, the center of gravity shifted to Alexandria and Egypt in general, whence the philosophically worked-on hydra of esoteric ideas spread to Rome and the rest of the Empire, insinuating itself into the Pauline and Jewish Christian churches while establishing independent circles.

From the mid- to the late-second century, the Alexandrian phase may have seen a broad divergence of sects into two major streams that, in their ferment, lapped into one another nonetheless: first, those sects stemming from, or associated with, the theologian Valentinus and, second, those sects with a more distinctly magical and libidinous character. One gets the impression that the Valentinian-related groups saw themselves as the master class of a superior, spiritual, esoteric Christianity, still expecting to be accepted as members of the church—albeit as its avant garde—while the Sethian, Naassene, Ophite, Simonian, Carpocratian, and Borborite groups appropriated broadly Christian material merely as it suited them; they were more likely to think of themselves as Gnostics, one suspects, than be bothered about recognition from the Catholic Church, which many of their number may have loathed anyhow. This generalizing picture does not include or place every possible sect, and we must suppose considerable overlap, morphing, and, probably multi-membership, in the way that eager Freemasons tend to join a number of orders in search of an ideal, or simply from curiosity or hunger for fresh experiences.

We might also suspect that some of the above names were used indiscriminately by heresiologists and may have been different names, or nicknames, for essentially the same group (who might well have called themselves something else), for if their gnosis was indeed "falsely so-called," as the heresiologists pronounced, there was no harm in the orthodox calling them according to their works. Hippolytus, for example, says that Naassenes "styled themselves Gnostics." Since *Ophite* comes from the Greek for serpent (*ophos*), and *Naassene* comes from the Hebrew for serpent (*nahas*), and since a veneration for the serpent of Eden was common among Gnostics, we are right to be cautious about naming names and believing in them too strongly. Spin-offs are rife where sects are concerned, and with so little respect for authority beyond the inner voice or superstitious awe for arcane mysteries, we must presume that sectarian splits were common. Too many novelties inhibit consistency. For Gnostics, dynamic imagination and variegated originalities were assets to be proud of; for the outraged orthodox, they indicated insanity.

SETHIANS, SEED-GATHERERS, AND SERPENT-WORSHIPPERS

Chapter 29 of Irenaeus's *Adversus Haereses* opens with a cry of alarm: "A multitude of Gnostics have sprung up and have been manifested like mushrooms growing out of the ground." Mushrooms traditionally appeared after a storm, and were associated with devils, so the metaphor may indicate the storm of Aurelian persecutions in Gallia Narbonensis in 177 CE that preceded Irenaeus's arrival in Gaul. Similar outgrowths had, however, already occurred in Rome under Bishop Anicetus (who served as bishop from ca. 157 to ca. 168), when the Carpocratian female magician Marcellina had "led multitudes astray" with "magical arts and incantations; philters, also, and love-potions . . . [and] recourse to familiar spirits, dream-sending demons, and other abominations,"[5] all employed to prove Gnostics had power over "the princes and formers of this world" and all things in it. We are in Simonian-type territory again.

Carpocratians, as we have seen, were taught that for the soul to be ultimately free, it had to undergo all experiences through successive incarnations (*cf.* the myth of Helena). If, as a reasonably responsible citizen, you didn't wish to commit criminal acts in this life, it was probably because you'd already done so in former lives. One suspects the doctrine was predominantly applied to sex and relationships, where it might be welcomed, for Irenaeus seldom refrains from portraying the Gnostics as both seducers and seduced.

According to the heretical doctrine favored by Marcellina, the sex instinct had to be fully experienced in all its facets, even exhausted, so souls could eventually come to indifference to it, for everything palls in the end, save the absolute desire of the soul, itself impassible to these passing affairs, however addictive might be one's desire for "salvation" via this path! The doctrine, of course, may serve to justify every failing, weakness, and surrender to temptation as education crying for tolerance—not at all far, I think, from the current, dubious notion of "moving on" after calamitous follies and crimes, with the unspoken suggestion that life is punishment enough. One is reminded of Dean Inge's uncharacteristically overgenerous logion: "The punishment for being a bad man is to be a bad man." But you won't ever recover the good man until you fully realize what being a bad man means. QED, says Carpocrates, above it all, with a wicked wink, indifferent to the damage done, for damage becomes the world.

Followers of Carpocrates, wrote Irenaeus, branded themselves inside the lobe of the right ear, an erotic locus, with what we now call a tattoo. Interestingly, with respect to this affectation, the Vatican's *Liber*

Pontificalis records that Bishop of Rome Anicetus ordered priests not to wear their hair long, possibly because that fashion prevailed among heretical teachers or followers in the city.

Irenaeus implies in chapter 29 of his work that the appearance of Barbeliotes, or Borborians, was a recent affair. No founder's name occurs.

Now "Borborians" can hardly be a group's self-designation, since the Greek word *Borboros* means "mud," "filth," "dung," and it would be as fair to translate *Borborian* as "shitty" as it would "filthy." The dung fly family *Sphaeroceridae* are also known as "Borborites." So we may be right in suspecting that the name for the "shitty people" is a severe, mocking pun on the name of the goddess whose story dominates heresiological accounts of their beliefs, namely Barbelo (sometimes Barbelos), whose opponents wish to stain the goddess's name indelibly with their opinion of the Barbelo-worshippers' practices. And since Barbelo appears in a variety of Gnostic works, especially Sethian works, we may see that this is a cultus or series of cults being viewed at something of a remove. It is notable that Irenaeus does not know the true meaning of the name *Barbelo,* even writing it as a masculine noun and referring to the figure as a "he." He is clearly thinking of the characteristic Gnostic tendency to ascribe bisexuality to heavenly powers. A heavenly Father is also a heavenly Mother (a growing movement of the period many discern in the Catholic assumption of the Virgin Mary, mother of God, to the heavenly realm as a soul-comforter, through the Holy Spirit, of course).

I shall save my research into the meaning of *Barbelo* for chapters 10 and 11, when my discoveries in this regard will make the most sense to the illuminated reader. For now, we shall see what we can learn about the sexual practices of the range of Barbelo-worshippers from Irenaeus, Tertullian, Hippolytus, and Epiphanius.

As far as we can discern, the Barbelo Gnostic wished to attain to the light of Christ through embrace of the divine Mother. That this could be enacted derived from the belief, related by Irenaeus,[6] that the Unknown Father wished to reveal himself, that is, be known, to his First Thought Barbelo, or Barbelos, a virgin spirit. A practical question is thus answered: *How do I receive the light?* Answer: *Attain to the virgin spirit; be cleansed of the Earth and the archons.* It helps enormously to see the myths of these Gnostics as serving to answer practical questions, "how-to" kinds of questions, related directly to ritual practices.

Irenaeus then tells us that the Ennoea (First Thought, or Mind) went forward and stood before the Father's face. This *going forward* idea is central to understanding Barbelo. She is a little precocious, to say the least: too quick off the mark at times. She asks the Father to his face for *prognosis,* or prescience, which the Father gives. They are face-to-face, and yes, we may think of sexual embrace. There are now two powers working together: Barbelo, the virgin spirit, and *Prognosis,* the power to prophesy. Able now to see in advance, to envision and create, together Barbelo and Prognosis request incorruption and eternal life to secure the purity of their vision. Barbelo is now well filled, overflowing with delight in her knowledge of the Father; she recognizes and experiences throughout her being the glorious bliss of the Father's previously unknown nature. The allusion is sexual. The myth specifies sacramental intercourse between male and female exalted to a plane above the world. Devotees may well have employed entheogens to stimulate rising to the divine embrace amid collective incantations.

Out of her stimulated excitement and amazement, she, Barbelo, generates a light, similar to the light characteristic of the Father's nature. But it is not the same: for though she has received the seed of the Father, it is combined with her own reflected light. (We may think of classical comparisons of significance given to male sperm and female sexual fluids.) Her light is, nevertheless, sufficient to generate all things. All things come from the light from Barbelo, and this light is effectively an invisible seed (*sperma*), the seed within the seed (*pneuma*), for in absolute spiritual light, no thing is seen. The Light is generative. This Light, followers believe, is also Christ, not the man Jesus (who *sows* the seed among men), but the Christ whom Jesus served to express and give temporary form to. The Light becomes discernible as Christ only after the Father, approving of, that is, *taking pleasure in,* the light-illuminating Barbelo, *anoints her generative light with his own grace.* The unmistakable suggestion here is one of divine fertilization: perfection of the seed. The account presented by Irenaeus as baloney probably served as the basis and justification for a sacrament of anointing within the Barbelite community. But . . . *Holy Mother of God!* What kind of anointing is this?

Christ in the light of Barbelo—she is his mother—requests *Nous* (spiritual Mind) of the Father to assist him. The Father also grants Logos (the generative Word). One can almost hear a Barbelite catechumen asking a priest: "What is meant by the words 'In the beginning was the Word, and the Word was with God'"? Think sacramentalized sperm.

The Ennoea is joined to the Logos, Incorruption (*Aphtharsia*) to Christ. Eternal Life (*Zōē Aiōnios*) is made a syzygy with Thelema (Will, or divine will; *cf.* "thy will be done on earth as it is in heaven"). Nous is paired up with Prognosis: Mind and Foreknowledge, the essence of prophecy. Were, I wonder, these syzygies enacted by couples in a secret collective ritual, combined with chanting?

By all of these supernal powers, the great light surrounding Barbelos is magnified. One can almost hear intoned solemnly Luke 1:46–47: "My soul magnifies the Lord and my spirit rejoices in God my Savior," a Gnostic solemnity that the orthodox would take for sheer satanic audacity, for the implication of a sexual sacrament, however innocently practiced, is luminously present in the Barbelo myth. This was not simply metaphysical philosophy run wild; *this was justification for spiritualized sex.* For Barbelo has effectively become the burning bush of the Simonians, from whose core the voice of God could be heard. We can tell this from Irenaeus's somewhat veiled statement following his account of the generation of the Barbelite aeons: "Hence also they declare were manifested the mother, the father, the son; while from

Anthrōpos [Heavenly Man] and Gnosis *that Tree* was produced which they also style Gnosis itself"[7] [my italics].

Gnosis is a tree. The significance of this will become plain in due course.

The branches extend downward, bearing fruit. In the descent, a breach in the harmonies occurs, as always in Gnostic systems. The result is the lower world the Gnostic must overcome, first by awareness of the dimensions of the predicament, then by sacraments, preenacting, and so preparing for, the eventual ascendance of the spirit when the body has passed away. Gnostics saw that the dark powers evident in the world of material generation, the shadow of spiritual generation, might overcome the alienated spirit, so divine characters enter the world under various names or guises.

But how had things gone wrong, and how could the way of escape be accounted for?

Barbelo sends the "Holy Spirit," whom, Irenaeus tells us, Barbelites also call Sophia (Wisdom) and Prunicus (which is not explained). Interestingly, Irenaeus uses the masculine pronoun for this figure, a figure we are used to regarding as feminine, and usually taken to be the same figure as Barbelo in most accounts of Gnostic systems. Irenaeus also uses masculine pronouns in reference to Barbelos, probably on account of the masculine form of the Greek noun ending (*os*). There may be another reason. He may want to distract his readers from the seduction of the ideas. By suggesting an androgynous, ambiguous, or masculine figure, the sensual resonance of the myth is obscured, and he can coolly expose it as subphilosophical claptrap.

On the other hand, the conclusion of the creation myth Irenaeus gives us next also suggests that there may have been a male counterpart to a feminine Barbelo, insofar as, though he does not say it, Barbelo was probably conceived of as androgynously bisexual, if only because she had absorbed the seed of the Father, for she had been given knowledge of him, face-to-face. These subtleties tend to get lost in many superficial accounts of the Gnostics.

Furthermore, in Irenaeus's account, the dual nature, or male nature, of Barbelos allows the myth to be concluded where the fallen Holy Spirit becomes also the Demiurge, an unusual, indeed unique, twist for a Gnostic system. This occurs because the mother Sophia leaves him because of his error.

> Next they maintain, that from the first angel, who stands by the side of Monogenes, the Holy Spirit has been sent forth, whom they also term Sophia and Prunicus. He [the Holy Spirit] then, perceiving that all the others had consorts, while he himself was destitute of one, searched after a being to whom he might be united; and not finding one, he exerted and extended himself to the uttermost and looked down into the lower regions, in the expectation of there finding a consort; and still not meeting with one, he *leaped forth* [from his place]; in a state of great impatience, [which had come upon him] because he had made his attempt without the good-will of his father. Afterwards, under the influence of simplicity and kindness, he produced a work in which were to be found ignorance and audacity. This work of his they declare to be Protarchontes [the Demiurge or first Archon], the former of this [lower] creation. But they relate that a mighty power carried him away from his mother, and that he settled far away from her in the lower regions, and formed the firmament of heaven, in which also they affirm that he dwells. And in his ignorance he formed those powers which are inferior to himself angels, and firmaments, and all things earthly. They affirm that he, being united to Authadia [audacity], produced Kakia [wickedness], Zelos [emulation], Phthonos [envy], Erinnys [fury], and Epithymia [lust]. When these were generated, the mother Sophia deeply grieved, fled away, departed into the upper regions, and became the last of the Ogdoad, reckoning it downwards. On her thus departing, he imagined he was the only being in existence; and on this account declared, "I am a jealous God, and besides me there is no one." Such are the falsehoods which these people invent. [my italics] (*Adversus Haereses*, I.29, 4)

Note again the *leaping forth* from his place by Holy Spirit-Sophia-Prunicus. There is perhaps the implication here not only of a feminine promiscuity but of a masculine premature, uncontrolled ejaculation, for the result is a poor child—a shadow of its mother, the neighbors might say: the universe into which the Gnostic soul has been born, asleep.

The way out is to regenerate the link with the Mother who had not fallen, but whose nature could be found, if awoken, within the fallen, lower regions. There may well be a pun there too. That which bound humankind to Earth held within it the seeds of salvation from the Earth, so long, that is, as the lower angels, or negative tendencies, could be, literally, overruled. This system is not without ethics, but they are probably to be applied quite specifically to effective, concentrated pneuma-sexual practice whose aim is union, or reunion: the healing of the wounded psyche or inner universe through uninterrupted concentration of the subject on a supercelestial objective. The climax may thus be expressed as the union of the microcosm with the macrocosm. The heresiologists were probably right to hold a magician as the *fons et origo* of the practice.

Irenaeus's rather confused account of the Sethians points out different twists of the basic mythic itinerary with which we are now familiar. We have offspring of Barbelo called Sinistra, Prunicus, Sophia, or "masculo-feminine." She/he, though lower than her source, is yet dignified by divine "besprinkling of light."[8] This suggests a visual analogue in the phenomenon of the stars in the otherwise dark cloak of night. The position of the stars, in those days note, dictated conditions of generation. However, the idea seems to be that what light exists in the dark universe is a fugitive light, the result of Ialdabaoth's curious envy of the besprinkled light—which he views rather like a savage gazing at alien cargo on the seashore—lavished on those above him, whom he is too blind to see. Knowing only his own work, he is "a jealous god."

Ialdabaoth is the Demiurge's name and the plural ending suggests its ultimate derivation from the Elohim (= "Gods") of Genesis, fashioner of earthly man. Perhaps the name is a pun derived from "begetter of Sabaoth" (= "the hosts": angels and/or stars), while combining Aramaic *ialad* for "child" and *baōth* for "chaos" into "child of chaos," is no more than suggestive. William Blake apparently concocted his demiurge "Old Nobodaddy" the "Ancient of Days" who as "Urizen" sets bounds to the universe out of the name "Ialdabaoth," finding therein puns on the Aramaic for "daddy" (*abba*), the Germanic and Old English "alt" or "eald" (for old), and the "Ia" or "Ja" denoting the shortened name of the Mosaic Law-giver and judge. Blake got the idea well enough.

Ialdabaoth is so jealous of his Adam that he makes Eve just to empty him, but Prunicus empties Eve of her power, so as to frustrate Ialdabaoth. We then find others coming to admire Eve and falling for her, and begetting children of her who are angels. This development is clearly inspired by the Genesis 6 story of the transgressive sons of God and Nephilim, a story transformed into the Watchers narrative in the first *Book of Enoch:* the primary literary origin, I suspect, of Gnostic archon theory.

Determined to get Adam and Eve to awaken from Ialdabaoth's soporific power, Sophia induces the serpent to ensure Ialdabaoth's command not to eat of the tree is transgressed. The serpent becomes thereby a symbol of Sophia's will, while, according to Irenaeus,[9] some other Sethians asserted that Sophia actually became the serpent. She thus implanted gnosis in men, "for which reason the serpent was called wiser than all others." These Gnostics even said our serpentine intestines through which food is conveyed revealed the "hidden generatrix."

Eve follows the serpent's advice as though from a son of God (note again the Genesis 6 reference), and persuades Adam to do likewise. On eating, they "attained to the gnosis of that power, which is above all, and departed from those who created them."[10] The Sethian is likewise to eat of the tree to depart from the grip of the mediocre powers of the world. Again, it must be understood that this is not all mythology for mythology's sake, as Irenaeus presents it. It is rationale for eating taboo substances: sexual therapy to reattain the powers of the Sethian seed and be reunited with the angel who is above and beyond this shadowy world, superior to all created things, including the fashioner of those things. This gnosis, Jesus-Seth had passed literally to his disciples: "Take, eat, this is my body which I give to you." It was probably part of Irenaeus's intention to sever deliberately the rationale from the practices themselves, lest he abet his enemies. Thus, accounts of Gnostic filth are presented primarily as blasphemous and fundamentally meaningless acts of deviance.

The Sethian take is, of course, very different. Prunicus rejoices in having proved that since the true Father is incorruptible, Ialdabaoth, who claimed to be the Father, was a liar. Irenaeus then adds an intriguing and rather odd, unexplored snippet. While the divine man (*anthrōpos*) and the first woman (presumably Barbelo) "existed previously," which seems to mean they were of eternity (aeons), Eve, the earthly reflection of her ultimate Mother, "sinned by committing adultery." The sin would in context appear to be paradoxical, for while, according to Genesis, the sin of Eve condemned her in the eyes of God to the cycles of painful birth and death, Eve's "adultery," her transgression of the command, assures her, in Sethian terms, of freedom. We may have here the first clear indication of romantic love being necessarily adulterous (*contra mundum*) love in the annals of Western literature, for this is a love that goes beyond the lusts of the body and the distribution of property. What Eve attains, she pays for by surrendering her chains. Marriage is clearly regarded then as part of the chains of the Demiurge, serving his intentions. This was as subversive in the second century as it is today to traditional social structures. These Gnostics are not Christians, shout the heresiologists, and it is difficult, on encountering more deeply their peculiar path to their enlightenment than has become widespread, to disagree with the heresiological position here.

Irenaeus's account now offers what we may suppose was given as guidance to new members of the Sethian community. *How do we tell ourselves apart from everybody else? Why are we, Sethians, superior? What's wrong with Mr. and Mrs. Average?*

While Adam and Eve originally had spiritual bodies, entry into the world made them opaque, gross, and sluggish. Now open to only mundane inspiration, their souls became feeble, languid. However, Prunicus, "moved with compassion towards them, restored to them the sweet savor of the besprinkling light."[11] Coming to remembrance of who they really were, they realized their nakedness, that they were enveloped in temporary material bodies. The body, subject to time, would be transcended; the imprisonment would be over. In the meantime, Sophia (like the "Peacock Angel" Melek Tawus of the Yezidis) taught Adam and Eve about food and carnal knowledge: so were born Cain and Abel. Unfortunately, their births brought to light the evil inherited from the substance of Ialdabaoth. But by the prognosis of Prunicus, Seth was begotten, beginner of the perfect race of aliens, strangers to the world.

Prunicus offers another Gnostic saint in the form of Norea, taken by Sethians as Noah's wife, and thus the ancestress of all races. *The Thought of Norea* is a work found in the Nag Hammadi Library. It is a prayer of Norea to the Father and Barbelo that she be rejoined to the "imperishable ones"; it is dated to the late second or early third century in Egypt. One may easily imagine her prayer being employed in a Sethian service.

However, Prunicus/Sophia is paying a high price for involving herself in the lower world. Distressed, cut off from her spiritual home, she invokes her heavenly Mother. One can again imagine the therapeutic value of this myth on disturbed or alienated women suffering in late antiquity. To Sophia is sent Christ into the world for the "besprinkling of light," announced by John, who prepares the baptism for turning again to God, and adopts Jesus, so Christ will have a pure vessel to appear through. Even though the man (qua man) Jesus is "son of that Ialdabaoth," Ialdabaoth will be outwitted as Christ announces "the woman." Christ clothes his sister in the "besprinkling of light," and with a strong implication of an erotic union of Christ and Sophia, "both exulted in the mutual refreshment they felt in each other's society: this scene they describe as relating to bridegroom and bride."[12] The Sethian allegorical Christology is intriguing. Jesus is begotten of the "Virgin through the agency of God" with the suggestion that the Virgin here is Barbelo. Because of this, Jesus was "wiser, purer, and more righteous than all other men: Christ united to Sophia descended into him, and thus Jesus Christ was produced."

On the Hermetic principle "as above, so below," this supercelestial union is mirrored on Earth in Gnostic circles in the special relations ascribed to Jesus and Mary Magdalene; there is no reason to imagine such relations existed historically, though history to the Gnostic expresses within its sundry patterns, drenched in illusions, a secret codex of the real. What had become obvious to the redeemed Gnostic was scarcely visible to the mundane disciples whose life in the synoptic gospels and in John was lived without benefit of holy pneuma, that is to say, in spiritual blindness.

There is evidence to suggest a pre-Christian Sethian system. In Hippolytus's account of the Sethians,[13] he mentions a book called the *Paraphrase of Seth,* wherein their secret doctrines are adumbrated, based on a trinity of Light, Spirit, and Darkness, whose mixture generated the cosmos (since the Darkness "knew not the Light," it attacked the Spirit). This work must have been very close indeed to the *Paraphrase of Shem,* found in the Nag Hammadi Library, for it concurs well with Hippolytus's account. However, in the extant version of the book, apart from the fact that the Seth figure has been transformed into the son of Noah whose name gave us the word *Semitic,* the savior figure is called "Derdekeas." However, the basic theme of a pure light that is also a seed, distorted through admixture, predominates.

The higher potential of the hidden light must be released from the grip of the demon that manifests through images of a false god. Thus, in this work, the Sodomites had knowledge of the true seed, and it was for this knowledge that Sodom was burned by the demon (an early example of "conspiracy theory"—itself virtually an invention of the Gnostics; odd then that contemporary evangelical conspiracy theories—"Illuminati" &c ad nauseam—blame Gnostics for everything!).

Author and scholar Frederik Wisse considers the *Paraphrase of Shem* important for the formation of early Christology, since it appears that Sethian, or Shemian, philosophy was Christianized to some degree. The question of the degree is significant. There are cunning references to John the Baptist's baptism, and therefore that of Christians generally, being of mere water and therefore of the demon, yet through this deficiency, the true baptism would be revealed. The work breathes a heady, rebellious spirit of transgressive liberation theory, and since Seth simply represents the transmundane seed, the Christian content is practically irrelevant, and I should think it post-Christian, since it parodies and ridicules the Catholic faith—including the theology of the first chapter of John's Gospel.

Something also tells me that we should not dismiss the suspicion that the "woman" beheaded, undoubtedly Wisdom, is also a possible stand-in for an arguably androgynous John the Baptist. While John the Baptist is claimed as the source of the testimony of "John's" gospel (John 1:19), John had his own Gnostic followers in this period (their probable descendants now widely known as the persecuted sect of "Mandaeans") and such could account for the work's apparently "pre" or non-Christian character or origin, since the Mandaeans venerate John as an "envoy of light" while eschewing any worship of Jesus.

The work is almost certainly based on a conceit that ordinary sex is unchaste because it deals only with corrupted matter, but an enlightened Sethian sex sacrament restores the power of the seed through the invocation of the spiritual light that is hidden in the sperm whose source is beyond this world. There is the woman who knows: "And they will behead the woman who has the perception, whom you [Shem] will reveal on the earth." This woman is apparently Sophia, among other names, elsewhere in the text called bluntly "a whore." "For the woman whom they will behead at that time is the coherence of the power of the demon who will baptize the seed of darkness in severity

that it [the seed] may mix with unchastity."[14] The enemy of the text is
nature, whose violent fire, precipitated by a struggle with Spirit in the
Darkness, is emitted from her "dark vagina," the echoing signs of which
are present in the womb of women who suffer the regular torments of
nature's bullying hysteria.

Curiously, further echoes of this idea are alluded to in Irenaeus, following his treatment of the Sethians: curious insofar as the foundation
of the Sethian seed was based on the assumption that that of Cain had
shown its evil root in the murder of Abel, and yet Irenaeus presents us
with what is apparently another Gnostic group called "Cainites."

Chapter 31 of *Adversus Haereses* asserts that the Cainites produced
a *Gospel of Judas,* which finally came to sensational public notice in
2006 (see my 2008 book *Kiss of Death: The True History of the Gospel
of Judas*). Since the revelation of Barbelo is a central feature of Jesus's discourse in that "fictitious history" (Irenaeus), it is considered by scholars
as a Sethian rather than Cainite work. Irenaeus himself distinguishes his
Judas gospel authors by saying they identified themselves with the *sinners*
of scriptural history since it was they who were "assailed by the Creator,"
albeit that none of them suffered injury, but the inclusion of Esau, anti-
Moses rebel Korah (Numbers 16:1–40), the annihilated Sodomites (*cf.
The Paraphrase of Shem*), and Judas Iscariot does not concur with the
claim, but it is probably spiritual injury that is referred to. Sophia "was
in the habit of carrying off that which belonged to her from them to
herself"—this being presumably their light. Judas apparently alone knew
the truth, and "accomplished the mystery of the betrayal," and by him
"all things, both earthly and heavenly, were thus thrown into confusion."
So Judas outwitted the Demiurge too: a concept of outwitting the "rulers of this age" doubtless derived from the incendiary writings of Paul (I
Corinthians 2:6–8) as well as the *Book of Enoch.*

That the Cainites practiced sexual magic is made explicit by Irenaeus
in his conclusion, and we might best conclude that there is no essential difference between Irenaeus's Cainites and the Sethians, for whom
Seth, as we have seen, could manifest in any number of transgressive

individuals, whose thing in common was the ability to excite the powers of the world to destroy them—hence Jesus is naturally included as a Seth. Since the Gnostics were opposed by the orthodox, that too clearly indicated they were on the right side, while the orthodox were the servants of Sakla the fool, keen to "behead" the woman, that is, deprive her of life and voice.

It is fascinating that in Irenaeus's brief exposition of Cainite writings, "Cainite" thought attributes the creation of the universe to Hystera, meaning "womb," whose works Cainites advocate abolishing. This may be a development on the Simonian Eden-paradise-womb discussed earlier. There is also an allusion to the prevalent Gnostic idea that women's menstruation reflects a primal wound in the heart of Sophia herself and her breach with the Pleroma ("Fullness") of God, below the navel, or Unity." Whether dysfunctions in the reproductive organs, giving rise to disturbed psychology, were implied originally—giving us our inherited word *hysteria*—is unknown, but its usage is suggestive of a possible therapeutic aspect to Sethian sexual rites, aimed at linking Gnostics to their transmundane angel beyond the pollutions of time, space, and matter, to recenter the troubled mind on its true Mother:

> They also hold, like Carpocrates, that men cannot be saved until they have gone through all kinds of experience. An angel, they maintain, attends them in every one of their sinful and abominable actions, and urges them to venture on audacity and incur pollution. Whatever may be the nature of the action, they declare that they do it in the name of the angel, saying, "O thou angel, I use thy work; O thou power, I accomplish thy operation!" And they maintain that this is "perfect knowledge," without shrinking to rush into such actions as it is not lawful even to name. (*Adversus Haereses,* I.31, 2)

We can probably name them now: sexual intercourse (predominantly heterosexual), cunnilingus, spermatophagy, manual and assisted masturbation, consumption of mixed vaginal fluids and sperm, consumption of menstrual blood, prolonged intercourse.

Put coldly like that, of course, we might want to reach for the heresiologists' bucket, but if we pause a moment, is it just possible to consider what our feelings might be if any of the above actions were shared equally with someone we truly loved, inwardly and outwardly, and whom we knew truly loved us—and whose spiritual aspiration to a beloved cause was shared also as the highest good? Sophia is, after all, understood by Gnostics then and now as the ever-existing archangelic wisdom of love. Her wisdom was also understood to reside in medicine and healing, in balms and herbs and ointments, and it may be that the story of Jesus's healing of the woman with the issue of blood indicated to Gnostics therapeutic possibilities for sexual healing, while the orthodox, on the other hand, accepted the Genesis account at face value that women's gynecological sufferings were the proper punishment for the sins of Eve and were intended to be endured as such. The Sethians, to the contrary, regarded the baptismal waters of the orthodox as unclean because they were *mixed,* when seen, that is, through the eyes of Shem, who was "from an unmixed power,"[15] and who was above the "darkness" that "was on the face of the deep" (Genesis 1). Seth, Shem, Jesus, Sophia—they came to heal: "For the knowledge of the things which are ordained is truly the healing of the passions of matter."[16]

HIPPOLYTUS ON THE NAASSENI

From Hippolytus, we first learn that it was priests of this persuasion who were called Naasseni (by whom?) but who subsequently "styled themselves Gnostics." We have the usual Gnostic inversion. That is, since the serpent, according to the orthodox Christian and conventional Jewish understandings, was condemned for the "error" that begat Adam's Fall, so the serpent must have been, for those in the know, the enemy of the one who deprived Adam of his birthright: spiritual knowledge, awareness, freedom. In opposing the Elohim (Demiurge), the serpent proved himself/herself Adam and Eve's friend. This made the serpent the revealer of their freedom: carnal knowledge, freedom of choice, self-knowledge. And the Demiurge showed his true colors by attacking Adam and Eve.

As revealer, the serpent is thus linked to Jesus, who, say the Naasseni, spoke to the three parts of man simultaneously—earthly, psychic, and spiritual—with the idea of the intellectually rational included in the latter. Each type, or part, of humanity hears a message pertaining to that nature. Naasseni got their message from the serpent's tongue directly and have created a superior church, for the three natures have manifested in three churches: angelic, psychical, and earthly. And clearly, once you accept this point, we can see there has been confusion, or mixture, in the other two; this more than compares with the three-principle primal conflict of the Sethians. Indeed, it is clear that we are dealing again with Sethian Gnostics, for Hippolytus advises readers requiring further elucidation on the Naasseni to consult the *Gospel of the Egyptians,* which by the miracle of the Nag Hammadi Library, has come down to us and may again be consulted. Therein, the figure of the great Seth predominates: "Then the great Seth came and brought his seed."[17] "And it was sown in the aeons, which had been brought forth, their number being the amount of Sodom." This is now familiar territory to us. Preserved in Sodom and Gomorrah was the seed of Seth: "This is the great incorruptible race, which has come forth, through three worlds to the world." We find again the male virginal spirit, Barbelon, and the uncallable virginal Spirit (unnameable also, presumably, Barbelo).

We also find in Hippolytus ample confirmation of what has been averred consistently, that the interest in Seth's seed evinces a concern with sexual rites interpreted as a transformation of mundane sexual fluids into holy sacraments.

Hippolytus notes the scandalous, staggeringly brazen manner in which the Naasseni quote from Paul's letter to the Romans regarding perversion of divinely instituted sexual relations into sodomy, lesbianism, and orgiastic excesses familiar to hedonistic pagans: "Wherefore also God gave them up unto vile affections; for even their women did change the natural use into that which is against nature." What, however, the natural use is, according to the Naasseni, we shall afterward declare. "And likewise also the men, leaving the natural use of the woman, burned in their lust one toward another; men with men working that which is unseemly" (Romans 1:26–27). Apparently, these very texts the heretics themselves used to assert that Paul had indicated "the entire secret of theirs, and a hidden mystery of blessed pleasure!" For to the Naasseni, sex had indeed been perverted. The devil of the world had perverted the true relations of man and woman, for he had deprived them of the true "washing," that is, seed baptism:

> For the promise of washing is not any other, according to them, than the introduction of him that is washed in, according to them, life-giving water [sexual fluids], and anointed with ineffable ointment into unfading bliss. But they assert that not only is there in favor of their doctrine, testimony to be drawn from the mysteries of the Assyrians, but also from those of the Phrygians concerning the happy nature— concealed, and yet at the same time disclosed—of things that have been, and are coming into existence, and moreover will be—[a happy nature] which [the Naassene] says, is the kingdom of heaven to be sought for within a man. (*Refutatio*, V, 2)

Fascinatingly, Hippolytus shows how these folk were employing the gospel according to Thomas, expressing themselves thus: "He who seeks me will find me in children from seven years old; for there concealed, I shall in the fourteenth age be made manifest" (*cf.* Nag Hammadi, *Gospel of Thomas,* logia 4–5). Hippolytus continues, correctly:

> This, however, is not [the teaching] of Christ, but of Hippocrates, who uses these words: "A child of seven years is half of a father." And so it is that these [heretics] placing the originative nature of the universe in causative seed, [and] having ascertained the [aphorism]

of Hippocrates, that a child of seven years old is half of a father, say
that in fourteen years, according to Thomas, he is manifested. This,
with them, is the ineffable and mystical Logos. (*Refutatio,* V, 2)

If it is not plain to the reader, the text is saying that those looking
for the living Jesus will find him in the sexual emissions that characterize the transition from physical childhood to sexual maturity. This,
to the Naasseni, is how the innocence of children manifested divine
wisdom. Hippolytus evidently understood something many theologians
and Gnostic commentators today have not grasped, that the *Gospel
of Thomas* is plainly a sectarian work, as can be discerned by anyone
consulting it, after having fully comprehended what the Sethians or
Naasseni were advocating, namely, spermatic rites. Once the taboo references are understood, many of the gnomic games with canonical texts
are exposed. This will shock many, I know. But serpents, even very old
ones, still bite.

Hippolytus goes on to explain how the Naasseni interpret any
and every philosophy that comes their way according to a phallocen-
tric principle, having found the primal substance in their groins. Thus
Hermes's, or Mercury's, golden wand is a phallic symbol, for this is the
transformative power, the giver of life and death. So also the phrase
"Thou shalt rule them with a rod of iron" plainly indicates the divine
erection to the initiated. This is the rod that can "awake the dead"; thus
do they interpret Ephesians 5:14: "Awake thou that sleepest, and arise,
and Christ will give thee light."

We should now be getting a vivid impression of the "besprinkling
of the light" as understood by Sethian Gnostics. The Naasseni condemn
"terrestrial intercourse." To indulge in sex in the ordinary manner is
to blaspheme a great mystery. The children of Israel must escape the
bondage of Egypt, that is, the body, before they can embrace the holy
Jordan, the life-giving waters, whose earthly direction, downward, must
be inverted so its properties are reassigned to heaven—possibly a specific
formula for retention of sperm, as has been practiced by Tantric yogis,

or taking sexual fluids orally rather than scattering them or leaving them to nature. The sexual fluids, anyway, must be redirected, as Jesus commanded the waters to go whither he willed them before transforming earthly water into spiritual wine, so prefiguring the true sacrament, administered by purified priests.

According to the Naasseni, those who return to Egypt—that is, those who engage in earthly intercourse—"shall die as men," even because "that which is born of the flesh is flesh, and that which is born of the spirit is spirit" (John 3:6). This, says Hippolytus, is for them the "spiritual generation," as opposed, presumably, to the "generation of vipers." Unredeemed seed is poison. The seed must be liberated from servitude to the power of the world, and this is not to be achieved, as with the Encratites, by abstaining from the precious substance, but by redeeming it in the secret chrism or anointing in the bridal chamber.

And lest anyone be in any doubt as to the sacramental intentions of the Naasseni, Hippolytus makes it very explicit when he asserts how "these most marvellous Gnostics, inventors of a novel grammatical art," have appropriated the Eucharist, in terms of the temple of the Samothracians wherein two naked men stand with penises erect, with both hands stretched upward to heaven, like the statue of Mercury on Mount Cyllene. These images, says a Naassene commentator, indicate the "primal man" Adam, the spiritual one who is born again, "in every respect the same substance as that man," so Jesus says:

> "If ye do not drink my blood, and eat my flesh, ye will not enter into the kingdom of heaven; but even though," He says, "ye drink of the cup which I drink of, whither I go, ye cannot enter there." For He says He was aware of what sort of nature each of His disciples was, and that there was a necessity that each of them should attain unto His own peculiar nature. For He says He chose twelve disciples from the twelve tribes, and spoke by them to each tribe. On this account, He says, "the preachings of the twelve disciples neither did all hear, nor, if they heard, could they receive. For the things

that are not according to nature, are with them contrary to nature."
(*Refutatio,* V, 3)

The grave is the body, and the resurrection is from the body, and the means of rebirth is the Holy Spirit. To receive it is to "enter through the gate of heaven."

One can only imagine that these people had discovered an ecstasy that conformed to their picture-making. Would it be going too far to suggest that something like what is today called kundalini yoga was central to their practice?

The Sanskrit adjective *kundalin* means "circular" and has been used as a noun for a snake, insofar as it is coiled. According to Hippolytus, one aspect of their "novel grammatical art" was to note that the Greek for *temple* (*naos*) was clearly (for them!) derived from *naas* meaning "serpent," so that *all* temples therefore worshipped the serpent without knowing it! And the serpent is "a moist substance," like water an originating principle, from which all things may draw on to live. Thus the Naassene serpent is a synonym for life at its source, soured by the darkness of the world, but capable of being redirected to the brain, which, according to Hippolytus, was understood by them as a metaphor for Edem, whence the four rivers flowed out into the world. As far as we can possibly know, no Naassene practitioners ever saw a single human sperm (from Greek *sperma* = "seed"), but had they done so, they would not have been surprised! Seen in terms of kundalini yoga, the Naassene myth is a positive redemption myth with the advantage of possible proof in practice.

An alabaster bowl of 22cm diameter has survived from third- to fifth-century Syria or Asia Minor whose intricate carving ties in with the Ophite perspective. On the inside of the bowl, sixteen naked adults of both sexes stand in a circle, some with one hand on heart, some with one hand raised openly upward from the elbow, others making both gestures, while other hands cover genitals or navels. At the center is a coiled serpent with little wings, surrounded by two concentric circles of what appear to be solar rays beaming out to the feet of the celebrants (*Journal of Hellenic Studies* 54 [1934]: 129–39, plate III).

KUNDALINI GNOSTICS?

Links to kundalini-type yogic practice are more explicit in Hippolytus's account of another Gnostic group, close in thought to the Naasseni, which he calls the Peratae, or Peratics, whose name is obscure, though Clement of Alexandria[18] says it derives from a place considered as being east of the Euphrates: Media or Persia—the latter since Sophronius of Jerusalem[19] speaks of the sect's alleged founder, Euphrates, with the Latin Persicus or Persia suffixed.

In chapter 12 (book V) of the *Refutatio,* Hippolytus, possibly oblivious to the fact, outlines the basic theory of how kundalini spiritual life-force energy, coiled at the spine's base, is induced by pranayama (breath discipline) to mount upward to the seventh chakra, called the crown, activating the golden cord linking the pituitary and pineal glands. Anyone familiar with this branch of yoga will recognize in Hippolytus's account an only slightly garbled version of something closely akin to the practice that, in its Hindu formulation, is recorded only from the fifteenth century CE:

No one, then, he [Hippolytus's source] says, can be saved or return [into heaven] without the Son, and the Son is the Serpent [a spiritual-physiological practice is likely being referred to here]. For as he brought down from above the paternal marks, so again he carries up from thence those marks roused from a dormant condition and rendered paternal characteristics, substantial ones from the unsubstantial Being, transferring them hither from thence. This, he says, is what is spoken: "I am the door." And he transfers [those marks] he says, to those who close the eyelid [meditate?], as the naphtha drawing the fire in every direction towards itself; nay rather, as the magnet [attracting] the iron and not anything else, or just as the backbone of the sea falcon, the gold and nothing else, or as the chaff is led by the amber. In this manner, he says, is the portrayed, perfect, and con-substantial genus drawn again from the world by the Serpent; nor does he [attract] anything else, as it has been sent down by him.

For a proof of this, they adduce the anatomy of the brain, assimilating, from the fact of its immobility, the brain itself to the Father, and the cerebellum [skull] to the Son, because of its being moved and being of the form of [the head of] a serpent. And they allege that this [cerebellum], by an ineffable and inscrutable process, attracts through the pineal gland the spiritual and life-giving substance emanating from the vaulted chamber [in which the brain is embedded]. And on receiving this, the cerebellum in an ineffable manner imparts the ideas, just as the Son does, to matter; or, in other words, the seeds and the genera of the things produced according to the flesh flow along into the spinal marrow. Employing this exemplar, [the heretics] seem to adroitly introduce their secret mysteries, which are delivered in silence. Now it would be impious for us to declare these; yet it is easy to form an idea of them, by reason of the many statements that have been made.

This leaves us with the possibility that such a practice may have originated in Media or Persia, transplanted to India possibly during the Sassanid invasions, or may have been transplanted to the Roman Empire via Persia, possibly from India, or even China. It is possible that an exponent of the knowledge came west during the second-century wars with Parthia.

Evidence for the portrayal of sexual intercourse as a divine mystery is not lacking in the period. A reference to "thrice-wretched people" may have been Clement of Alexandria's joke at the expense of followers of Hermes Trismegistus (Thrice-Greatest Hermes), or even of Sethian priests when he wrote in *Strōmateis* (III, 4):

There are some who call Aphrodite Pandemos [sexual intercourse] a mystical communion. This is an insult to the name of communion. To do something wrong is called an action, just as also to do right is likewise called an action. Similarly communion is good when the word refers to sharing of money and food and clothing. But they have impiously called by the name of communion any common sexual intercourse. The story goes that one of them came to a virgin of our church who had a lovely face and said to her: "Scripture says, 'Give to everyone that asks you.'" She, however, not understanding the lascivious intention of the man, gave the dignified reply: "On the subject of marriage, talk to my mother." What Godlessness! Even the words of the Lord are perverted by these immoral fellows, the brethren of lust, a shame not only to philosophy but to all human life, who corrupt the truth, or rather destroy it; as far as they can. These thrice wretched men expound like hierophants carnal and sexual intercourse as a sacred religious mystery, and think that it will lead them upwards to the kingdom of God.

Clement reckoned it would simply carry them to the brothels, perhaps a knowing reference to the place where Simon found his queen of heaven, Helena. Nearly two centuries later, Bishop Epiphanius would have agreed wholeheartedly with Clement's point. For Epiphanius, finding an antidote to the heresies of Barbelo-worshippers, had entailed him in an unhappy flirtation with the fleshpots of Egypt.

EPIPHANIUS ON BARBELIOTES AND BORBORITES

Epiphanius's detailed account of Gnostic heresy is frequently discredited in scholarship, but while he has no qualms about expressing his total disgust, and naturally has no pretensions to "objectivity" in the modern sense, he nonetheless gives forth what he thinks are the facts of the practices in the expectation that decent people will hardly be interested in the interpretation of those practices once they are aware of the practices themselves. Thus he speaks of the "filthy people" (Borborians):

> For after having made love with the passion of fornication in addition, to lift their blasphemy up to heaven, the woman and man receive the man's emission on their own hands. And they stand with their eyes raised heavenward but the filth on their hands and pray, if you please—the ones they call Stratiotics and Gnostics—and offer that stuff on their hands to the true Father of all, and say, "We offer thee this gift, the body of Christ."
>
> And then they eat it partaking of their own dirt, and say, "This is the body of Christ; and this is the Pascha, because of which our bodies suffer and are compelled to acknowledge the passion of Christ."
>
> And so with the woman's emission when she happens to be having her period—they likewise take the unclean menstrual blood they gather from her, and eat it in common. And "This," they say, "is the blood of Christ."
>
> And so, when they read, "I saw a tree bearing twelve manner of fruits every year, and he said unto me, "This is the tree of life," in apocryphal writings, they interpret this allegorically of the menstrual flux.
>
> But although they have sex with each other, they renounce procreation. It is for enjoyment, not procreation, that they eagerly pursue seduction, since the Devil is mocking people like these, and making fun of the creature fashioned by God.
>
> They come to climax but absorb the seeds of their dirt, not by implanting them for procreation, but by eating the dirty stuff themselves.
>
> But even though one of them should accidentally implant the seed of his natural emission prematurely and the woman becomes pregnant, listen to a more dreadful thing that such people venture to do.
>
> They extract the foetus at the stage, which is appropriate for their

enterprise, take this aborted infant, and cut it up in a trough with a pestle. And they mix honey, pepper, and certain other perfumes and spices with it to keep from getting sick, and then all the revellers in this herd of swine and dogs assemble, and each eats a piece of the child with his fingers.

And now, after this cannibalism, they pray to God and say, "We were not mocked by the archon of lust, but have gathered the brother's blunder up!" And this, if you please, is their idea of the "perfect Passover."

And they are prepared to do any number of other dreadful things. Again, whenever they feel excitement within them they soil their own hands with their own ejaculated dirt, get up, and pray stark naked with their hands defiled. The idea is that they can obtain freedom of access to God by a practice of this kind.

Man and woman, they pamper their bodies night and day, anointing themselves, bathing, feasting, spending their time in whoring and drunkenness. And they curse anyone who fasts and say, "Fasting is wrong; fasting belongs to this archon who made the world. We must take nourishment to make our bodies strong, and able to render their fruit in its season."

They use both the Old and the New Testaments, but renounce the Speaker in the Old Testament. And whenever they find a text the sense of which can be against them, they say that this has been said by the spirit of the world.

But if a statement can be represented as resembling their lust— not as the text is, but as their deluded minds take it—they twist it to fit their lust and claim that it has been spoken by the Spirit of truth. (*Panarion,* 26, 4:6–6:2)

The details about cannibalism of aborted fetuses seem not only utterly scandalous, but also far-fetched in the extreme. However, in Roelof van den Broek's study of Epiphanius,[20] van den Broek is prepared to accept the possibility that Epiphanius's account may be based on experiences he had in Egypt when female members of a sect tried to seduce him into it, as Epiphanius maintains, though he does not state that he either observed such horrors or learned about them directly from members. It is always a possibility that some followers went beyond relatively harmless (arguably) symbolic acts and practiced enormities in secret. However, Epiphanius uses the information to tar every Gnostic sect with the charge, itself unproven in a Roman court. Outlandish things are always told of exclusive sects because the very suspicion works to condemn all and repel all.

The details about consumption of sexual fluids as a Eucharist chime in with other reports noted hitherto. There is the suggestion of a parallel between sexual passion and the passion of Christ, not entirely without a hint of masochism in both men and women, according to a pun on the Hebrew *pascha* (Passover) with the Greek *paskein* "to suffer" and the substantive *pathos* "passion."

Sexual passion is equated with suffering, regarded as a means used by the Demiurge to enslave the soul to the chains of the body. This equation stems in part from the whole corpus of ideas about Sophia's yearning to know the Father. Her passion ultimately leads to exile and the aborted cosmos in the basic Gnostic myth, mostly associated with Valentinus but by no means confined to his followers. That we have at once the idea of a spiritual yearning for knowledge and a passion of the heart and flesh for the flesh and heart transmuted brings us into the kind of explicit romantic territory explored in the spiritually heterodox Symbolist movement in art (late nineteenth–early twentieth century), itself inspired by such music as the aching, if rather sickly, intensity of the Liebestod in Wagner's *Tristan und Isolde* that threw French Occult Revivalists, and later, Salvador Dalí and his decadent ilk, to distraction. Religious aspiration and the sex instinct become fused, or are taken as being fused, resulting in an erotic religion far from the cultural mainstream's taste.

And certainly not to Epiphanius's: his take on spermatophagy and the like is simple. The "so-called gnosis" begins when a heresiarch makes excuses for his own uncontrollable lusts and burdens theology with them in self-justification. Thus, Epiphanius says the followers of Nicolaus, the Nicolaitans (condemned in Revelation 2:6, 15), were caught up in their progenitor's lust for his beautiful wife, which he could not control, and instead of being ashamed and repenting for his incontinence, he declared instead that eternal life needs daily sex, while insulting his wife, imagining that men lusted after her as he did. While discussing Nicolaus, Epiphanius explains why the Borborians do what they do:

> But others honor one "Prunicus" and like these, when they consummate their own passions with this kind of disgusting behavior, they say in mythological language of this interpretation of their disgusting behavior, "We are gathering the power of Prunicus from our bodies, and through their emissions." That is, they suppose they are gathering the power of semen and menses. (*Panarion,* I, section 2, 25, 3:2)

We have seen in our investigation of the range of Sethian convictions that these Gnostics considered the divine element in human beings to exist in the procreative power: "In the beginning was the Word," and the Word is understood as the potential of the seed, which is pneuma, whose virtue is, as the profoundly heretical *Gospel of Thomas* has it, spread out upon the world "but men do not see it."[21] No doubt, many scholars of gnosis have missed the point, including this one on many occasions!

Salvation is realized by bodily emissions offered to God, reminiscent of the Old Testament conviction that "without the shedding of blood [understood by heretics as life/semen] there is no forgiveness" (Hebrews 9:22). Epiphanius is quite blunt about why Prunicus is called the whore. She keeps appearing before the archons in beautiful form and "through their lust-caused ejaculation robs them of their seed." She does this to recover her power "sown in" some of the jealous archons.[22]

According to Epiphanius, Nicolaitans followed Prunicus in this gathering process: "We [Nicolaitans] gather Prunicus's power from our bodies through their emissions."[23] Virginity is defined by these Gnostics as those in touch with untainted seed, like their heroine Noria, beloved of Barbelo, the Great Mother, sometimes virgin daughter of Eve—as in the Nag Hammadi *Hypostasis of the Archons* (*Reality of the Rulers*)—sometimes wife of Noah or Shem. The central interest is always the same: the destiny of the seed and the redemption of it from the corrupting powers of the world. According to Epiphanius's accurate reading of Gnostic priorities:

> For Noah was obedient to the archon, they say, but Noria revealed the powers on high and Barbelo the scion of the powers, who was the archon's opponent as the other powers are. And she let it be known that what has been stolen from the Mother on high by the archon who made the world, and by the other gods, demons and angels with him, must be gathered from the power in bodies, through the male and female emissions. (*Panarion,* I, section 2, 26, 1:9)

According to one of the sect's favored texts, *The Greater Questions of Mary,* the ritual was instituted by Jesus in Mary's company, presumably the Magdalene. In a twist on the birth of Eve, Jesus took Mary up a mountain, produced a woman out of his side, then had intercourse with her before consuming the resultant fluids, saying: "Thus we must do, that we may live."[24]

When Jesus says to the disciples in their text: "Except ye eat my flesh and drink my blood," the disciples back off: "Who can hear this?" they say. That's why they were disturbed and fell away; the teaching was too exalted for them! They couldn't get high enough, as Mary could on the mountain. The men were inhibited by the archons: "uptight" to use the argot of the *Hair*-brained hippies of the late '60s and early '70s. Transgression was "where it was at." Followers should learn to take their clothes off as prefiguring the divesting of the body: soul to soul, man. They should strip with the innocence of children, as the *Gospel of Thomas* urges[25] (*cf.* the effect on Jim Morrison of Julian Becks's *Living Theatre* productions).

The Gnostics quote Psalm 1:3: "He shall be like a tree planted by the outgoings of water that will bring forth its fruit in due season" to indicate that the fruit of the tree is the moment of emission: the orgasm is the fruit. The imagery of fruit and trees was in the marrow of the sect's beliefs, as we shall see. Barbelo, we may recall, is the root and life of the tree that is the gnosis. Its fruit contains its seed. Among the "Barbelites" (better I think than the rather clumsy "Barbeliotes") the seed is given up for the restoration (Greek: *apokatastasis*) of wounded being (the Pleroma). The wounds or passion of Barbelo and her daughters (particularly Sophia) are allegorized, then particularized as menstrual blood, representing the passion for God as well as the pain of the world under the law of the archons. The pain is healed by semen, the Word from above comes to redeem and makes fruitful the barren one, spiritually speaking.

It may be inferred that union leading to fertility stops the bleeding, becoming a higher passion in which the material self is surrendered and transcended in union, thus "healing the passions of matter." Ordinary sex, on the other hand, is for Barbelites a surrender to nature, a victory for the archons, and a careless casting away of seed among the "weeds" and "dry land," to be gobbled up by "the beast" (that is, the fleshly body). Epiphanius makes no distinction. Sex presupposes filth. He treats sacramental sex as sex disguised by perverts. Encratite in orientation, Epiphanius views bodily fluids as "dirt." If you had asked him, "Who made these fluids?" he would doubtless have said, "You had better ask what they were made *for*." He would then tell you they were made for procreation for the sinful many, as part of God's dispensation for Eve's sin, though the stronger spirits, the elect, would continue to abstain from sex because the Devil used it to ensnare and to corrupt. Some readers may feel driven to repeat the question Zoé Oldenbourg put in the introduction to her book *Massacre at Montségur*. What is the practical difference between a world made by God and perverted by the Devil, and a world made by the Devil whose denizens could be saved by God? Well, to Epiphanius, there was no difference at all. You do not achieve correct doctrine through blasphemy and lust.

The Gnostic might reply, "It depends what you're 'blaspheming.'" St. Paul said the cross outwitted the "rulers of the world." The tree trapped them. He who was hung on a tree, according to Jewish custom, was accursed. If the "rulers of this world" had known what they were doing, they would never have crucified the Lord of Glory (I Corinthians 2:8). Paul supported the idea of the "messianic secret," the ultimate salvation of humankind kept in the dispensation of Wisdom since before time, for God had prognosis: the eyes that see before we see. Jesus, according to John's Gospel (8:23), was "not of the world." He was "from above," his enemies "from beneath." Jesus knew about the archons, the rulers of the world; his mission was to execute God's judgment upon them. As for lust, that is a travesty of what sacred sex is all about. Was it lust in the ordinary sense of the word that made the woman touch the hem of Jesus's garment in order for her fountain of blood to be healed (Matthew 9:20)? And would not the Barbelite see the word *garment* and think "body"? If the Barbelite recognized that the "hem" or "tassle" of a priest's garment was particularly sacred, he would doubtless particularize what part of the body the initiated interpretation of the text suggested.

The Barbelites had an X-rated *Gospel of Eve,* from which Epiphanius quotes:

> They begin with foolish visions and proof texts in what they claim is a Gospel. For they make this allegation: "I stood upon a lofty mountain, and saw a man who was tall, and another, little of stature. And I heard as it were the sound of thunder and drew nigh to hear, and he spake with me and said, I am thou and thou art I, and wheresoever thou art, there am I; and I am sown in all things. And from wheresoever thou wilt thou gatherest me, but in gathering me, thou gatherest thyself." (*Panarion,* I, section 2, 26, 3:1)

Thus the Barbelites explained all biblical references to gathering and lost sheep; Barbelites saw themselves, literally, as *life*savers. We may recall that Simonians saw Helena as Simon's lost sheep. We seem to be seeing a development of that idea. And it would seem the idea went on being developed for the *Gospel of Eve*'s description of that which is distributed in all things, but which is also absolute self-knowledge, would in time be applied to the philosopher's stone of the alchemist, if indeed such was not already the case, as legendary Persian alchemist Ostanes left a famous quote that there existed such a stone in Egypt; and what is it that exists at the heart of lush fruit?

Similarly, metaphors of harvesting and cutting of fruit from the tree were interpreted by Barbelites as the saving of the seed from falling to earth. Epiphanius insists Barbelites eschewed procreation, for it involved enveloping the seed in archon-made, corruptible flesh. This does seem somewhat contradictory of the notion of sacramentalized fertility. As we shall see when we come to approach the Valentinian obsession with holy seed, it was possible to hold such ideas and aim for the preservation of the seed within children raised spiritually within the community.

In *Panarion* I, section 2, 26, 16:4, Epiphanius says Barbelites "forbid chaste wedlock and procreation," while having sex to suit themselves, and in doing so "hinder procreation," a phrase which, while favoring contraception (possibly confining sex to the menstrual period where possible), is not as extreme as aborting every inadvertent fetus as a matter of course. However, we may suspect Barbelites shared the widespread Christian belief that virginity was the ideal to be venerated. However, their idea of virginity was peculiar. Epiphanius says they called their women virgins, a usage with a somewhat ironic twist on the usual understanding, since they were having sacramental sex, and pregnancies occurred when coitus interruptus was not interrupted for the gathering of the seed. How seriously we must take Epiphanius's account of abortions and consumption we have discussed already. Of course, we might note that today we do not consume aborted fetuses ritually, accepting or reintegrating the products of fleshly unions; they are left with strangers to be disposed of clinically.

In the Barbelite view, losing one's virginity meant to contribute willingly to the reproductive cycle of the archontic rule. This seems to have opened up an area of spiritual validity for homosexuals, otherwise condemned by Christians and Jews. According to Epiphanius, the sect had a class of Levites, who, he says, practiced homosexual sex, though there is no account of which I am aware to suggest that Levites were unmarried. Perhaps it was because the tribe of Levi was the only tribe at the conquest of Canaan denied landownership rights "because the Lord God of Israel is their inheritance" (Deuteronomy 18:2); also Levites are so by patrilineal descent, and the priesthood is thus literally passed from man to man.

Epiphanius offers a fascinating glimpse of actual conditions when he describes encountering real live Barbelites in Egypt in 330 CE. Highly attractive women attempted to seduce him, in both senses:

> For I happened on this sect myself, beloved, and was actually taught these things in person, out of the mouths of people who really undertook them. Not only did women under this delusion offer me this line of talk, and divulge this sort of thing to me. With impudent boldness moreover, they even tried to seduce me themselves—like that murderous, villainous Egyptian wife of the chief cook—because they wanted me in my youth.
>
> But he who stood by the holy Joseph then, stood by me as well. And when, in my unworthiness and inadequacy, I had called on the One who rescued Joseph then, and was shown mercy and escaped their murderous hands, I too could sing a hymn to God the all-holy and say, "Let us sing to the Lord for he is gloriously magnified; horse and rider hath he thrown into the sea."
>
> For it was not by a power like that of Joseph's righteousness but by my groaning to God, that I was pitied and rescued. For when I was reproached by the baneful women themselves, I laughed at the

way persons of their kind were whispering to each other, jokingly if you please, "We can't save the kid; we've left him in the hands of the archon to perish!"

(For whichever is prettier flaunts herself as bait, so that they claim to "save"—instead of destroying—the victims of their deceit through her. And then the plain one gets blamed by the more attractive ones, and they say, "I'm an elect vessel and can save the suckers but you couldn't!")

Now the women who taught this dirty myth were very lovely in their outward appearance but in their wicked minds they had all the devil's ugliness. But the merciful God rescued me from their wickedness, so that after reading their books, understanding their real intent, and not being carried away with it, and after escaping without taking the bait, I lost no time reporting them to the bishops who were there, and finding out which ones were hidden in the church. Thus they were expelled from the city, about 80 persons, and the city was cleared of their tare-like, thorny growth. (*Panarion*, I, section 2, 26, 17:4–9)

We get the picture. Epiphanius had always been a good boy. He just said no. One wonders if one of the bishops responsible for exiling the heretics might have been Athanasius, who occupied the see of Alexandria from 328 to 373 CE (with interruptions). If so, Epiphanius might just have been a catalyst for Athanasius's Festal Letter of 367 CE, which was a possible cause of the burial of the Nag Hammadi Library, without which you would not be reading and I should not be writing this.

Roelof van den Broek has made the important point that two Gnostic texts, earlier than the *Panarion,* are forthright in condemning practices like those Epiphanius draws attention to.[26] In *Pistis Sophia* (*Faith Wisdom*), Thomas says to Jesus:

We have heard that there are some upon the earth who take male semen and female menstrual blood and make a dish of lentils and eat it, saying: "We believe in Esau and Jacob." Is this then a seemly thing or not?

At that moment, Jesus was angry with the world and he said to Thomas: "Truly I say that this sin surpasses every sin and every iniquity. Men of this kind will be taken immediately to the outer darkness, and will not be returned again into the sphere." (*Pistis Sophia*, 147)

The *Second Book of Jeu*, 43, insists that no mysteries will be given to servants of the seventy-two evil archons: "neither give them to those who serve the eighth power of the great Archon, that is, those who eat the menstrual blood of their impurity and the semen of men, saying: 'We have come to true knowledge and pray to the true God.'" "Their God, however, is bad." These are important testimonies to a gnosis not dependent on the conflation of spiritual and physical seed. Van den Broek recognizes the polemical character of Epiphanius's dismissive discourse but reckons the *Panarion* "may harbor some truth in these allegations." The difficulty is that while we get quite a good idea of the way Epiphanius interpreted many of the practices, based on the heretics' own writings, we do not know the precise context, especially the ritual context, for the acts described.

My own view is based on what I consider the inescapable likelihood that while one might abhor the literalism of the Eucharistic practice, it may not be entirely the parody it at first appears to be. Or certainly, not a parody without spiritual value for its adherents, though corruption of an original scheme may well have taken place. There is, I think, the plain inheritance of a theory, or several theories, of sexual magic, derived from a number of possible sources: Simon Magus, Persia, India, Egypt herself. Magicians tend to be eclectic: "if it does the trick, use it." A potentially magical substance is charged sacramentally. This may be called sexual alchemy, and that might be what is really at issue here; it is hard to say with certainty. However, if we are dealing with magical sacramentalism, and I strongly suspect we are, the question of whether the nature of the Barbelite sexual practices is predominantly erotic or sacred seems beside the point, insofar as, for the magic to operate in the imagination of late antiquity, it would need to be both.

Remarkably, perhaps, sects of the Barbelite type survived in southern Asia, Syria, and Armenia, beyond the time of the bishop of Salamis, even when the Eastern Roman Empire had been completely Christianized, from the official point of view, and the state exercised a hand in the condemnation and punishment of heretics. Imperial legislation targeted them in the fifth century when Gnostic heretics were forbidden to hold services or erect churches.

One of the heretics' late influences may have been connected to the persistent cults to elevate the Virgin Mary. In this regard, we might note that to Barbelites a virgin was someone who related to the Great Mother, rather than the material world, someone like Mary Magdalene, who offered herself to Jesus's service. The growing enthusiasm for representing the Virgin Mary as a heavenly power or even a goddess for all intents and purposes, suggests a possible fusing of ideas of the Mother of God and the persistent Barbelo, Great Mother whose fruit was Jesus who promised the thieves hung on the tree that they would join the Son in paradise, identified by Sethian Gnostics as the womb, or gateway. Such ideas may have occurred both as a reaction to orthodox Mariolatry, and as an encouragement to it. Either way, Catholic Christianity has not been able to thrive without the woman and many now believe their future to be in her hands.

SIX

TANTRA—
REMARKABLE PARALLELS

What God hath cleansed, let no man call unclean.

ACTS OF THE APOSTLES 10:9; *cf.* ROMANS 14:14

This is a timely point to recognize that treating gnosis in terms only of Christian heresy and deviation from orthodoxy involves misunderstanding its essence, that is, what the Gnostic schools may have been to themselves. It is hard not to get swept up in the heresiologists' basic attitude to gnosis. They make a witty appeal to sense and morality. However, if we step aside for a while from Christianity and look at another, remarkably similar tradition, we may feel that orthodox apologists have deliberately sidestepped a vital point about Gnostic group identity.

A transgressive approach to acculturated norms of behavior is also a glaring feature of those traditions associated with Hinduism and Buddhism, generally known as Tantra, or the left-hand path. That is to say, a certain "decadent" antinomianism may constitute a valid spiritual path, replete with practices that disgust outsiders, not practiced in pursuit of disgust but in order to overcome the limitations of the bases of disgust, so as to reveal otherwise hidden properties, indeed glories, "in the world but not of it." We have seen this idea in the context of Gnostic antinomian Carpocrates, and perhaps we should also recognize that Jesus, according to canonical accounts, was "numbered with the transgressors," keeping company with harlots, tax collectors, and "sinners." He was outrageous and was ministered to by women "of their substance" (Luke 8:3).

If we now examine some important features of Tantric traditions, I think we shall be amazed at illuminating parallels with the hostile patristic (church fathers') reports of the "filthy ones." Indeed, we may, on the basis of these parallels, be disposed to conclude that Gnostics and Tantrics at least share common roots, if only in the mind of humankind.

Hugh Urban, an authority on the exposition of Tantra to Western scholarship, informs us that the word *tantra* comes from the Sanskrit *tan,* occurring in the earliest Vedic texts (ca. 1200 BCE–500 BCE), when referring to a particular text. It means only "to weave, stretch, or spread": an exposition. The word *veda* itself is more suggestive to us, for veda means "knowledge" or "wisdom," and the earliest texts of the Vedas include hymns, incantations, and mantras, the kinds of things heresiologists condemn as wicked practices among Gnostics. The implication is that "Tantriks" worked from written, revelatory traditions, interpreting them in practice.

According to Urban, Tantra is "a rather messy and ambiguous term used to refer to a huge array of texts, traditions, sects, and ritual practices that spread throughout the Hindu, Buddhist, and Jain communities of South and East Asia from roughly the fifth century [CE] onward"—that is, from about the time the Barbelite Gnostics seem to disappear from Western history.[1]

In Tantric traditions, we are straightaway met with a parallel figure to Barbelo, namely Shakti; understanding Shakti may help us to understand the Mother of Wisdom. Shakti is energy; she creates and she destroys the universe. We all know that in Tantra she is worshipped through sexual union (*maithuna*). According to the medieval *Kularnava Tantra:* "If liberation could be attained simply by having intercourse with a [female partner], all living beings in the world would be liberated just by having intercourse with women."[2] Technique is central, as is knowledge of what is involved, for Tantra's tolerance of ritual transgression is directed at nothing less than gathering the universal Shakti into the worshipper's being. Shakti flows through everything, but is principally most fruitful in the creative juices of man and woman, which, while "unclean" to ordinary worshippers are reconceived as vehicles of divinity to Tantriks, to be adored, venerated, and "saved."

Suddenly, Epiphanius's "filthy people" begin to appear in a different light.

While some Tantric schools advocate retention of semen in the manner of certain Taoist practitioners, sublimating the passion completely or generating an inner orgasm, members of one of the oldest extant Tantric schools, the Kaula—from *kula,* meaning "lineage" or "family"—consume ejaculated semen and uterine blood orally. This practice is very much set within a context of a Eucharistic rite ("giving thanks"), where the combined juices, transmuted in praise and ecstasy are, as it were, consumed by the delighted goddess herself, who has a vested interest in gathering the precious seed of creation. In gratitude for this worship, the goddess offers supernatural gifts to satisfy the needs of her worshippers.

Hugh Urban draws attention to the fourteenth-century *Brihat Tantrasana* (*The Great Essence of the Tantras*), where the combined fluids, transmuted through the sacramental act, become the *kula dravya,* the "clan substance," binding the Tantric family into communion with her through her eternal communion with Shiva (the Father force), her consort. Shakti, like Sophia, involves herself with the things of Earth, but remains ever pure with regard to them. To paraphrase the Gnostic "gospel," she may walk in filth but her garments are not soiled (*The First Apocalypse of James*): hence she is virgin, pure and houri divine, most worthy of worship. The sacred substance, raised in ecstasy, divine delight, is now the potent "remnant" (*nachishta*) of the "sexual sacrifice." We have here a clear intrinsic link between "passion" and "suffering," or self-offering. As the *Great Essence* puts it: "[. . .] he should worship the Goddess in the vagina [. . .] with incense, lamps, and food offerings, the Kula adept should honor her in various ways, and then he should [consume] the remnants himself" (Agamavagisha, *Brihat Tantrasana*, 703).

Benefits from consumption of the nectar are not practical only; awakening is also involved. Thus, the Tantric-Buddhist *Hevajra-Tantra* associates semen with the "thought of awakening" (*bodhicitta*), and we may be reminded of the Gnostic text: "It is those who are awakened that I have addressed." The Buddha of the *Hevajra-Tantra* is quite direct: "I dwell in the Sukhāvatī [Land of Bliss] of the woman's vagina in the name of semen."[3] The fifteenth-century Tantrik, Krishnananda Agamavagisha, advocates putting all reserve aside in a matter so important: "The one who is hesitant in drinking [wine] or is disgusted by semen and menstrual blood is mistaken about what is [in fact] pure and undefiled; thus he fears committing a sin in the act of sexual union. He should be dismissed—for how can he worship the Goddess, and how can he recite Chandi's *mantra*."[4] The same Tantrik master declares this "nectar of life" to be of the "nature of the Supreme Brahman" and the partaker of the sacrificial vessel imbibes "the eternally blameless state free of all distinctions."[5]

This substance is not that which outsiders imagine, any more than the body and blood of Jesus consumed in Catholic sacraments constitute the act of cannibalism hostile pagans believed it to be. The clan substance consumed outside of the sacrificial vessel, consecrated by the Goddess, would lead to hell. Strictly for worship, it is transformed into *amrita,* the nectar divine. In Gnostic terms, such would be considered the fruit of Barbelo's tree, glorious and transformative.

The practice gains immeasurable stimulus from its transgressive characteristics, albeit within strictly defined contexts. Its practitioner is a hero (*vīra*) who has dared to transcend the limitations of ordinary human beings and embraced the lawless power that comes from transgressing the bounds of impurity; eccentric appearance and behavior are associated with Tantriks, such that, as Jeffrey J. Kripal asserts in his study of the Bengali saint Ramakrishna: "Too often scholars have equated Tantra with a philosophical school . . . and have ignored the popular connotations of the term Tāntrika, almost all of which revolve around the notions of magical power, strangeness, seediness, and sex."[6] This makes one think immediately of Simon Magus and of his spiritual descendant, Aleister Crowley (1875–1947) who asserted, tellingly, in his diary in 1920: "I recognize Magick as concerned to *reverse* any existing order."[7]

Crowley's friend and sometime disciple, Gerald Yorke, wrote with regard to Crowley's antinomianism—Crowley once ate his mistress's excrement at her command to prove he could practice what he preached in terms of "everything partakes of God"—"Crowley didn't enjoy his perversions! He performed them in order to overcome his horror of them."[8]

Alexis Sanderson's *Purity and Power*[9] refers to the Tantriks' attainment of an "unfettered super-agency through the assimilation of their lawless power in occult manipulations of impurity," for with the practice may come the *parergon,* or by-product of *siddhis:* reception of exceptional spiritual wisdom, Gnostic insight, or apparently miraculous phenomena.

The sixteenth-century *Kaulavalinirnaya* advocates behavior like that described by Irenaeus of the Gnostic magician, Marcus, follower of Valentinus, namely, having adulterous intercourse for magical purposes: "The Goddess is fond of the vulva and penis, fond of the nectar of vulva and penis. Therefore one should fully worship the Goddess with the drinking of the virile fluid and by taking pleasure in the wife of another man, as well as with the nectar of the vulva and penis." While such assertions, typical of the Tantrik vīra, suggest to most Westerners a mere worship of sex, Hugh Urban insists that "in most Asian traditions

Tantra is generally understood less in terms of 'sex' than in terms of power or energy. That is, it is a series of teachings and techniques aimed at awakening, harnessing, and utilizing the spiritual power believed to flow through the entire cosmos and the human body."[10]

We cannot, however, avoid noticing that the embrace of the lawless power is very much in tune with the Gnostic attack on the god of the law who binds his dupes to the Earth, preventing consumption of the fruit, and who works through the lowest level of created existence, manifest in the unredeemed genitals that under normal circumstances, waste seed or push it into unhappy reproductions of unredeemed souls.

It is also important to recognize then that in Tantra's consciousness of kundalini (the serpent), we may see the Gnostic itinerary placed firmly within the human body, as it may be supposed members of Gnostic groups did as well, judging by what we have seen. Much of what the heresiologists took to be crazy physics, cod theology, perverted scripture, and barmy creation structures were almost certainly taken by the cognoscenti of the movement as codes and metaphors for physical practices coupled to a nascent psychology—as Carl Jung recognized and strongly believed.

The whole drama of the Gnostic creation and redemption myths can be seen as taking place not in the objective, arguably illusory, universe, or even beyond it in spatial terms, but chiefly within the awakened being of the Gnostic, wherein paradise is in the genitals, the unknown Father is accessed through the crown of the head, and the serpent-Sophia redeems the seed that comes from on high and brings it back up the spinal column (tree) through the aeons, corresponding to the "cakkras" (*chakras*) to its source, from which the precious pearl of creation has dripped to the lower regions, governed by a dark ignorance, enslaved to the cycle of birth and death. The way to eternal life is up, and it takes a lot of courage to make the journey; the world doesn't want you to do it. The world wants you to do as you're told. The world wants you scared, for your "own good" (an offer we are not meant to refuse). Hence the Tantrik master is a hero and his mistress a heroine, for she in-personates Shakti, as he in-personates for her Shiva, whose symbol is the erect shiva lingam. Now perhaps we can see what the worship of Simon and Helen was all about, once we remove the skin of eighteen hundred years of orthodox smothering.

Gordan Djurdjevic has written most effectively concerning the Tantric use of decadence as a spiritual technique for ascending from the lowest cakkra (chakra) ("wheel" or "flower"), the *mūlādhāra,* at the genitals, to the highest cakkra where supreme joy awaits the successful practitioner: "According to Tantric theory, the semen, which in its original state [and situated at the top of the head], has ambrosial properties, turns into poison when it reaches the lower parts of the body [*cf.* the Demiurge and the unredeemed seed] specifically the genitals. For this situation to be remedied, the semen needs to be brought back to the top of the head."[11]

Practices for achieving this have involved the voluntary retention of semen and imaginary rechanneling of its essence up the spine, and even sucking back the combined fluids from the vagina after quite extraordinary yogic training. These practices are generally regarded as later developments of Tantric practice. The Kaula method is thought to be the most ancient. Oral consumption of semen (*bindu*), menstrual blood (*rajas*), and vaginal sexual fluids (*yonitattva*) conferred divine status on participants. Such may account for the claims of Simonians that their followers possessed eternal life. Walter O. Kaelber's account of Vedic asceticism in ancient India informs us how "Male seed is also capable of generating spiritual rebirth and immortality."[12] Understood from this perspective, Ireneaeus's and Epiphanius's taunts fired at Gnostics' belief in their eternal life register as the carping of ignoramuses. It is an ancient belief of the Indian subcontinent that loss of semen contributes to disease, aging, and premature death, for semen is life and the promise of fertility.

The North Indian Tantric tradition of the Nāth Siddhas, credited with developing hatha yoga, considered that while bindu carried immortality, its perpetual dripping from the crown depletes energy by its being consumed in the stomach's digestive fire or through ejaculation, which, to be at its holiest, must rather be fertile of the spinal lotuses opening them up to induce spiritual awakening as the spirit rises home. Analogies (at least) with Gnostic claims for "realized resurrection in the body" can hardly go unnoticed. Tantriks hold that oral consumption offers rejuvenation as well as enlightenment, for the nectar of the gods is also the elixir of immortality, amrita, or the divine liquor *soma,* giving the drinker "eternal life in heaven on earth."[13]

We may also wonder about the tendency in Gnostic thought to emphasize Jesus's other body, which watches the crucifixion at a distance in the Nag Hammadi *Apocalypse of Peter* and in *The Second Treatise of the Great Seth.*[14] Normally attributed to the heresy of Docetism (Jesus only *appears* as human), the emphasis on Jesus's being outside of his body may also be attributed to a common store of ideas implicit in Tantra, wherein the gross body conceals a subtle body, and a goal of alchemy is to refine the subtle from the gross. Thus, the subtle body extends invisibly from the genitals via the spine to the crown of the head. When we consider the spine in terms of the Barbelite tree, we may be able to make fresh sense of the following utterance of Jesus in the *Apocalypse of Peter,* which might as well have been called the awakening of Peter:

> He whom you saw on the tree, glad and laughing, this is the living Jesus. But this one into whose hands and feet they drive the nails is his fleshly part, which is the substitute being put to shame, the one who came into being in his likeness. But look at him and me. But I, when I [Peter] had looked, said, "Lord no one is looking at you. Let us flee this place."

No one is looking at the spiritual body. That was the Gnostics' complaint, so preoccupied with flesh were the fleshly materialists that they failed, from the Gnostic point of view, to see what was really happening: the spiritual glory of the living Jesus, not the death of the fleshly tunic.

In worshipping the man, they blinded themselves to themselves. The last words of the *Apocalypse* are: "When he [Jesus] had said these things, he [Peter] came to himself." That is the point. He came to himself.

John 3:14 seemed to Gnostics to give the game away: "And as Moses lifted up the serpent in the wilderness: even so must the Son of man be lifted up." For Tantriks, of course, the primal spiritual energy is the snake coiled at the base of the spine. Was Tertullian, I wonder, cognizant of this idea when, in *Adversus Valentinianos* (II.76), he mercilessly parodied the supposed esoteric "wisdom" of the Valentinians' serpent:

> To sum up, the dove used to reveal Christ; the serpent used to tempt him. The former from the first was the herald of divine love; the latter from the first was the thief of God's image. Therefore, innocence by itself can easily both recognize and exhibit God. Wisdom by itself can rather attack and betray him.
>
> Now, let the serpent hide himself as much as he can; let him twist his entire wisdom into the windings of his lairs. Let him live deep in the ground, push into dark holes, unroll his length coil by coil; let him slither out—but not all of him at once, the light-hating beast. Our dove, however, has a simple home, always in high and open places toward the light since this symbol of the Holy Spirit loves the sunrise, the symbol of Christ. Just so, truth blushes at nothing except being hidden away, because no one is ashamed to listen to her, to learn to recognize as God the one whom nature has already pointed out to him as God, the one whom he sees daily in all his works.

For Tantriks, who would easily qualify for Tertullian's lesson, *kundalinī śakti* is the microcosmic correspondent of the Great Goddess, whose divine partner Shiva has his esoteric home on the top of the human head. One can hear Tertullian's reaction to this: "Microcosmic correspondent! *Microcomic,* more like!" Heresy, remember, began in Eden, so the Carthaginian lawyer would have no truck with the idea that when Shiva and Shakti appear separate, the world appears illusory, pain-ridden: the world of ordinary people whom, Tertullian asserts, Christ came to save, not with esoteric subtleties ("for the serpent was more subtle than any beast in the field"), but with the truth delivered plainly. But the Gnostic might reply to the Tertullian tirade: "Did not the dove whom you say is the Holy Spirit alight upon the top of Jesus's head at the baptism, when Jesus emerged from the waters below, and was not the voice heard: "This is my beloved Son, in whom I am well pleased"?

In his book *Kālī's Child*, Jeffrey J. Kripal urges us not to see Tantra as a philosophical, text-based school, but as a "dirty path" to ontological truths that are as terrifying as they are profound."[15] Djurdjevic quotes Alexis Sanderson on the benefits of decadent rejection of rules of purity: "The conscientiousness essential to the preservation of purity and social system was to be expelled from his identity by the Tantric Brahman as impurity itself, the only impurity he was to recognize, a state of ignorant self-bondage through the illusion that purity and impurity, prohibitedness and enjoinedness were objective qualities residing in things, persons and actions."[16]

Tantra is quintessentially about a kind of marriage, and the *sādhāna* (sexual rite) is often today performed within otherwise conventional marriages. As we shall see when we investigate Valentinian practices, a kindred setting was enjoyed among Valentinians enjoined to celebrate a kind of mystical marriage involving something like an alchemy of the bodies of the married couple that thoroughly internalized the idea of marriage while transforming it into its spiritual essence. In Tantra, it is the human body that is the setting and the means of achieving gnosis. And when we speak of alchemy, we shall be on the right lines to consider what is intended by a base metal that can be transformed into gold, for as the alchemists have never ceased repeating, the first matter of the Great Work is something universally diffused, but universally unvalued. He was in the world, and the world was made by him, but the world knew him not.

Who is he? What is he?

SEVEN

BE MY VALENTINE

Longing for the light of the Father, my relation and companion of my bed Sophē, anointed in the bath of Christ, with imperishable unction, you went to see the faces of the aeons, the angel of the Great Council, the true Son.

MEMORIAL TABLET, FIFTEEN INCHES HIGH,
ERECTED BY A GNOSTIC HUSBAND FOR HIS WIFE
FLAVIA SOPHĒ IN ROME, THIRD CENTURY CE

The association between the Gnostic teacher Valentinus with what we call romantic love is both ancient and profound. The moving words of the solitary inscription above testifies not only to extremely rare evidence for the genuine Gnostic presence in Rome in the third century, but to a spiritual love bond that characterized, and characterizes, couples who have embraced a Gnostic conception of everlasting love.

We tend to take romantic love for granted, but it was not always so. Marriage was, and still is in many parts of the world, primarily an arrangement of property, both in what the wife brings with her to the husband's estate, and the husband's to the wife's family, and the disposition of the woman herself, as the husband's property. The longing of love that typifies romantic dreams was primarily a matter of adulterous or premarital life: the object of desire was generally unobtainable in a quite literal way, since he or she was already "promised in marriage." In the bitterly ironic words of Sgt. Francis (Frank) Troy in Thomas Hardy's *Far from the Madding Crowd:* "All romances end in marriage."

Western culture is, however, aware of another idea of the "love unobtainable" something remote and spiritual, an unfleshly ideal, to which lovers are called, *contra mundum.* This apotheosis of love appeals to the imagination and has been prized for its ability to transform the physical pleasures of romance into an ecstasy unfathomable, a union of souls, something rare, unspoiled by the filth and duplicities of the world: the knowledge of the heart.

Such a love is properly associated with an Egyptian-born poet who came to Rome in about 136 CE and caused a stir with his startling ideas and charisma during the primacy of Bishop Hyginus. A native of Phrebonis in the Nile Delta, Valentinus (ca. 100–ca. 160 CE) very nearly became bishop of Rome himself. His disappointment at being passed over was held by detractors such as Tertullian to explain Valentinus's embarking on founding a heretical school of "gnosis falsely so-called." Even enemies rated Valentinus's intellect highly, while naturally denigrating intellectualism in the process.

Clement of Alexandria recorded that Valentinus's followers, educated in an Alexandrian culture of Hellenized Jews, claimed their master had received a secret, inner teaching from Theudas who had received the gnostic teaching from Paul (*cf.* 2 Corinthians 12:2–4). According to Tertullian's *Adversus Valentinianos* (IV), Valentinus eventually retired from Alexandria to Cyprus and had Bardaisan for a pupil, having already given sufficiently as to turn into teachers and developers, or perverters, of his doctrines pupils Heracleon, Ptolemy, Marcus, Theodotus, Florinus, Secundus, Colorbasus, and Axionicus. Tertullian insists, however, that only Axionicus of Antioch kept true to his master's teaching; all the others disavowed owing anything specifically to Valentinus and objected to being called Valentinians. Tertullian is emphatic that among his followers, personal insights were regarded as revelations, signs of gnosis. Therefore, originality and personal judgment were prized over consistency or respect for authority.

Since Valentinus's thought is mostly known after percolation through the minds of his pupils, it is hard to know precisely what Valentinus's own doctrine was, for so much of Valentinianism's superstructure—and even this may not have been his work—appears at first sight distinguishable only in incidentals and scale from much of the Simonian, Basilidean, and Sethian strains of emanated coteries of aeons, comprising the remoteness of the incomprehensible Father from the lower creation of the Demiurge. However, close reading of texts gives grounds for confidence that certain features, being common to all his pupils, may be regarded as inspired by their teacher.

These features include a poetic approach to philosophical questions answered through elegant mythic devices, and, perhaps above all, a seductive doctrine of celestial marriages. Furthermore, the Nag Hammadi Library has furnished us with a previously lost text—the *Gospel of Truth*—that may be substantially identical to a text referred to by this name by Irenaeus,[1] employed by Valentinians as scripture, and therefore, possibly the work of Valentinus himself. (For a convincing argument, see Jan Helderman's *Die Anapausis im Evangelium Veritatis*.)[2] It is indeed a work of some sophisticated subtlety, authoritative in tone and fundamentally different from other extant Valentinian works, such as the *Gospel of Philip*, but that does not mean Valentinus wrote it.

In his seventieth year, the late Dutch theologian and historian of Christianity, Gilles Quispel (1916–2006), shared with me his considered opinion that such was Valentinus's appeal, after his death, kept alive in the memory of his followers, and such the power of his dangerous heresy, that the church had to invent its own St. Valentine to confuse and trounce the memory and reputation of the arch-Gnostic.

Quispel's suspicion is perfectly plausible. The figure generally accepted as St. Valentine is supposed to have died a martyr's death in the mid-third century, but his name did not appear in Roman martyrologies until very late in the fifth century, over a century after the Roman emperor Theodosius I had declared Christianity the religion of the Empire in its orthodox form, calling deviants from orthodoxy foolish madmen liable to persecution. By then, who would dare to stand up publicly for a condemned heretic? Quispel reckoned the Catholic Church thus absorbed a major rallying figure celebrated by heretics and gave the name its extremely mild, even vapid version of a romantic connotation with the story that Catholic martyr Valentinus, whose acts, as Pope Gelasius I said in 496 CE when establishing February 14 as his day, "were known only to God" (that is, unrecorded in history), though his name was justly reverenced by men. Legends grew that this martyr priest had married Christian couples to prevent them from being drafted into the army. It would be fitting that orthodox Christian marriage would be the story to slap onto a figure that had advocated a form of Christian marriage very different from that preached by the celibate clergy of the fifth century.

Curiously, the more intense forms of romantic love around the feast of Valentine were much amplified in English literary circles around Geoffrey Chaucer in the thirteenth century and associated with the remnants of courtly love—over a century after the Catholic Church had through propaganda neutralized the power of the adulterous troubadours with approved songs to the Virgin—clearly unobtainable!—and cleaned up love codes that would make even a nun smile wistfully. Intuitive persons might see that there's something in this; conceivably the phenomenon speaks eloquently of the strange manner in which suppressed traditions manage to work their way back through the vicissitudes of time. The truth will out!

The original Valentinus would probably be dismayed by the modern idea of erotic and sentimentalized love dressed up very often as something romantic when it is only lustful fascination lathered in manufactured scent and plastered with cosmetics. However, not all of Valentine's card-sending children have sunk to the abyss of bump-and-grind "lurve, baby." Spiritually minded souls know intuitively that there is love, and there is spiritual love, and spiritual love does not necessarily mean chaste in the expression of the flesh, but chaste in the intention of the heart and mind, with reservations about losing sight of the fullness of love, and each other, in lust and self-service.

Spiritual eroticism can be noble, that is to say, of the head, the glittering crown with a channel to eternity, beyond the stars, and may involve transmutation of the lower nature through the higher magic of spiritual union. It may also be described as mysterious and to those outside its garden, certainly esoteric. That is to say, if lovers of today and tomorrow wish to bask in the light of Valentinian love, we must look forward to rising in love, not falling into it. We should also bear in mind perhaps that the name *Valentine* comes from the Latin valens, which means "strong," "worthy," "healthy," "potent," "worthwhile." These qualities are the essence of virtue, vital for the promotion of spiritual values, with spiritual love, their crown and seal.

Not at all misty-eyed, Valentinian lovers have come out of the fog that obscures the mountaintops of aspiration; they are involved in a response to a clear call for which clarity of vision is an essential requirement. Which brings us to the philosophy, or perhaps, as I have dubbed it elsewhere, erosophy of this innovative genius.

What I think is special to the *idea* of the Valentinian system is the way that its progenitor seems to have glimpsed a psychological truth within the mythic scheme that, presumably, came to him through Basilides, Menander, and Dositheus, although pertinent Jewish conceptions had been current in Alexandria for some three hundred years.

According to Tertullian, the questions that made people heretics were: "From whence springs evil, and what is the cause and principle of it? What was man's original, and how was he made? And what Valentinus hath last of all proposed, whence is God?"[3]

Meeting Hans Jonas in New York in 1986, the venerable "*alte meister* of Gnostic studies" expressed to me his conviction that the church had lost much by condemning the Gnostic movement. It had lost perhaps a spirit of daring, of creativity, of intellectual adventure and imagination in the formation of doctrine. While Catholic doctrines became rigid, unimaginative, and inflexible, the Gnostics had found "ways to answer all of this [questioning] together and wrap it up into one grand scheme."

Clearly, Professor Jonas was thinking of gnosis in terms of its philosophical content, something the heresiologists immediately recognized and, insofar as they could identify the philosophies of Plato, Aristotle, Heraclitus, Anaximander, Parmenides, Zeno, Epicurus, and the poetry of Homer and others within it, gave but greater force to their condemnation of it. In Valentinus, though, there was recognition that they faced a sterner problem, for Valentinus was a creative theologian advocating Christianity, as he saw it, apparently from within the church, or more particularly, he was presenting an apologia for Christianity from the inside as a philosophy, though a highly exclusive one—one we might today call a theosophy, since it is so theocentric. Valentinus's effort, in the first instance, might have appeared a useful service, because it might bring unbelieving philosophical and speculative types to faith on the basis that there was *more to it* than faith. However, on examination of Valentinus's method, there was bound to be consternation.

Whereas, Jewish and Christian teachers accepted the fundamental philosophy of Moses as revealed in the Pentateuch, namely, that the creation of the universe was an act of divine will (*Fiat Lux!*—Let there be light!), Valentinus posited the idea of *materiale ex passione:* material creation from passion, from feeling, pain, suffering: waves disturbing mind, like ripples and shadows on a pool, unsettling repose. A corollary of this premise—*Spiritale ex imaginatione,* Spirit from imagination— was arguably even more shocking. In this fundamentally transgressive idea lies, I think, the perennial attraction of Valentinianism because its premise, while appalling to the traditional rationalist, is so deeply related to the experience of creative and imaginative people (that ought to be all of us!), and to the life of the heart.

•••

We are now generally disposed, through observation and interest in artists, be it a van Gogh or a John Lennon or a Michelangelo, to recognize that creation may be experienced as a product of pain. The artist suffers; he or she may write, draw, paint, carve, etch, compose, invent, design, and so on: first the imagination, then the coagulation of thought into visible object. The cynic might say, "You want art from this artist? Put him in a garret on short rations until he's filled it with canvases." If we translate this idea to that of the creation of the universe—which is more or less what Valentinus did—we must subject the potential initiator of the creative process to pain. Pain makes things happen, for suffering induces reaction, and the Valentinian concept of creation is a kind of chain reaction, set off with a spark that, *in the process itself,* is turned from metaphor into spiritual substance, thence to materialization.

Being a good Platonist, Valentinus cannot have the ultimate God suffering, since, as Aristotle taught, God is the "unmoved mover." There can be no suffering in absolute being, for absolute being is absolutely perfect. Suffering, on the other hand, suggests deficiency. So there has to be a shift of responsibility for the ability to suffer or feel to take place, and this shift comes about due to the reflexive thought of the One. This thought is a potential of perfection, but, of course, in the reflection, there comes into being a further potential, albeit at a conceptual remove from its perfect impassible source. God's First Thought is God's virgin Spirit, and she can get involved, and from this involvement with the Depth of Divine Being, she receives seed.

How can we acquire wisdom if we cannot suffer, that is to experience pain and pleasure? For both require passibility: hence the mysterious duality of passion. Valentinus's originality was to see this passion as creative, in the macrocosm and the microcosm, and creative both positively and, necessarily, negatively.

From the initial seed that is the spark begins to grow a tree, a tree of gnosis. The spark that is the passion becomes the spirit or sap of the tree, whose root is the passion of Sophia, the passion of Wisdom endeavoring to know the unknowable Father, instead of being true to herself (that is, conforming to God's will with respect to her), that is, wise, wise enough to accept that the ultimate nature of being is not subject to rational understanding, even enough to use the word *ultimate* or *nature* of *something* or someone that may just as rationally be called "nothing," for reason is exhausted in the futile effort of understanding the unknown God. Humankind inherits this passion of Sophia from that source, and with it a tragedy. Though few are awake to it, it is literally in our blood, *bound up* with the perennial itch of lively loins. Here is the brilliance. The truth of our predicament is an inheritance of the source of that predicament. We are profoundly involved in the divine scheme; we are called to awaken. If we awaken, we may rise up through the life of that tree. Our bodies are hung on that tree, and through it, we must rise to paradise beyond the body. As the Valentinian *Gospel of Philip* has it: "he [Christ] came crucifying the world." As St. Paul had declared, the wood of the tree on which Jesus was hung was a trap sprung on the archons, and the plan to outwit them thereby had been held in Wisdom's bosom since the beginning of time.

This is a philosophy, but also, as we have seen, the itinerary for a specific practice of union, where the spinal column is the tree and the gateway to the Pleroma the pineal gland.

It is possible that Valentinus got his basic insight from Paul's clue and further contemplation of Jesus on the cross. Knowing that in classical philosophy, the highest being is impassible, Valentinus could not argue with that conception until he saw an evident (to him) truth in the image of the Savior nailed down, bleeding. The Savior appeared to be suffering, and from the suffering came a new creation: the Christian church with its opened path to the aeons, eternal life, a new beginning for the human race, begun on the third day. His "blood" was the essence of life, given to all who could take it.

Jesus had created a new world, through his "death," that is to say:

he did not will it; he had accepted a will through knowing himself. The new creation had come as a product of the divine humanity exposed to feeling: the passion had been inherited from the true Mother of Christ, desirous to redeem lost pneuma.

Valentinus then looks to earthbound man's existential plight. We are in a fog, lost as regards knowledge of ultimate truth, our origin, our true place in the cosmos, and out of it. The result: We suffer. Effect: a yearning for truth, understanding, knowledge; out of this parallel yearning, the true church is also created. Love is creative. Love and suffering are experienced together. Passion can change everything. Why then cannot passion create everything? For is that not what we see in human life every day? Passion generates matter. If a yearning for knowledge can begin the soul's healing, if it can be satisfied, is it not because the anguish of matter derived from a yearning for knowledge, unsatisfied?

The Universe contains evil because it is filled with the passion of its creation.

As the author of the *Gospel of Truth,* possibly Valentinus himself, writes:

> This [is] the gospel of the one who is searched for, which [was] revealed to those who are perfect through the mercies of the Father—the hidden mystery, Jesus, the Christ. Through it he enlightened those who were in darkness. Out of oblivion he enlightened them, he showed [them] a way. And the way is the truth which he taught them.
>
> For this reason error grew angry at him, persecuted him, was distressed at him, [and] was brought to naught. He was nailed to a tree; he became a fruit of the knowledge of the Father, which did not, however, become destructive because it was eaten [as when Adam and Eve ate in Eden], but to those who ate it, it gave [cause] to become glad in the discovery. For he discovered them in himself, and they discovered him in themselves, the incomprehensible, inconceivable one, the Father, the perfect one, the one who made the all, while the all

is within him and the all has need of him, since he retained its [pl.] perfection within himself which he did not give to the all.[4]

Perhaps we can now begin to understand how passion, yearning, and love played such an important role in the spiritual-sexual lives of those who constituted the awoken elect who partook of the fruit of the tree and "received from the Father of truth the gift of knowing him, through the power of the Word that came forth from the Pleroma."[5]

It was not only Valentinus's tragic myth of creation that made him, in the words of Gilles Quispel, "one of the most original thinkers of the Christian tradition." Valentinus, according to Quispel, "discovered the mystical conjunction of spiritual man and his guardian angel or, in other words, of the conscious Ego and the unconscious Self. His system resembles that of the kabbalistic Zohar and the idealistic philosophy of Hegel. All this he [Valentinus] says he owes to Christ, who manifested Himself to him in the form of a child, the Logos, and thus inspired him to design his "tragic myth."[6] To add to long-belated plaudits, Quispel praised Elaine Pagels of Princeton University for having demonstrated Valentinus to have been "the only man in the whole Judaeo-Christian tradition who was wholeheartedly for sex and marriage, and explicitly taught the equality and complementarity of the human male and the human female."[7]

When modern writers of the last forty years or so have attempted to make a fresh case for the significance of the Gnostic tradition, it is almost always to Valentinian-type works they have principally gone. There are no Borborians there, no obvious instances of spermatophagy; instead we have a tragic Sophia related directly to the struggle of the soul in the world. Such resonant features of female soul-suffering have been seized on by advocates of the divine feminine, that is to say, feminist theologies, as offering a spirited tonic against the effects of patriarchy, historically in the church, and in modern societies in general. Valentinus seems to speak to us. That he was a radical freethinker stands him in good stead with the post-'50s liberal consensus; that he has been condemned makes him a martyr for truth.

When it comes to *The Da Vinci Code* bandwagon, including a possibly passionate relationship or implied eroticism between Jesus and Mary Magdalene, it is upon the Valentinian *Gospel of Philip* that advocates have principally drawn for selective source data (along with the *Gospel of Mary* from the Berlin Codex). Meanwhile, new theologians and broad-consumption esoteric commentators find much to admire in the "whore and the holy one," the radical antipuritanical, sex-friendly goddess of *The Thunder, Perfect Mind*,[8] linked rather freely to the Sophia-Mary of Valentinians.

Not surprisingly, you won't find the barest hint of any value ascribed to Valentinus's work in Irenaeus, Tertullian, Clement of Alexandria, Hippolytus, or Epiphanius. As Tertullian expressed the matter bluntly, Valentinus not only accused "us"—Tertullian and his nonpneumatic, non-Gnostic brethren, a.k.a. the "Christians"—of worshipping a brute and a failure for a God and Father of the Lord Jesus Christ, but, to cap it all, all those unable to scale the heights of pneumatic consciousness, that is the Catholic orthodox and the rest, were destined at death to be chucked back into the savage jaws of the God of this world, to be obliterated and/or recycled in the dark ecology of an abortive universe. Valentinus may have saved his baby, but he'd thrown the possibility of universal salvation out with the dirty bathwater. There was good news for a minority who owned the truth; for the rest the news was a tabloid catastrophe. How accurate a picture this is of Valentinus's prognosis, we shall try to uncover in due course.

What can we learn from the heresiologists regarding the sexual priorities of Valentinus and his pupils?

EIGHT

A QUESTION OF SEED

Some of them, moreover, are in the habit of defiling those women to whom they have taught the above doctrine, as has frequently been confessed by those women who have been led astray by certain of them, on their returning to the Church of God, and acknowledging this along with the rest of their errors. Others of them, too, openly and without a blush, having become passionately attached to certain women, seduce them away from their husbands, and contract marriages of their own with them. Others of them, again, who pretend at first to live in all modesty with them as with sisters, have in course of time been revealed in their true colors, when the sister has been found with child by her [pretended] brother. (Irenaeus, *Adversus Haereses*, I.4, 3)

Irenaeus commences his attack on Valentinians with a tirade against the followers of Ptolemy. Active *circa* 170 CE, Ptolemy's following was familiar to the bishop of Lyons who accuses them of running ordinary Christians down, claiming to be "the perfect, and the elect seed."[1] Asserting that they had received grace (*charis*) from above by indescribable conjunction, they recommend practicing the mystery of conjunction as a continual necessity. Truth requires loving a woman, taking sexual possession of her, as a priority. However, this benefit only operates for the spirituals. The animal men (men of soul, but not spirit) should practice continence and good works, and then only in hopes of finding an intermediate habitation, that is, a second-class location outside of the Pleroma, apparently. Ordinary people are not fit for the spiritual sex experience.

Good conduct is not an issue for the *pneumatikoi* (the spirituals) for their way to the Pleroma relies solely on the bringing to perfection of the seed that, although derived from the Pleroma, entered the world in a feeble, immature state, a state rectifiable by regular observance of the mystery of conjunction. When all the Pleromic seeds have been perfected at the end-time, their primal Mother (Achamoth) will reenter the Pleroma from the intermediate place to take the Savior as her spouse: bridegroom and bride. This primal Mother is Sophia[2] and the Pleroma is the nuptial chamber. In this great wedding feast, all the perfected seeds, divested of animal soul to become intelligent spirits, will become brides to the angels that wait on the Savior.

As Gilles Quispel pointed out in a review of Jan Helderman's *Die Anapausis im Evangelium Veritatis,*[3] the word *repose* (anapausis) is significant to Valentinians, a significance evinced not only in the *Gospel of Truth* but also in Irenaeus's account of Ptolemy.

At the end of the material catastrophe, the Demiurge will move into the intermediate place, where also the souls of the righteous will find repose, but no animal (soul) nature will enter the abode of the perfect in the divine Fullness (Pleroma). Once this acosmic rescue has been accomplished, the fire hidden in the world (note the possible usage of a Simonian idea) will blaze forth and finish everything else off, including itself.

It was for Valentinians probably more important to experience repose through conjunction in this life, that is, to be a resurrected, fully realized seed while on Earth, than to be overly obsessed with the end of the world. The guarantee of ultimate salvation was the realization of immanent salvation. The fruits of this seed are wisdom, prophecy, and the inevitable jealous fascination for these powers shown by the Demiurge.

In chapter 8 of book 1 of *Adversus Haereses,* Irenaeus is keen to emphasize that the three kinds of men—material, animal (psychic or soulful), and spiritual—are no longer all found in one person but constitute three ineluctable classes, typified as Cain (material), Abel (animal), and Seth (spiritual). However, in the same paragraph, Irenaeus seems to contradict this distinction by making the point that Ptolemy further held there were good animal souls and others evil by nature. The good had the capacity to receive spiritual seed, while the evil in nature could never receive it. One suspects that views on this critical matter were diverse and subject to elaboration in Valentinian groups, some of whose adherents may have doubted at sundry times who did and did not have the seed.

SENSELESS AND CRACK-BRAINED

If Ptolemy is presented as a merchant of lechery, Irenaeus pictures Marcus as the new Simon Magus. Chapter 13 (book 1) has him "a perfect adept in magical impostures," craftily drawing a large male following and "not a few women" into his enchantments. Irenaeus describes Marcus, not without a sense of absurdity, as the "precursor of Antichrist." He describes Marcus ceremonially dropping a precipitate into a cup of wine so that its color changed, calling it the bloody effulgence of Charis (Grace), and that from above: trickster, juggler! The mystified throng is enjoined to drink of the Grace set before them, having the cups consecrated by the women. The magician then produces a larger cup and does a trick, making it look as if it has overflowed from the contents of the smaller cup, while intoning words that Charis fills the "inner man" and sows the "grain of mustard seed in thee as in good soil." Irenaeus says this performance goads the women to "madness." Perhaps there was more to the precipitate than a dye.

Irenaeus says Marcus goes after wealthy, well-dressed women, using a familiar spirit to prophesy, and seduces them, saying:

"I am eager to make thee a partaker of my Charis, since the Father of all doth continually behold thy angel before His face. Now the place of thy angel is among us, it behooves us to become one. Receive first from me and by me [the gift of] Charis. Adorn thyself as a bride who is expecting her bridegroom, that thou mayest be what I am, and I what thou art. Establish the germ of light in thy nuptial chamber. Receive from me a spouse, and become receptive of him, while thou art received by him. Behold Charis has descended upon thee; open thy mouth and prophesy."

On the woman replying, "I have never at any time prophesied, nor do I know how to prophesy;" then engaging, for the second time, in certain invocations, so as to astound his deluded victim, he says to her, "Open thy mouth, speak whatsoever occurs to thee, and thou shalt prophesy." She then, vainly puffed up and elated by these words, and greatly excited in soul by the expectation that it is herself who is to prophesy, her heart beating violently [from emotion], reaches the requisite pitch of audacity, and idly as well as impudently utters some nonsense as it happens to occur to her, such as might be expected from one heated by an empty spirit. [Referring to this, one superior to me has observed, that the soul is both audacious and impudent when heated with empty air.] Henceforth she reckons herself a prophetess, and expresses her thanks to Marcus for having imparted to her of his own Charis. She then makes the effort to reward him, not only by the gift of her possessions [in which way he has collected a very large fortune], but also by yielding up to him her person, desiring in every way to be united to him, that she may become altogether one with him. (*Adversus Haereses* I, 13, 3)

Whatever the truth as to the seduction charge, the words give us some notion of ideas Marcus may have used or twisted from a different context to his advantage. The "angel" is brought into the woman's "nuptial chamber" (presumably her genitals) by his agency. He has "the germ [seed] of light." The transmission of seed somehow brings

the angel into her presence. It is unclear whether the "angel" (her ultimate bridegroom) is actually within the seed Marcus offers through his
inflamed phallus, or whether the angel becomes a celestial, but spiritually immanent, witness to the sexual act of consecration—even invoked
or conjured by it—wherein *she* becomes *him* (male: joined spiritually to
the bridegroom), and where, most interestingly, he becomes what she
is: bride. This male into female reverse subtlety is often missed in comments about the Valentinian bridal chamber.

Though the seed gives males the advantage, the sacrament of the
bridal chamber involves the male wholly in the feminine dimension of
the spirit. The suggestion is one of androgynous union through which,
and only through which, women are enabled to enter the kingdom, the
Pleroma, through the grace transmitted by the male, which makes the
woman male, and therefore able to enter the holiest of holies. This is
the elect way for the woman to make contact with Pleromic intelligence
while in the female body. This classic Valentinian escape clause from
the Encratite prohibition on sexual contact with women suggests the
influence of Jewish priorities in a Greco-Egyptian setting. The woman
has to be brought back, or redeemed, into man. We should be grateful
to Irenaeus for preserving Marcus's little seduction number, for it helps
us at last to make good, literal sense of the otherwise notoriously difficult logion 114 of the *Gospel of Thomas*:

Simon Peter said to them, "Mary should leave us, for females are not
worthy of life." Jesus said, "See, I am going to attract her to make
her male so that she too might become a living spirit that resembles
you males. For every female [element] that makes itself male will
enter the kingdom of heaven."[4]

Such also is the redemption of Sophia, for she cannot be restored
to the Pleroma until she is wed to the Savior: a nuptial prefigured in
Valentinian literature by the spiritual relationship established between
Jesus and Mary Magdalene: terrestrial stand-ins for the aeons, or

perfected intelligences, Sophia and Savior. Since it seems to be understood that the virgin spirit is androgynous (*cf.* the Mother and "male virgin" variants: Barbelo, Barbelos, and Barbelon; *viz.* the *Gospel of the Egyptians*[5]), then spiritually speaking, the bride is also the bridegroom and vice versa, for the ultimate aim is to become altogether one, for two as divisible units only came about in the created realm of manifestation where objects appear separate, for the creation is separate from the unknown God who is absolutely One.

We can see why consecrated sexual intercourse was so crucial to Valentinians; it was preparation for the ultimate divine union, sanctioned by Sophia, as healing the ruptured harmony of the precosmic Pleroma. Obviously, the system was open to abuse, as is every system.

Irenaeus accuses Marcus of using love potions to make the women open themselves to him. Perhaps it was the case that herbal stimulants were used to heighten consecrated intercourse, inducing a consciously sensible experience of the mysterious. Irenaeus says that some of his former female "crack-brained" dupes had thankfully returned to the Church of God, saying their being defiled derived from a "burning passion" for him. This makes Marcus appear rather like Lord Byron to his besotted acolytes, such as poor Lady Caroline Lamb led to the slaughter. Irenaeus cites the case of an Asian deacon whose beautiful wife fell under Marcus's spell and went around with him until "converted" by the brethren; she was thereafter engaged in regular public confessions, lamenting her shameful defilement. Quite a warning!

According to the bishop, it wasn't only Marcus, but his male followers who pulled the same seductions and claimed to have "imbibed the greatness of the knowledge of that power which is unspeakable," having "attained to a height above all power." We are in Simonian territory with these claims, I think, though they can be found as phrases throughout Gnostic literature, whence, I suspect, Irenaeus culled them.

He mentions a specific type of spiritual experience Marcosians have undergone to generate such gigantic pride in their spiritual enormity.

He calls it the redemption (*apolytrosis*) and it is also connected to sexual practice.

We find the redemption, boldly enough, in the third century *Gospel of Philip*: "The Lord [did] everything in a mystery, a baptism and a chrism [anointing] and a eucharist and a redemption and a bridal chamber."[6] On the following page of the extant Coptic papyrus, we have, I'm sure, ample confirmation that this redemption required sexual union on a spiritual plane: "When Eve was still in Adam death did not exist. When she was separated from him death came into being. If he again becomes complete and attains his former self, death will be no more." The female nature must be swallowed up back into him; sexual rites prefigure the ultimate union and actualize the realization on Earth of the Gnostic truth.

Male and female are aspects of one spirit. "Through the Holy Spirit we are indeed begotten again, but we are begotten through Christ in the two. We are anointed through the Spirit. When we were begotten we were united."[7] If this were not sufficiently explicit, see the following page of the original text: "But the woman is united to her husband in the bridal chamber. Indeed those who have united in the bridal chamber will no longer be separated. Thus Eve separated from Adam because she was never united with him in the bridal chamber."[8] The redemption is effected by Christ: "Christ came to repair the separation which was from the beginning and again unite the two, and to give life to those who died as a result of the separation and unite them."[9] Jesus, himself the fruit of the Pleroma, wants joyous lovers to join and save the seed. The divided must become one; when all pneuma is no longer divided in and through matter, but is restored to itself, the cosmos will cease. Sacramental sex is then the image for the entire Valentinian philosophy of being. Passion is the cure for the "passions of matter."

Irenaeus says that such is the perfected ones' platinum card entry status to the Pleroma that were they to be brought before the judge (possibly a Roman judge holding them guilty of an illegal religion), they need only pray to their Mother who will make the illusory trial situation unreal so that their spirits, invisible to the judge, may be caught up by the Mother and taken to the real world of the bridal chamber (in heaven presumably) to be be handed over to their consorts, that is, their angelic counterparts: the gilt-edged prize of the redeemed seeds. This was the Valentinian take on the canonical accounts of the trial and passion of Jesus; its seductive power ought to be obvious.

Irenaeus adds a stinger. Some of the shamed women taken in by Marcus and his team have quit, not infrequently in such a state of confusion that they have apostatized from the Christian faith completely, while others hover in a state "neither without nor within." Such, says Irenaeus, is all they have to possess "as the fruit from the seed of the children of knowledge." This is a devastating critique, to be sure. In that latter phrase, he shows he has grasped the linguistic world of his opponents and their august-sounding symbolism. These women seem like today's cult victims coming out of deprogramming, disoriented.

That Marcus's beliefs seem informed, directly or indirectly, by the *Book of Enoch*'s interpretation of Genesis 6's account of the sons of God sexually possessing the beautiful daughters of men, so engendering a race of giants, may be confirmed by a poem about Marcus by a "saintly elder" included in Irenaeus's survey. Therein, Marcus's powers are attributed to Azazel, who, in the *Book of Enoch,* is the invisible prince of this world and ruler of the rebel celestial Watchers who have brought both knowledge and corruption to the world, and whose judgment and binding to the world Enoch prophesies in the seminal apocryphal work that bears his name.

> Marcus, thou former of idols, inspector of portents,
> Skill'd in consulting the stars, and deep in the black
>   arts of magic,
> Ever by tricks such as these confirming the doctrines
>   of error,
> Furnishing signs unto those involved by thee in
>   deception,

Wonders of power that is utterly severed from God
  and apostate,
Which Satan, thy true father, enables thee still to
  accomplish,
By means of Azazel, that fallen and yet mighty angel,
Thus making thee the precursor of his own impious
  actions.[10]

Regarding the specifics of the Marcosian redemption, Irenaeus declares in chapter 21 (book 1) that there is no consistent doctrine on the matter, as his followers all invent methods and theories to suit themselves. There are common ideas, however. The chief of these is that Jesus brought the baptism of water—John's baptism—for remission of sins, but there was a further baptism. Paul calls this the baptism of fire, or the Holy Spirit, but Marcosians go further. The Aeon Christ that descended on Jesus brought the baptism of perfection, which, unlike the water baptism, was spiritual. This powerful baptism, we shall not be surprised to discover, was, in some cases, performed via a nuptial couch or bed:

> For some of them prepare a nuptial couch, and perform a sort of mystic rite (pronouncing certain expressions) with those who are being initiated, and affirm that it is a spiritual marriage which is celebrated by them, after the likeness of the conjunctions above [the syzygies of the Pleroma].
>
> Others, again, lead them to a place where water is, and baptize them, with the utterance of these words, "Into the name of the unknown Father of the universe—into truth, the mother of all things—into Him who descended on Jesus—into union, and redemption, and communion with the powers." Others still repeat certain Hebrew words, in order the more thoroughly to bewilder those who are being initiated, as follows: "Basema, Chamosse, Baoenaora, Mistadia, Ruada, Kousta, Babaphor, Kalachthei." The

interpretation of these terms runs thus: "I invoke that which is above every power of the Father, which is called light, and good Spirit, and life, because Thou hast reigned in the body." Others, again, set forth the redemption thus: The name which is hidden from every deity, and dominion, and truth which Jesus of Nazareth was clothed with in the lives of the light of Christ—of Christ, who lives by the Holy Ghost, for the angelic redemption. The name of restitution stands thus: Messia, Uphareg, Namempsoeman, Chaldoeaur, Mosomedoea, Acphranoe, Psaua, Jesus Nazaria. The interpretation of these words is as follows: "I do not divide the Spirit of Christ, neither the heart nor the supercelestial power which is merciful; may I enjoy Thy name, O Saviour of truth!"

Such are words of the initiators; but he who is initiated, replies, "I am established, and I am redeemed; I redeem my soul from this age [world], and from all things connected with it in the name of Iao, who redeemed his own soul into redemption in Christ who liveth." Then the bystanders add these words, "Peace be to all on whom this name rests." After this they anoint the initiated person with balsam; for they assert that this unguent is a type of that sweet odor which is above all things.[11]

It appears from Irenaeus's account that the baptism of perfection actually succeeds where Sophia failed. For the Marcosians believed that those with knowledge must of necessity "be regenerated into that power, which is above all."[12] Thus they interpret a pun on the Valentinian name of the Unknowable Father. He is called Bythos (in Greek), which means "Depth" or "Abyss," in the sense of an unfathomable ocean. Into this depth the Gnostic is baptized, believing it a baptism instituted for the elect by Christ, prophesied by John to supersede the water baptism for those who could stand it. Irenaeus says some do this as a mystic rite on a couch or bed; others are led to water; still others are anointed on the head with oil and water, or with balsam: this being the redemption. Others, however, regard any rite as unsuitable insofar as they are mixing the incorporeal with the corporeal: gnosis "of the unspeakable Greatness is itself perfect redemption."

Irenaeus also explains how some practice anointing with oil and water on those near death as a means of securing the ascent of the spirit through "the principalities and powers" while their animal soul is headed for the Demiurge (such practices may be the ancient remote origin of the famous Consolamentum administered to believing, unperfected Cathars, before the moment of death, recorded in France and northern Italy from the twelfth to the fourteenth centuries).

As far as Irenaeus is concerned, this baptism is in fact a baptism out of the Church of God and into a nightmare of error.

TERTULLIAN
ON THE VALENTINIANS

It is interesting in the face of modern ideas to note that a major bone of contention between Catholics and heretics was the Gnostics' belief that, as Tertullian puts it: "our flesh cannot be restored after Death," that being "an opinion maintained by every sect of philosophers," whereas the "church has acknowledged but one God, the creator of the universe; it hath believed in Jesus Christ his Son born of the Virgin Mary, and it hath taught the resurrection of the flesh."[13] In the words of the old song: "Dem bones, dem bones gonna walk around; dem bones, dem bones gonna walk around; dem bones, dem bones, dem *dry* bones; now Hear the word of the Lord!"

For the Catholic, orthodox teachers, all the Valentinian talk about a spiritual Pleroma; immortal aeons; the division of mortal soul, inanimate body, and immortal spirit simply denied God's role as judge and creator of all things while permitting practically any physical excess to be justified as a spiritual symbol, with bodily continence a spiritual impertinence. Only the seed counted, its fruit to be gathered at the harvest, or destruction of the material universe.

In chapter 36 of his "prescription," unmoved by Gnostic priorities,

Tertullian takes a fascinating swipe at Gnostic ideas of the holy seed, using Romans 9:16–25 as his parallel source:

> For as from the stem of a pure and rich and natural olive tree springs the wild olive tree, and as from the seed of the most delicious and grateful fig tree branches out the wild fig tree, so also do heresies arise from our stock, though of very different race and nature from us; they grow up from the seed of truth but through the poison of falsehood become corrupt and degenerate.

This needs a little explaining. St. Paul had said in his epistle to the Romans that the tree of God's salvation was holy and pure, but some branches had been cut away from it (Jews who denied Jesus was the messiah), while a "wild olive tree" had been grafted onto the holy stem. The wild tree referred to Gentiles, outsiders to the Mosaic covenant, who had heard the call of Christ and followed. Tertullian seems aware that Gnostics had taken Paul's metaphor to another level altogether (see also Clement of Alexandria's *Excerpta ex Theodoto* 56–60, which shows the Valentinian Theodotus's use of Paul's olive tree parable).

For many Gnostics, the *wild* fruit tree was that which had begun to grow outside of the Pleroma, growing downward. For Valentinians, the Mother of that tree was Sophia, who had erred, but the tree nonetheless bore the fruit of the Father's seed she had inherited, being his First Thought and infused with spermatic Word (Logos). For Sethians, as we have seen, that seed, the Mother's seed, infused with the Father's Word, was the great Sethian seed that had not been corrupted by the lord of this world and his archons.

Tertullian won't let them get away with that. Tertullian says that the new wild fig tree of the heretics owes its origin to the old stock of the now grateful Gentile tree that bore the fruit of honest faith. The Gentiles' wild olive tree grafted onto the pure tree still bore kinship with the old seed from the wild days; Tertullian means the philosophies of Plato, Heraclitus, Epicurus, Aristotle, Zeno, and so on: the lumber of Athens, unfit for the holy Jerusalem. The heresies came as a wild outgrowth from the Gentile stock that had accepted Christ, and the new wild fig was assuredly wild stock, growing wild and wilder still, unconnected to the promises of God's holy tree.

Tertullian mercilessly parodies Ptolemy's emanating tree in *Adversus Valentinianos* (XX):

> Ptolomaeus certainly remembered his childhood babblings, apples growing in the ocean and fish on trees. In the same way he assumes nut-trees grow in the sky. Of course the Demiurge acts in ignorance and perhaps he does not know that trees are supposed to grow only in the ground.

Such profusion of tangled conceptions come, says Tertullian, from a "very different race": almost certainly a dig at those Gnostics who claimed to be the immovable, "alien" race of the tree of Barbelo. In other words, the so-called holy seed of the heretics is bad seed! Consume it at your peril, whether on couch or bed or among the branches of the Pleroma! Tertullian was too modest to suggest the repentant converts who returned to Irenaeus's church would spend the rest of their lives trying to cough it back up.

In a magisterial piece of polemical sarcasm, Tertullian's *Adversus Valentinianos* (XXX) draws attention to the lasciviousness of Valentinians, basing their libertine attitudes on the unpleasant idea that while ordinary church members should bear the full weight of the demands of righteousness, being but souls in need of strict guidance, they the spirituals went scot-free and could "prove their nobility by the dissoluteness of their life and their diligence in sin."

And for such lives, they could expect, says Tertullian, to be the sole entrants to the prize of the Pleroma once the world below and all in it were destroyed. Tertullian completely "disses" the heavenly feast of brides and bridegrooms, of spirits and angels. For him, it's just the continuity of the earthly orgy begun in their imagined illusion of this life:

These men then, men destined to enter the Pleroma, are unclothed first; to be unclothed means to put aside the souls with which they are only apparently endowed. They return to the Demiurge these souls which they received from him. They become spirits entirely metaphysical, immune to restraint or detection; in this fashion they are received invisibly into the Pleroma—secretly, if this is the way it is! What then? They are handed out to the angels who accompany [the Aeon called] Savior. As sons, do you suppose? No. As valets perhaps? Not even this. As ghosts? I wish even this were the case! What, then, if you are not ashamed to say? *As wives!* For marriages they will play "Rape the Sabines" among themselves. This is the reward for being "spirit-like"; this is the prize for believing.

These are proper little stories; for example, you, Marcus, or you, Gaius, at present bearded in this body and in this soul a stern husband, father, grandfather, or great-grandfather certainly masculine enough—then, in this harem of a Pleroma, by some angel you might be . . . by my silence I have already said it. Anyway perhaps you might give birth to some new aeon. In place of the usual torch and veil I imagine that famous mysterious fire will blaze out to solemnize the ceremony, and will devastate the entire universe, then be reduced to nothing, after it has incinerated everything. That will be the end of their myth. But I am certainly the rash one for betraying, even in jest, such a great mystery.[14]

In Tertullian, the variegated followers of Valentinus had met their adversarial match!

CLEMENT OF ALEXANDRIA AND THEODOTUS

It is significant that Clement of Alexandria, uniquely, finds reason to praise the Valentinians. This may not be so much because Clement did not share Tertullian's and Hippolytus's hostility to Plato, but because the Valentinians were not permeated by the Encratite "hatred for the flesh" that led them to reject marriage (*Strōmateis,* III, 7, 60). Clement noted that the Valentinian "delight in marriage" derived from their emulating the life of the syzygies above. The surviving inscription to Flavia Sophē in Rome proves this as a passionate feature of Valentinian Christian life.

Clement contrasts the Valentinians with the "carnal and wanton" sexual acts of the Carpocratians, and this distinction alone should warn us from letting the use of terms like "Gnosticism" blind us to the very distinct kinds of experience possible within a "Gnostic" spectrum; that they were all condemned does not make them all the same by any means. Clement recognized that Valentinians did not use symbolism as a smokescreen for cynical and libertine enjoyments. Writing in *Strōmateis* (III, 29), Clement opined of other Gnostics: "if these people performed spiritual intercourse (*pneumatikas koinonias*) like the Valentinians, perhaps one could accept their view."

By spiritual intercourse, Clement seems to have indicated marital sex for procreative purposes, controlled by the will, not performed as lust took the participants. According to Clement, "we are children not of lust but of will [*thelematos*]." It is hard to think Clement would have caviled at the watchword of Aleister Crowley's Thelema system: "Love is the law, love under will." *Strōmateis* (III, 58) reflects knowledge of Valentinian "marriage guidance": the husband should love, not lust after, the wife "that he may beget children with a chaste and controlled will." Lust should be restrained, not surrendered to as if it did not matter on account of an alleged superior, invisible, unfelt, and remote Self. Since, to Clement, spiritual life converged on the divine Logos, if the ultimate Self was holy, then the path there must be too, regardless of the distractions of the world and its darker aspects.

Clement of Alexandria's *Excerpta ex Theodoto* gives us a more intimate, considerably less caustic, insight into the exegetical acuity of one of Valentinus's followers, Theodotus. Clement quotes from Theodotus's otherwise unknown works and does not try to twist what he finds with sarcasm to paint his subject in the worst possible light.

A native of Byzantium and an adoptionist (the view that Jesus the man was adopted by the descending Christ, who used his body), Bishop Victor excluded Theodotus from the Church in Rome between 189 and 198–199 CE.[15] The work makes it clear that there were at least some Valentinians not committed to orgiastic excess dressed up as sickening sacramental piety, as Tertullian asserts. The picture here is one of Valentinian married couples taking the spiritual education of their offspring very seriously as their duty to pass the precious seed on to the eternal aeons in its highest state: perfected Christians, above the law insofar as they fulfilled it in love and acts of purified love. Theodotus believed it important to protect the children from zodiacal powers that swayed children's dispositions at birth; one means being for the parents to be regularly in communion with the higher powers through the bridal chamber:

"When we were in the flesh," the Apostle says [Romans 7:5], as if he were already speaking without the body. Now he [Theodotus] says that he [Paul] means by flesh that weakness which was an offshoot of the Woman on high [Sophia]. And when the Savior says to Salome that death will reign as long as women bear, he does not speak in reproach of birth *since it is necessary for the salvation of the believers* [my italics]. For this birth must be until the previously reckoned seed be put forth. But he is alluding to the Woman on high whose passions became creation when she put forth those beings that were without form. On her account the Savior came down to drag us out from passion and to adopt us to himself.

For as long as we were children of the female only, as if of a base intercourse, incomplete and infants and senseless and weak and without form, brought forth like abortions, we were children of the woman, but when we have received form from the Savior, we have become children of a husband and a bride chamber. (*Excerpta ex Theodoto*, 66–67)

The powers that govern fate are nullified through spiritual baptism, according to Theodotus, a baptism of the soul through the symbol of rising from water. Spiritual baptism generates rebirth whereafter the new being is "higher than all the other powers."[16] Now this rationale gives a much more reasonable idea of the vaunted, and much ridiculed, Gnostic superiority. One is to rise beyond the inhibiting powers of the lower realms to prevent them from distorting the character of the children:

> Until baptism, they say, Fate is real, but after it the astrologers are no longer right. But it is not only the washing that is liberating, but the knowledge of who we were, and what we have become, where we were or where we were placed, whither we hasten, from what we are redeemed, what birth is and what rebirth. (*Excerpta ex Theodoto*, 78)

Theodotus believed that children of perfected parents entered the world with the weaknesses inherited from their spiritual Mother. As Sophia had to be saved by Christ, so the seed also had to be completed, or perfected, transformed from the female unformed seed to the male. The eternal welfare of the child motivated the care for the seed:

> So long, then, they say, as the seed is yet unformed, it is the offspring of the female, but when it was formed, it was changed to a man and becomes a son of the bridegroom. It is no longer weak and subject to the cosmic forces, both visible and invisible, but having been made masculine, it becomes a male fruit.
>
> He whom the Mother generates is led into death and into the world, but he whom Christ regenerates is transferred to life into the Ogdoad [the eight or four primal syzygies of the principal Valentinian Pleroma]. And they die to the world but live to God that death may be loosed by death and corruption by resurrection. (*Excerpta ex Theodoto*, 79)

A NEW PICTURE
OF VALENTINIAN SEX

Valentinians' concern for their children has recently been highlighted brilliantly in April DeConick's remarkable study "Conceiving Spirits: The Mystery of Valentinian Sex."[17] Her achievement is to make a decisive shift of emphasis in understanding Valentinianism from the spiritual-philosophical to the spiritual-sociological perspective. Professor DeConick has moved the traditional emphasis from the superior pneuma to the insecurity of the sperma, the seed: a factor that, frankly, has been staring scholars in the face for decades if not centuries, but has been strangely avoided. Her study places the seed as spirit-particle squarely in the realm of reproduction.

As we have been finding in our investigation, it is, as DeConick observes,[18] seed that guarantees the acquisition of gnosis. She attacks thereby the view of Valentinians as either conservative snobs or libertine egotists, as the church fathers and much subsequent scholarship have painted them. According to DeConick: "For some strange reason, most scholars have misunderstood the Valentinian call for gnosis as a call for pursuing intellectual and philosophical knowledge when, in fact, this could not be any further from the crux of the matter."[19] DeConick insists that the Valentinians were emphatically not elitists "concerned only with their own salvation." Rather, they were "brilliant exegetes," seeing in Romans 8:29, for example, the goal of universal salvation while giving account also of Paul's picture of those "predestined to be conformed to the image of his Son."[20] They were true believers in the grace and love of God. Making their starting point the human condition itself, they were driven by their theological inheritance into worry over the integration of spirit (seed) and soul during the testing time of terrestrial exile in a world of filth.

From this shift of emphasis, a very different image of Valentinians emerges, and, I should say, a considerably stranger one than we are used to, carrying almost obsessive interest in the value of their seed just a touch reminiscent of Sterling Hayden's bizarre Col. Jack D. Ripper in Stanley Kubrick's dark comedy *Dr. Strangelove or: How I Learned to Stop Worrying and Love the Bomb:* a military nut so obsessed with his "precious bodily fluids" that he is prepared to spark a world war to preserve their purity.

Chapter 15 (book VI) of Hippolytus's *Refutatio* attributes the emphasis on the eventual mass return of the mature seeds to the Pleroma to Basilides, an inheritance allegedly passed on to Valentinus, who added his own details concerning the nakedness of the seeds at the conjugal feast. DeConick's study indicates just what a momentous emphasis this would become for Valentinus's followers. The destiny of the seed, highlighted by the parables of the sower, the famous speech of John the Baptist concerning the apocalyptic harvest of first fruits, even the implied use of the parable of the Good Samaritan—who fell among thieves—but was saved by one who did not "walk on the other side" with the servants of the law, became the essence and rationale for Valentinian practice. The pleasure of the bridal chamber was not denied but massively accentuated by the thought of there doing the will of the highest God.

We can now see the Valentinian experience from the inside in a way never before possible, so coated were its features by the hostility of the heresiologists. Thanks to the stimulus of DeConick's insight, we can now assemble a completely fresh vision of Valentinian marriage.

NINE

THE VALENTINIAN MARRIAGE

At the heart of Valentinian marriage was an august conception of the inheritance of the seed, and the desire to redeem it to the life above.

The sower went forth to sow. At the point of the seed touching the earth, the seed of the spirit dwells in every soul, enlivening it. The real Valentinian heresy (from orthodox believers in the resurrection of the body) lay here: that the real Self is neither the body nor the rational soul as created, but the deepest aspect of a person, an aspect of the heart, or inner core of the soul (think of a peach stone surrounded by the flesh; within the flesh is the marked stone; within the stone is the smooth kernel containing the essential power of its germination). The spirit animates human beings; the spirit is an embedded seed in the soil of the soul. This seed idea is not simply a metaphor, as in orthodox interpretation; it is truly generative. It is the hidden dimension of sperma, the "pearl of great price" that is in the world but the world knows not its true value. It holds the key to reunion with the unknown God, the power of the radiant Logos. As DeConick puts it: "This Self was God in Exile."[1] Its presence within us causes the unsettling grief of our condition, the longing for a home, out of touch; it colors the life of the world with a sense of tragedy or tragic necessity:

it encourages compassion. It speaks of a distance from nature and its gods.

This seed was dormant in humanity. It needed to be awakened. That's what being a Gnostic was all about. This seed was God in us. Awakened, it has a will of its own: to be done "on earth as it is in heaven." The seed required cultivation; this was the duty of the awakened Christian, to transform the seed from the raw germinal state into the being of glory that at the end of time would be united to the angelic "twin" or holy guardian angel within the pure light choir of the Pleroma.

The Gnostic, male or female, is the twin and true companion of the living Jesus, as Jesus Christ is the twin and true companion of Sophia redeemed, prefigured on Earth in Jesus's relationship with the "redeemed whore" Mary Magdalene who has taken in by the mouth Jesus's holy pneuma-sperma (breath-seed), awakening her true wisdom, wisdom the stupid disciples ought better to attend to, according to the Gnostic *Gospel of Mary.*

The bond reveals the hidden meaning of sex.

Seen in this light, the powerful attraction of the Valentinian solution to the dilemma of mortal, material existence is revealed. *Valentinians had found the hidden meaning of sex:* the truth of their freedom. We can also recognize why it was then that the state of mind of husband and wife during sexual intercourse leading to its climax was so vital a consideration.

In one form of the Valentinian salvation myth, Sophia's generation of spiritual seeds is actually excited by her focusing attention on the dazzling angels that descended with Christ (the anointed) on his way down to Earth (a disgusted Tertullian poured prurient scorn on this myth). In the ancient world, there was a clear magical link between contemplation and procreation; we must be careful what we wish for. The *Gospel of Philip,* for example, makes much of the idea that if a woman is thinking of an adulterous lover when engaging in intercourse with her husband, this adultery will show in the resemblance of the child produced to the lover. Hence, they deduced, Jesus's instruction that thinking about adultery is spiritually on the same level as practicing it. The object of thought during intercourse determines the kind of being that results from it. Therefore, we must suppose that in the Valentinian rite of the marriage chamber, the participants were to concentrate their thought on the image of the Son (see Romans 8:29), reflected in the sprinkling light emanating from the aeonic marriage, for the Son inherits the will of the Father, as the *Gospel of Philip* observes emphatically. To be an heir of Christ means to establish the seed in its fullness: to inherit eternal life (literally, the life of the aeons) whose kingdom is not of this world.

Arguably, it was absurd for the heresiologists, as it is for modern ecclesiastics, to dismiss Valentinian gnosis on the grounds of its becoming apparent after the time of the apostles when every essential precept to its practice can be exegetically discerned from the canonical Gospels and Pauline letters! This is doubtless what so enraged the heresiologists and explains why Tertullian insisted that the heretics in general had no right even to gain access to the scriptures, as the heretics were, he believed, intent on perverting them to paint an alien scheme. In the case of the Valentinians, we can rarely be entirely sure that they have interpreted wrongly, only that the interpretation was inconsistent with much of the traditional understanding. There are moments when one does wonder if Valentinus did, as was claimed, have access to a secret teaching of Paul's, especially where the significance of spirit-baptism was concerned. However, it may be argued that one would be unlikely to come to Valentinian-type conclusions if referring to the canonical texts alone; some outside stimulus was obviously necessary to come up with the distinct slant, "gag," and underlying theosophy. The heresiologists are emphatic that Valentinus simply got his essential models from Greek philosophers, Plato and Pythagoras in particular—and they were heretics—for, as we noted earlier, heresy began in Eden! (Clement of Alexandria and Justin Martyr were exceptions to this rule; they both saw prefigurements of Christian truths in ideas promoted by these philosophers: Christians, as it were, before Christ.)

For Valentinians, Plato's idea of the universe as a shadow or copy of the eternal world of things in themselves meant that, for them, the universe was an image, a deficient image, of the Pleromic world above. Tertullian jibed, probably cheaply, that with so many images abounding, one might speculate as to whether the Valentinians themselves were not imaginary! Hence marriage, Valentinian human marriage, on the principle of "as above, so below" or "on earth as it is in heaven" must be itself an image of the aeonic marriages beyond.

Consciousness-raising during intercourse was a sacramental necessity for those who cared about the seed, for they were the true Christians who had heard their name called, not "hylics" whose materialism smothered the energy and light-potential of the seed. The elect had been redeemed and must go on redeeming the lost sheep. If one could not practice the rite properly, it was better to be celibate than procreate error and give food to the prince of this world who had tried and failed to nail down the essential Christ to his will, revealing only the wondrous fruit on the tree that Gnostic vision, and Gnostic vision alone, could see.

This injunction that the psychics (the soul-conscious) should follow Paul's exoteric advice and shun carnal relations if at all possible led to the accusation that Valentinians practiced one thing and preached another to their "inferiors": possibly a calumny in many cases, for Paul was responsible for making distinctions between Christians worthy only of the milk, but unready for the spiritual meat, which he claimed to own but would not reveal in publicly read letters. Paul would keep the high mysteries to the intitiated. He would be simple for the simple, though he had as much knowledge as anyone on Earth, for he, or someone or something intimate to him, had experienced the "second heaven," whether in or out of the body, he knew not (II Corinthians 12:2). The Valentinians could say: It's all there in the scripture if you read it with the light on, but if you are blind, you won't even know the light has been switched on, and this is the ordinary light of the world, that only the spiritually enlightened see the light; don't blame us, that's just how it is. The light emanates from the seed, but not all men can see it.

Thus it was that, for Valentinian couples, the marriage bed was a locus of awed, sacred practice. There the spirit of God joined with the Christian Gnostic souls and enacted the creation of a new Adam or Eve in the paradise of the womb. If the parents got it right, the child would be inclined to the light and could participate consciously in the redemption of the fallen Sophia and the loss experienced in the soul. For those whose souls were in love with God, sex was a wonder, a miracle, performed not in the dark as an act of shame, but in the light, with the wine and fragrance of spiritual joy suffusing the light of a new day. This was their daily bread to be consumed with thanks. Those unable to see the spiritual glory profaned the very thought of the act; those who failed to see the light in the act were the filthy ones with unclean minds. Such persons would never understand; they were living in the outflow of the condemnation of Adam and Eve, not in the light of the redeemed promise of eternal paradise. Gnostics accepted that they were living in a completely fresh dispensation that had surpassed the "way of the world." There could be no backsliding.

It is supposed that Valentinians did attend ordinary services of the church, but also additional lodges (perhaps an unfortunate term, as this was not Freemasonry as we know it!), where pneumatic instruction could be shared with sacraments of anointing (chrism) and *apolytrosis*. Gilles Quispel has described Valentinians as "the children of the knowledge of the heart" (*Gnostics*, C4 TV series, 1987, ep. 1). Such is evinced in their writings, most particularly the *Gospel of Truth*.

THE KNOWLEDGE OF THE HEART

In the sophisticated text that is the *Gospel of Truth*, Jesus is "knowledge and perfection," who proclaims "the things that are in the heart."[2] The

Coptic word used for *heart* is *het,* and it is "the heart of the Father" that pneumatic Christians come to know. The Valentinian receives "the fruit of his heart and an impression of his will."[3] This is not an intellectual approach. They must understand from the heart the knowledge that is within them. They must feel its light. This kind of emphasis on the sensation of the heart and its knowledge—that reason does not know— looks forward to the continental Pietist movement that grew out of the sixteenth-century Reformation when pre-Reformation spiritual currents began to flow back or emerge into the German, French, and, to some extent, English churches, thence to be replanted in America by the Moravians, Schwenckfeldians, and other Pietist communities. Its most noted proponent was, of course, Jacob Böhme, (1575–1624) whose admirers, Abraham von Franckenberg (1593–1652) and Gottfried Arnold (1666–1714), believed Böhme to be in the spiritual orbit of the Valentinian Gnostics.

While Valentinians were, as DeConick observes, interested in "knowledge that," but probably primary in their concerns was "knowledge how." It was not enough to think about God; one had to experience God, and God could be experienced directly in the love celebrated between husband and wife. The experience of divine love was to take them further than merely an idea or concept of God (whose substance all Christians were to have faith in); they were to discover the reality beyond the idea or concept: God realization was the aim—direct gnosis. Total and complete perfection was still reserved for the eschaton, or end-time, when they would move from an intermediate plane, divest themselves of their garments, that is the soul element, and naked, that is as pure spirit, would be conjoined to their angelic counterparts: the archetypal fathers of their seed, in everlasting joy beyond time. The bridal chamber prefigured the ultimate experience when the Pleroma itself would become a vast chamber of divine union. The sacrament of the bridal chamber also sealed the ultimate experience as an immanent, if temporary, reality. *Resurrection Now!* Visionary planes of experience were associated with the Valentinian sacraments, for the common state of consciousness had been raised, as Moses raised the serpent in the wilderness that healed the exodus children from the vipers of the world.

As we have seen in our comments on Irenaeus's presentation of Ptolemy's followers, there has been some doubt as to whether Irenaeus was consistent in asserting that ultimate salvation was denied to all but the pneumatics. Irenaeus himself says that Valentinians subdivided "animal souls" into those with good tendencies and bad tendencies, and the good might still receive the seed while the hylics, not hearing the call, would never receive it and were damned with the totality of what they thought was real: the world.

Considering all relevant texts, the philosophy in theory was likely to have been practiced in the sense that where there was a possibility of turning to Christ, Christ would know what to do with good souls. Those who had awakened, however, need not entertain any doubts at all about their spirits' eventual destiny, though they would eventually leave their active souls behind them (what this meant in terms of psychology of the self and personal identity at the "end" is still unclear). The perfected Gnostic had found repose.

Now this state of repose mitigates against the cartoon of Gnostics provided by their enemies that they strutted around like proud cocks doing as they fancied while looking down on everybody else. This may have been a projection born of their enemies' disquiets and insecurities. On the other hand, the possibility of inflamed, unbearable egos is with us always—they prance about many corridors of power—and the fusion of the sense of seed and the awareness of the "Big I AM" was always, one must suspect, a moral, if not mortal, risk in Christian-Valentinian life, even when the strutting Demiurge picture was understood as the false god or self of the all. Having said this, many of us can point to distressing cases of rampant egotism dressed up in religious pieties in every religious tradition: the identification of the ordinary ego with God is not uncommon; the egotist or, when lost to extremes, the psychotic, knowing only himself, mistakes this for self-knowledge. It is always a horrible sight. False humility is as sickening as real pomposity, probably a lot more so. "Hold on to your ego!" by all means, as Brian Wilson sang, but don't worship it; don't be overwhelmed by it!

The parable of the sower, even in orthodox interpretation, presupposes that some of the seed fell on stony ground, or was choked by thorns, and, bearing no fruit, could be left to die or be burned up in the harvest fire. Obviously, the orthodox view of the seed is understood as a metaphor for the message of the messiah, or the call to repentance of God Almighty, not the spermatic word of the Gnostics. But reception to either means that the orthodox attack on privileged salvation among Gnostics only emphasizes the Catholic concern that they might not be saved: the rest of the unbelieving pagans and unredeemed sinners could still all go to hell—indeed, the orthodox had no compunction about consigning Gnostics to the same agonized oblivion.

For Valentinians, the whole experience of procreation incarnated important powers of the seed, powers that could in their maturity discarnate the Gnostic from the power of the world. Being the marrow of the soul, the seeds were likened to leaven, Jesus's "light of the world" that raises it. The seeds bound the soul to the body, which itself suggests that they must have supposed the seed existed *in potentia* in every human, or else they would not be human, though they, like us, might doubt that when confronted by a real beast.

There was seriousness for the Valentinian couple, for the seed was called forth for the divine imperative of harvest. Reading John the Baptist's sermon on the coming harvest conflagration from a spiritual point of view, the Valentinians observed the distinction of the wheat from the tares, the latter destined for the fire. Thus the crisis of the coming judgment would bring forth the divine pneuma, condemning the temple of flesh. This was their "gospel" or even "secret book" of John. Valentinians described the hylic dimension of the soul as a tare naturally, and as seed of the devil, being of his substance, for the Valentinian soul seems to be a demiurgical copy to some extent of the spirit that the archons cannot grasp; it is what they're made of: deficient substance, unredeemed, for it came out of the disturbed tendencies (*enthymesis*) of Sophia, acting without her syzygy (one might therefore suppose at least some Valentinians' uneasiness with masturbation, unless it could be justified as gathering seed and then consumed sacramentally). The soul, anyway, was tarnished by the dark powers of the created world, like the crater-scars of the moon, or the external marks of the peach stone that belie the spherical perfection within it.

THE GOOD SPERMARITAN

Valentinians were concerned that bad spirits lived in the soul, and it is likely then that exorcisms were performed in apolytrosis rituals, from time to time, to preserve the heart, the core of the soul, from contamination. They might have had their own explanations and ways of dealing with overly cocky or overbearing members. They had to live with what was the natural soul condition, subject to negative tendencies. The cure was the Eucharist of the indwelling Son, who sanctified the heart with his light, banishing the darkness and subduing the tempests of the world, so that the heart might find repose, rest, and peace unutterable. These benefits came from grace, the sprinkling light of the Savior, come to Earth but not of the Earth. "You walked in mud but your garments were not soiled, and you were not buried in their filth, and you were not caught" (*First Apocalypse of James,* NHL V, 3, 28).

The Nag Hammadi work known as the *Valentinian Exposition* attributes the natural corruptions of the soul to Sophia's passions;[4] these too could be healed by the sexual *apolytrosis* of the Valentinian marriage chamber. The wounds of the Sophia could be bound by, if I may be forgiven the transposition, the "Good Spermaritan" who took pity on the one who fell among thieves. Valentinians valued baptism to remove demons and unction to invoke the Holy Spirit. And if you consider me presumptuous for making the link with the famous Good Samaritan parable, look at the Gnostic work the *Exegesis of the Soul,* where the soul, which may justly be compared to the redeemed whore Helena of Tyre, is tracked in her descent to Earth: "when she fell down into a body and came to this life, then she fell into the hands of many robbers, and wanton creatures passed her from one to another [. . .] they defiled her."[5] The Father redeems her defiled state by anointing (chrism) and by baptism. Valentinians had no problem understanding why the gospel Jesus was often in the company of prostitutes; he *understood*.

The *Exegesis of the Soul* directly relates the blessing of the seed of the redeemed soul's beloved with the importance of rearing good children: "and when she had intercourse with him, she got from him the seed that is the life-giving Spirit, so that by him she bears good children and rears them. For this is the great perfect marvel of birth. And so this marriage is made perfect by the will of the Father."[6]

For those who wish to dismiss the Valentinian attitude as spiritual elitism, again it must be said that the cause of the distinction very much lies in the legacy of Paul. It was Paul's opposition to James, the brother of the Lord, that ignited the distinction between the psychic who must obey the principles of good conduct, and the pneumatic who has become a "law unto himself," having the image of the Son in his heart. James advocated *zedek* and *hesed*, "righteousness" and "loving-kindness," that is, good works as the means to salvation. Paul regarded these as the means of the old covenant, challenged now by the appearance of the fire of the spirit and the spirit-baptism, vouchsafed to the wild olive tree that was the Gentile Christian family. The wild sowing of the seeds denoted for Valentinians the gift of salvation to the Gentiles; their tree had grown wild, outside of the covenant of Moses, who, they suspected, was inspired by the Demiurge. Paul taught his disciples that the spiritual man is superior as spiritual fire is to water. Therefore, pneumatics were saved by this nature that was within them; those who followed the rational path of law would be content with the blessings that mercy showed toward the people of good works; they would need to earn their passage.

Valentinian couples would have been eager to partake of the ordinary Christian Eucharist, for the Eucharistic symbols brought the soul and its tendencies into conformity with the image of the "Perfect Man," Jesus, though they knew of a higher intimacy than the partaking of bread and wine, which for themselves prefigured the commingling of the life-giving substance of the sexual rite. Their experience of Eucharist would have belied the image of their partaking of the elements together with ordinary church members. Again, this dichotomy doubtless enraged the bishops: "with us, but not of us," they could say. The aim for the orthodox was to prevent any commingling, and to isolate the Gnostics. They succeeded pretty well, while taking in and transforming a number of Gnostic spiritual symbols in the process. Hence it would seem that the Gnostic Valentinus, whose heart-image was the hidden light of God, became the sentimental spirit of romantic gifts, rarely spiritual.

Many reading this will wonder if the church did not lose something of its own soul in extricating the heretics from its numbers, tarring all groups with the same brush of utter disdain and moral horror. As for the Valentinians, their inspiration came from the scriptures, enlivened by spiritual imagination, transmuted by an exalted eroticism, and inspired by a sense of a new creation of a wholly spiritual character. Thus when they read of the birth of Seth, after the catastrophe of Cain and Abel, they saw, at the moment of Seth's conception, as Adam embraced his wife Eve with love and hope and faith, Adam's soul raised to the heights of heaven, there to find the image of the true Son for the formation of the hoped-for child. As with Seth, so with their own offspring: to make a holy generation whose house was built in heaven. As April DeConick expresses this vision: "It was this form of lovemaking that the Valentinians considered sacred and believed would lead to their own redemption, which was nothing less than the redemption of God himself" ("Conceiving Spirits" in *Hidden Intercourse,* 46).

At last we can clearly and unequivocally see the gnosis specifically as the liberation of the captive seed through the sexually harmonious contemplation of angelic beings. For Valentinians, acts of love heal the heart and prepare the seed for reunion.

TEN

IN SEARCH OF THE MYSTERY OF PROUNEIKOS AND BARBELO IN ALEXANDRIA

O ne of the many mysteries that still surrounds the origins of the Gnostic impulse is that of the names given to the Gnostic goddess or, better, archangelic, figure known to Valentinians as the aeon Sophia (mother of the angels), but known among Ophite and Sethian followers of the gnosis as Barbelo, Barbelos, Barbelon, or Barbalo, the virgin spirit.

While in some texts, Barbelo seems intimately identified with or even identical with Sophia, both roles being maternal and primal, Sophia is perhaps best understood in most texts as the somewhat wayward, self-willed daughter of the androgynous progenitrix Barbelo. However, Barbelo, her/himself is just as eager to know God the Father face-to-face, and to receive his reflection (seed) as an image. However, Barbelo asks first and then receives. For Barbeloites (or, as I prefer, Barbelites), heavenly man is engendered in the image of God (Barbelo) by divine spark. Sophia is apparently not the type, or archetype, to ask. As wisdom, of course, she is already supposed to know. She is proud.

In the *Apocryphon of John,* Sophia is called the "Sophia of the Epinoia"[1] (epinoia means "insight," "thought," "purpose," "design," "intent"), whereas Barbelo, who emerges first from the depth of the Pleroma, is the androgynous pronoia ("forethought" or prognosis) of the Father (he/she is also "man" and receives the Father's seed to produce Christ, he anointed with virgin light); Sophia then appears as an emanation or daughter of the androgynous Barbelo, being the wisdom aspect of mother-father Barbelo's foreknowledge.

One reason for the somewhat awkward complexity of this father-mother-daughter-son generative process is that the Gnostic myth-makers were trying via a myth or story to satisfy philosophical objections to insolubles and imponderables, such as: How could perfection generate anything imperfect? And, indeed, why should a perfect Monad (God as "One") need to generate anything at all? The essential myth purports to show that the process emanated, or was dynamized, from an irresistible necessity of the nature of the Monad: its mysterious, incomprehensible heart, a loving generosity of spirit inseparable from its being and thus carried on in its much-desired seed.

Irenaeus tends to identify Barbelo so closely with the figure Prunicus (in Latin) or Prouneikos or Pronikos in Greek (a name that does not appear directly in the Nag Hammadi Library) that they appear practically identical, as Sophia and Barbelo also function identically in many texts. However, Prouneikos's characteristics seem most fitting for the myth of Sophia and her exile, as well as that of the unnamed "whore and the holy one" of the Nag Hammadi text, *The Thunder, Perfect Mind.*[2] If we are to stay in tune with the paradoxical characterizations of Gnostic wisdom, we must accept that the Mother is in the Daughter and the Daughter is in the Mother, for the Father's fertile seed is in the Mother. The question is: Which one of them errs like the lost sheep?

In order to begin our search for the meaning of Barbelo and Prouneikos, we need to go back to the Jewish community in Alexandria two centuries before the time of Jesus. We are in the time when Egypt was governed by senior Greek army officers intermarried with Egyptian aristocracy, for Alexander the Great had taken Egypt and founded his city Alexandria in 331 BCE. In response to the overwhelming influence of Greek culture, the legend goes that Greco-Egyptian pharaoh Ptolemy II (d. 246 BCE) commissioned seventy or seventy-two Jewish scholars to translate the sacred Hebrew texts into Greek for inclusion in his great library at Alexandria. Begun in the third century BCE, the work was completed by the late-second century BCE. The Greek Bible is known collectively as the Septuagint (or Book of the Seventy). Translating Hebrew into words comprehensible to Greek-speaking people had a profound effect on the development of thought among Jews, and among educated Gentiles interested in Jewish culture.

There is another significant aspect to the translation of one culture into another. Things inevitably look different when you create a linguistically homogenous text. By translating the Hebrew word for wisdom, *hokhmah,* for example, into the Greek *sophia,* or *logos,* you launch the Hellenistic mind onto an associative exercise that links Hebrew accounts with quite "other" philosophical and mythological contexts. You take it that you're dealing with the same thing as what has become familiar to you when encountering this word; meaning becomes expanded, diversified, and, inevitably, somewhat distorted from its primary resonance.

Alexandrians concerned with history and philosophy had a chance to look at the Hebrew inheritance as a whole; that goes for Jews as well as Gentiles. Greeks could get inside something that had previously been entirely alien or closed to them. The Five Books of Moses (the Pentateuch) could be, and were, considered as philosophy, as were the wisdom books such as Proverbs. As philosophy, compared to other, alien philosophies, syncretism became inescapable. Different approaches could be applied to the Jewish texts, operating from wildly different premises from those that motivated the original authors. The texts attracted questioning and debate, whereas previously they had simply been respected as sacred records.

It would become necessary for Jewish savants to comment on their works for Gentile consumption, so that the Greek-speaking inquirer got the right idea or could at least begin to understand the Jewish spiritual and intellectual outlook, as far as the commentator understood it. In this process, of course, the traffic of ideas journeyed in both directions. Seen from a Hellenistic perspective, the meaning of Jewish texts expanded to Jewish commentators as well. They had not been known as philosophers before, and while religious purists balked at such a pagan encumbrance, urban sophisticates could revel in it.

Above all, what did the corpus of Hebrew sacred literature communicate as a whole, as a continuum? While to the Jewish people, their literature told an epic of salvation history, of how, through abiding by covenanted promises with the personal God Jahveh, the Jewish people had survived the tremors of historic epochs, and how, through disobedience to their God, highlighted by the prophets, they had suffered disasters and, intermittently, foreign yoke. But faith was justified; faith was wise; the beginning of wisdom was the fear of God: the essence of wisdom was the knowledge of God.

There was another story, or way of telling that story. Jewish commentators in Greek could tell how God had created the universe with his wisdom, and wisdom to the Greeks was both an intellectual concept and a goddess, or inherent absolute, or law, in nature. So you start in Genesis ("In the beginning") with a pure idea: an unspoiled canvas of divine will; God made the *kosmos* with wisdom ("let us make") and "saw that it was good." The Platonic good would have immediate resonance: optimistic, naturalistic, positive. Well and good. But then we find that this good picture enters a process of phase upon phase of deformation: Adam and Eve fall; Cain slays Abel; Sodom and Gomorrah; the Great Flood; the Tower of Babel and the division of peoples; the splits between Isaac and Ishmael, between Jacob and Esau; the enslavement of the Hebrews by Egyptians; the corruption of the covenant by apostasy to Canaanite gods and goddesses; the division of Judah from

Israel; the destruction of the Temple; the Babylonian exile; the conquest by Persians, then in the second century BCE the conquest by the descendants of Alexander's Greek-speaking generals (the Seleucids), followed by a war of liberation under the Maccabean family of Judas, the Hammer (post-167 BCE). How could all this be understood? How could it be portrayed?

On the one hand, we begin with a virgin—Wisdom—timeless, eternal, perfect. Then this divine idea is brought into contact with creation, and with men whom she adores and teaches. And what happens? Wisdom is progressively defaced, distorted, ignored, reviled, assaulted, and enslaved—though Wisdom in herself remains pure, of course. Insofar as the First Temple is defiled, Wisdom is successively, figuratively, raped by the powers of the world and their gods, whom, we should realize, were regarded by Jews as rebel angels: the genii of the nations. But in the end, she is justified, as are those who have loved and love her, and her imageless image is seen by the blessed as pure again.

At the opening of the second century BCE, the Jews had their Second Temple, and right worship was devoted to their God in Zion, and the nations were hearing of their faith. But Wisdom's place was not entirely secure; there were cataclysms to come.

Seen in this manner, the violent itinerary of Simonian mythology in the first century CE, after the Roman conquest of Samaria and Judea and the Roman-backed imposition of alien, Herodian-Idumaean rule over the Temple, bears more resonance than being presented merely as a creation myth. It is a culture myth as well, and the abuse of the divine consort, forcing her into prostitution and oppression, mirrors the destiny of God's chosen vessels: the temporal passage of Wisdom through the hands of the dark angels of foreign control. The name *Helen* means "shining light" or "torch": light in the darkness. The vertical fall from on high is reflected in, and corresponds to, the linear, horizontal passage of time: as above, so below. As long as time continued, Wisdom would alternately suffer, that is, experience, and be vindicated: "for wisdom has been proved right by all her children" (Luke 7:35). The Septuagint told the story and promised its eventual resolution, for those with eyes to see.

It is not surprising then that it was at Alexandria where the personified Lady Wisdom of the Proverbs received speculative attention in works like *Ecclesiasticus* ("The wisdom of Jesus the Son of Sirach") and the *Wisdom of Solomon*. Along with Proverbs, these works contain the seeds for the development of the Barbelo-Sophia myth into full Gnostic bloom when Gnostics followed Jewish Platonists in trying to turn divine epithets into Platonic ideas, mythologizing them to anthropomorphic levels.

Hear the words of the Jewish sage in Egypt, Jesus, son of Sirach, and note how he develops ideas from Proverbs that Wisdom is a fruit-bearing *tree:*

Who can find out the height of heaven, and the breadth of the earth, and the deep, and wisdom? Wisdom hath been created before all things, and the understanding of prudence from everlasting. The word of God most high is the fountain of wisdom; and her ways are everlasting commandments. *To whom hath the root of wisdom been revealed?* Or who hath known her wise counsels? *Unto whom hath the knowledge of wisdom been made manifest? And who hath understood her great experience?* There is one wise and greatly to be feared, the Lord sitting upon his throne. He created her, and saw her, and numbered her, and poured her out upon all his works. She is with all flesh according to his gift, and he hath given her to them that love him. [. . .] *To fear the Lord is the beginning of wisdom: and it was created with the faithful in the womb. She hath built an everlasting foundation with men, and she shall continue with their seed.* To fear the Lord is fullness of wisdom, and filleth men with her fruits. She filleth all their houses with things desirable, and the garners with her increase. [. . .] Wisdom raineth down skill and knowledge of understanding standing, and exalteth them to honour that hold her fast. *The root of wisdom is to fear the Lord, and the branches thereof are long life.* [my italics] (*Ecclesiasticus* 1:3–20)

The author would already have been familiar with Proverbs 3:18–20:

She is a tree of life to them that lay hold upon her: and happy is every one that retaineth her. The LORD by wisdom hath founded the earth; by understanding hath he established the heavens. By his knowledge the depths are broken up, and the clouds drop down the dew. [my italics]

It is interesting that Irenaeus ridiculed Gnostics for being absurd enough to imagine that the rain and waters of the world were signs of the tears of Sophia, and yet here are the canonical Proverbs attributing the rain to the foundation of the Earth by Lady Wisdom.

Attributed in its prologue to the grandson of Shimon ben Yeshua ben Eliezer ben Sira of Jerusalem, the author of *Ecclesiasticus,* Jesus ben Sira, went to Egypt in the thirty-eighth year of Energetes, an epithet of Ptolemy III Energetes (247–222 BCE) and of Ptolemy VIII who reigned from 170 to 117 BCE. If the latter pharaoh is referred to, the move to Egypt might have been occasioned by Judas Maccabeus's violent revolt against the Seleucids (167–160 BCE). Antiochus IV put a Greek temple on the Temple Mount in Jerusalem, profaning the Second Temple's altar with pagan sacrifices.

The author writes of a personified Wisdom in chapters 1 and 24. Wisdom is eternal: "From eternity, in the beginning he created me, and for eternity I shall not cease to exist" (24:9; cf: Proverbs 8:22: "The Lord possessed me in the beginning of his way, before his works of old"). Wisdom came out "from the mouth of the Most High"; she is the "firstborn of God" (24:3a; *cf.* Colossians 1:15 where the firstborn creator is identified with the "dear Son" of God).

In 24:18–19, Wisdom (Sophia) tells her listeners to come to her: "I am the mother of fair love, and fear, and knowledge and holy hope: I therefore, being eternal, am given to all my children who are named of him. Come unto me, all ye that be desirous of me, and fill yourselves with my fruits." Again, the inspiration seems to come from Proverbs 8, which follows a passage warning the would-be son of Wisdom against the low whore of the city of the world who would drag a young man down to fruitless destruction. By contrast, Wisdom, also pictured as a female figure on the streets, calls for attention: "She crieth at the gates, at the entry of the city, at the coming in at the doors. Unto you, O men, I call; and my voice is to the sons of man" (vv. 2–3). "For wisdom is better than rubies; and all the things that may be desired are not to be compared to it" (v. 11). "I love them that love me; and those that seek me early shall find me" (Proverbs 8:17).

Wisdom then is a kind of holy whore, generous with herself and her secrets, eager for men to stop by her; though she is worth more than riches, she gives herself to those who love her, and stays forever pure: for she is the path that leads away from destruction to righteousness and the high places: "My fruit is better than gold, yea, than fine gold; and my revenue than choice silver. I lead in the way of righteousness, in the midst of the paths of judgment" (vv. 19–20). "Come, eat of my bread, and drink of the wine which I have mingled. Forsake the foolish, and live; and go in the way of understanding" (Proverbs 8:5–6).

Taking root in "an honorable people, even in the portion of the Lord's inheritance" (*Ecclesiasticus* 24:12), Sophia was exalted "like a cedar in Libanus, and as a cypress tree upon the mountains of Hermon" (24:13), and "was exalted like a palm tree in En-gaddi, and as a rose plant in Jericho, as a fair olive tree in a pleasant field, and grew up as a plane tree by the water" (24:14). "As the turpentine tree I stretched out my branches, and my branches are the branches of honor and grace. As the vine brought I forth pleasant savor, and my flowers are the fruit of honor and riches" (24:16–17). She is the tree that bears the best, most fragrant fruit. Those who would be fruitful had best eat and drink her in.

We may note also in Proverbs that Wisdom has a distinctly forward character; she delights in the company of men and is the delight of the Lord also, for she is deeply involved in the creation of the world:

The Lord possessed me in the beginning of his way, before his works of old. I was set up from everlasting, from the beginning, or ever the earth was. When there were no depths, I was brought forth; when there were no fountains abounding with water. Before the mountains were settled, before the hills was I brought forth: While as yet he had not made the earth, nor the fields, nor the highest part of the dust of the world.

When he prepared the heavens, I was there: when he set a compass upon the face of the depth: when he established the clouds above: when he strengthened the fountains of the deep: when he gave to the sea his decree, that the waters should not pass his commandment: when he appointed the foundations of the earth: Then I was by him, as one brought up with him: and I was daily his delight, rejoicing always before him: Rejoicing in the habitable part of his earth; and my delights were with the sons of men. (Proverbs 8:22–31)

Gnostic speculators clearly asked themselves these questions: Did Sophia delight a little too much in her glory? Did she try to make herelf equal to God? To delight, to play so much among the sons of fallen men, had she too fallen from grace? If she had such a role in creation, might that explain its imperfections, imperfections that God her Father could never have been responsible for?

The *Wisdom of Solomon* is generally believed by scholars to have been written in Alexandria during the second or first century BCE, most likely as late as the reign of Caesar Augustus, formerly known as Octavian. Octavian sanctioned Herod the Great's rule over Judea while establishing the imperial *Pax Romana* over Egypt by force, having defeated Cleopatra and Mark Antony at Actium in 31 BCE.

Appearing in the Protestant Apocrypha (deutero-canonical in the Catholic Church) and known also as the *Book of Wisdom,* or simply *Wisdom,* Sophia is presented as "the breath of the power of God," as "everlasting light, the unspotted mirror of the power of God, and as "the image of his goodness" (*Wisdom of Solomon* 7:25–26). Sophia is swift; she has gone through, that is, penetrated, everything: "For wisdom is more moving than any motion: she passeth and goeth through all things by reason of her pureness" (7:24). This moving and penetrating characteristic is very significant, and did not pass Gnostics by, as we shall see.

Sophia is conceived in terms of Middle Platonism and as the logos of the Stoics. She is "the worker of all things" (what makes them tick); she is "subtle, lively, clear, undefiled" (7:22); she is the "mother" of good things (7:12). The author, speaking as Solomon, declares:

> I loved her and sought her out from my youth, I desired to make her my spouse, and I was a lover of her beauty. In that she is conversant with God, she magnifieth her nobility: yea, the Lord of all things himself loved her. For she is privy to the mysteries of the knowledge of God and a lover of his works. . . . Therefore I proposed to take her to me to live with me, knowing that she would be a counsellor of good things, and a comfort in cares and grief. (*Wisdom of Solomon* 8:2–4, 9)

Sophia is even presented as the agent of salvation, an immanent messiah; through her, men are saved. Her ability to inspire men to reform their crooked ways is linked directly to the Holy Spirit (9:17–18). She even brought Adam out from his "fall"; she taught him what he needed to know: "the power to rule all things" (10:1–2). Indeed, this latter passage could easily have been viewed by a Gnostic exegete as a plain indication of Sophia's role in permitting the Demiurge to do the work of creation, for Adam, unnamed, is called "the first-formed father of the world" (*patera kosmou*) and the title could be taken for the craftsman-angel: "She preserved the first formed father of the world, that was created alone, and brought him out of his fall, And gave him power to rule all things" (Wisdom 9:18). Even if this passage did not stir such a radical gnosis, we cannot help noticing that it is Sophia who picks up Adam after his fall, effectively undoing much of the punishment meted out to him and his wife, while giving the condemned "power to rule all things," something, unless we are mistaken, offered also by the serpent with the fruit of the tree of knowledge of good and evil.

When God was angered by the descent of humankind into unrighteousness and brought the Flood to wipe them out, Wisdom preserved the world "in a piece of wood of small value" (10:4) (note the redemptive link between *wood* and *tree* and later, of course, in the hands of Paul and the Gnostics, with *cross:* the wood that sprung the trap on the prince of the world). When the righteous is oppressed by his brother, she shows him the path to the "kingdom of God" and "knowledge of holy things" (*gnōsin hagiōn:* 10:10). Sophia saves. When Joseph's brothers cast him into the pit, Sophia goes down into the pit with him, and rescues him, and brings him up to the path of glory (10:13). She has the capacity to enter fully into the world, even the darkest places, but remains forever unspoiled, radiant, shining, beautiful.

We can feel the power of the Septuagint in this work, for the salvation history of the Jewish people is represented plainly and systematically as the work of Sophia, saving the righteous from destruction time and time again through her holy knowledge and spirit. She illuminates the path to the kingdom of God, and, as Jesus says in Luke's Gospel, Sophia is "proved right by all her children." She is the "incorruptible Spirit" "in all things" (12:1). She is the mother who brings the wise to the knowledge of the Father: an immanent savior.

PHILO OF ALEXANDRIA (CA. 20 BCE–CA. 50 CE)

The Jewish philosopher Philo is very important to understanding how Greek speculative structures were applied to Jewish religious convictions in Alexandria. A contemporary and elder of Jesus and Paul, Philo comes very close in his thinking to that of the Gnostic heresiarchs at certain points, though he never loses faith that the creator of the world is the absolute God; however, *he* may not have been working alone.

Philo does not appear to have seen gnosis as a salvific principle in itself, but he does see the essence of God as being even beyond the identification of him as the Monad (or the One), and the creation of the world, though his work, essentially, was undertaken by subordinate powers and where there were imperfections in human judgment, they might be attributed to humans themselves. This thought in itself, to a speculative frame of mind, already opens a can of worms. And Philo encouraged speculation because he identified Plato's eternal ideas as God's thoughts, and the power of thought resided in Man.

Philo expressed the link between the transcendent God and the lower creation as being effected by the Stoic word *Logos,* the Word, a kind of intermediary, binding power and intelligence, present, like the Sophia of the *Wisdom of Solomon,* in all things. As Professor Henry Chadwick has noted,[3] the personified Hokhmah, Sophia, is never far from Philo's thoughts when he writes of the Logos, to whom is given many epithets, such as "the first-begotten Son of the uncreated Father," "second God," and even "the man of God."[4] Such ideas would flower in the prologue to John's Gospel, of course. It is odd to think that Jesus and Philo might have passed one another in the streets of Alexandria when Joseph and Mary took Jesus from Judea following Herod the Great's threats against the House of David.

We can see how the masculine character of the Greek noun *logos,* and the feminine noun *sophia* automatically suggest an androgynous characteristic both in the masculo-feminine Barbelo, and in the relations between the feminine and masculine Gnostic aeons Sophia, Christ, and Logos, for the Logos comes from the primal heavenly, androgynous *anthrōpos,* the heavenly man as reflected image of God: the seed in the Mother, Barbelo.

In Valentinian speculation, of course, the deficiency of the cosmos comes from Sophia's attempting to create from her passion alone. Only the uncreated Father can create perfection alone; powers of perfect creation are a grace of the Father. Thus we can see Plato's statement that "Time is the moving image of eternity" (paraphrased from *Timaeus*, 37 c-e), blending mythically with Sophia's precocious presumption, for in trying to create her image of eternity, through her ungovernable passion to know the Father, her rogue tendency creates only the deformation of eternity into time, which is finite and ultimately destructive. The mystery of time lies precisely in its deformation. Sophia is naughty; she sets One at naught. She denies the rights of the One, and creates the many, for as Plato accounts for the distinction between time and eternity, things that move, like time, do so by number, whereas eternity rests in unity. And Sophia, as the *Wisdom of Solomon* maintains, "is more moving than any motion" (*Wisdom* 7:24).

This highly significant statement would have immediately alerted Valentinus to its implication: Sophia already had something of the character of the world in her. Not content with repose in unity, she, like time, moved. She is the moved mover. She moves the Pleroma; that is, her antics move the aeons to compassion, which itself is a move from the state Philo regards as divine perfection, namely *apatheia,* the "absence of passions:" God does not need the world. How, asks the Gnostic philosopher, could the apathetic transcendent God have got to the stage where it could be said he "so loved the world that he gave his only begotten Son" (John 3:16) so that believers could have the life of eternity? Sophia rocked the boat; out of passion came the corruption of the world; out of passion comes salvation from it through the love of God.

This, of course, makes this precocious, outspoken feminine power a real heroine, not only for all she has suffered, but for initiating the opportunity she has given for people to experience the *life of the aeons:* eternal life, to transcend time and the corrupt creation.

Philo saw Genesis 1:26—"Let us create man in our image, after our likeness"—as referring to the creation not of the earthly Adam, but the heavenly man, while Philo supposed it was Genesis 2:7 that referred to the earthly Adam who, though of dust, has breath of life breathed into him. In thus distinguishing earthly from heavenly Adam, Philo reconciled Plato's distinction between the intelligible and the sensible worlds, the eternal ideas from the finite copies or images: material that bore the stamp of the superior impress. Philo's identification of the Logos, as archetype of heavenly Mind, with the heavenly Adam also leaves only a small gap to cross in order to regard Wisdom as a heavenly archetype who has got herself involved in the lower creation.

Philo calls the Logos bread (he is again thinking of Sophia) or manna, God's heavenly food for mankind to be consumed in the wilderness (a salvific image within the *Wisdom of Solomon*). Again, we are not very far from the Gnostic allegory of bread and seed: the Stoic *logos spermatikos,* where the Logos is both sower and sown, and eaten by the elect.

Philo, as we have seen, believed the aspirant to the life beyond the finite body must advance to a complete absence of passion, and this helps us to understand what was intended by Valentinians when the seed rises to the Pleroma, which, on entering, is divested of its garments, that is, the psyche. For the psyche is the home of the passions, which as the spirit rises toward home are progressively divested and handed over to hierarchies of governing angels: rendering unto Caesar, as it were, what was theirs from the beginning.

For Philo, the cardinal sin was pride, that is, the lust to become equal to God was the root of sin. Valentinus, hardly alone, saw this pride in the Mother of heaven, for what Mother in such a place would not be proud?

Philo does foreshadow the Gnostics' conception of the bad creation, for his interpretation of Genesis 1:26 gives the transcendent God the get-out clause for any imperfections, such as the painful fact of humanity's mortality. Philo sees the creation of humanity as an act shared with necessarily inferior angels. Philo has perhaps been reflecting on Plato's Timaeus (41) where we hear of a "craftsman" or *dēmiourgos* (literally a "public worker") who does his best to fashion the solid from the ideal (the mechanical never matches up to the pure thought of a thing; machines always need to be repaired). Jewish speculation on the evil angels and their prince who fell from grace—speculation based in part on Genesis 6 and flourishing in the *Book of Enoch*—gave this figure and his fellow archons a considerably more sinister, and no less unflattering, connotation.

Now that we have a reasonable idea of the swirl of philosophically legitimate ideas that circulated in Alexandria at the time of Simon Magus's heyday and doubtless beyond it (and many that had circulated for at least a century before him), we shall, I think, understand much better how we may understand those mysterious names: Prouneikos and Barbelo.

ELEVEN
The Lascivious One

Liddell and Scott's *Greek-English Lexicon* gives us the masculine noun *prouneikos,* or *prounikos,* as meaning a porter, or hired porter: one who bears another's burden. The suggestion here perhaps, at least in our context, is of someone who has been "put upon"; it doesn't seem strong enough to warrant an epithet for Mother Wisdom, or strong enough as a euphemism for *whore,* though Sophia, according to Gnostics, has suffered for our sakes and carried the brunt of salvation and cultural history, as the *Wisdom of Solomon* asserts.

A secondary meaning is offered by Liddell and Scott, based on the *Anthologia Palatina* and the *Anecdota Graeca* of August Immanuel Bekker (1785–1871). The former source is a collection of Greek poetry and epigrams discovered in the Palatinate Library in Heidelberg, Germany in 1606 (*Codex Palatinus 23*), based on the lost collection of rare Greek literature from the seventh century BCE to 600 CE, gathered by Constantine Cephalas in the tenth century CE. *Anecdota Graeca,* published in three volumes (G. Reimeri, Berlin, 1814–1821) contained German philologist August Immanuel Bekker's investigations into practically all known ancient Greek literature, excluding the tragedies and lyric poets.

From these sources,[1] Liddell and Scott deduce a usage of *prouneikos* as being from the Greek *propherēs,* and also suggest the secondary translation of "lustful" and "lewd." Since *propherēs* means "carried before," "placed before," "excelling," "superior," "eldest," "precocious (of young persons and plants)," and "premature," while the verb *propherō* means "I bring forth," a more suggestive picture does emerge, though we may still be guessing since the aeon in question is not called "Propheros." Nevertheless, early authorities derive *prouneikos* from the aorist of *propherō*.[2]

Checking the index of volume 3 of Bekker's *Anecdota Graeca* (1821, p. 1415), I found the passage in which *prouneikos* appears. It is an extract from Choeroboscus, interpreting the testimony of Demetrius and Alexis (first century CE) that the word referred to young servants or slaves who carried trade articles out of the agora (city center) and who had to deliver the goods before getting their reward.[3] Unlike Epiphanius of Salamis who leapt to the conclusion that *prouneikos* meant "lascivious," the context of the word here concerns masters, service, and honorable reward. The word qualifies *misthos,* which means "reward," "hire," "wages," and "punishment," so the suggestion is of "one for hire," "one for rent," or a "wage earner." We seem to be back with the carrier or hired porter again.

Liddell and Scott seem to have gotten their lewd and lustful from a combination of the *Palatine Anthology* (12.209) and from the biased heresiologist Epiphanius (on "Prunicus" in *Panarion* book I, part 25). The passage in the *Palatine Anthology* comes, interestingly, from the world of Greek comedy, from Strato of Sardes's epigram *Mousa paidikē* (= "Boy-Muse" or "Boy-love," ca. 125 CE). Strato addresses a youth with a long face, inciting him to get into the fun of the game and show a bit of passion. The word *prouneika* qualifies "kisses" (*philēmata*). The boy is asked where are the (lewd?) kisses to vie with the opening games, bickering, and debate. The context suggests something like the kisses should be "cheeky," "forward," "lusty," or "tempting" and "encouraging." And yes, possibly "arousing," "lewd," or "leading" (as in "leading on"). The comic use of the word should be noted; the suggestion is of an entertaining type of behavior and a theatrical character.

Epiphanius says that the word means "wanton," "lustful," or

"lascivious." He would; that's how he thought of all heretics. He bases his interpretation, for he is guessing, on a Greek phrase, *Eprounikeuse tautēn,* referring to someone who has debauched or importuned a girl. Epiphanius's undoubtedly biased twist—one surely that Irenaeus or Hippolytus would have used if they'd known of it—may only find confirmation in the later (end of fifth century CE) lexicon of Hesychius of Miletus.

In interpreting the Greek *skitaloi* ("lewd fellows," "lechers," or "lascivious ones"), Hesychius uses the phrase *aphrodisiōn kai tēs prounikias tēs nykterinēs.* This is most interesting for *aphrodisiōn* means something belonging to the goddess of love—we recall that *Aphrodite* was a euphemism for sexual intercourse. Nectarines are, of course, peaches, and peaches, believed to have come from Persia, were sacred to the goddess Isis and the peach-tree branch to her son Harpokrates, patron of mystical secrets in Egypt and elsewhere. Love is not necessarily lewd. *Prounikias* denotes a quality within the nectarines, likely to promote love. The English word *cheeky* keeps springing to mind, but we may not have the exact correspondent to the word's meaning in English.

According to Anne Pasquier,[4] Hesychius applies the word to someone overzealous or forward in gaining sexual pleasure. This would, of course, fit very well the yearning of Sophia to know the Father and acquire his seed: someone anxious to secure the attention of men— as Sophia is presented as being in *Ecclesiasticus* and the *Wisdom of Solomon.*

Patriarch of Constantinople, Photios I (ca. 810–893 CE), used Hesychius for his own *Lexicon,* which was aimed at providing interpretations of words in classical literature that had lost their meaning. Photios objected to Hesychius's interpretation of the word, noting that it seemed to have been diverted from its former meaning.[5] Photios reckoned the word could mean "overzealous," "eager," or "fiery," suggesting being too "forward" in reward-seeking, implying perhaps a hired porter greedy for a tip.

The function of the word seems to be primarily comic, linking the ideas of peddling and precosity. Pollux, writing in the second century, informs us that "Ancient comedy calls *phortakes* those who carry supplies from the market whereas the poets of the new comedy call *prounikoi* the paid porters." The word might then mean "loaded one," as we might say of a rich person "he or she is loaded," for, according to Pollux, the epithet was applied to Byzantines in general.[6]

Hesychius says *prounikoi* (plural) refers to "those who in return for a reward carry the supplies from the market, that some call young boys: runner, quick, hasty, changing, impetuous, wage-earning [or hireling]." The word *quick* is a word we find for Sophia in the *Wisdom of Solomon*: Sophia's a fast mover, quick off the mark, maybe a little too quick, but with shades here of Hermes with winged feet darting between worlds, and not a little mischievous. This all suggests the English word *fast*, as in a "fast woman." Is Prunicus then the "Fast Lady"? Sounds promising.

Such ideas chime in well with the myth of Sophia throwing herself forward, wishing to be face-to-face with the Father, as Barbelo is, and that she has sprung from Mind—her Mother being the Father's First Thought—somewhat violently (in the sense of violation) exceeding the limits of the Pleroma: an unruly, sparky child (*cf.* also, the Egyptian god Seth whose mythic birth has him literally tearing himself from his mother's womb. I have elsewhere indicated my conviction that the "Seth animal" in Egyptian art is based on an Egyptian desert hare [the ears!]. The birth of a hare is precocial: born with eyes open and covered in fur).

I think the word *ripe* in the older English understated sense of "bold" or "hot," or ready to burst with fruitiness, fits the aggregate context, where fruit is clearly a persistent image-locus for the word. Then we might conclude that Prouneikos is the "Ripe One" or even the "hot totty": the fruit of the tree most succulent and ready to be picked, and ready and willing to fall. There could be a pun here on the Greek *proumnē* (feminine): a plum tree, or *proumnon* (neuter), a plum.

Anne Pasquier[7] deduces from Choeroboscus[8] that the term might be a synonym for hubris in the immature: acting like a lord, and could be used in reference to a function or a personality: that overconfidence that in aiming too high invites disaster. We might think of an "artful dodger," a "spiv," or a "likely lad" if we were referring to a male: someone exceeding his station or rushing out of bounds. She may have gone "too far" or been "bold as brass."

We seem to be getting closer to Irenaeus's Prunicus, who certainly goes too far and is very hot indeed. For in *Adversus Haereses* I.30, dealing with Ophites and Sethians, we find that the Mother of the Living "was unable to carry and contain the extreme Greatness of the Light, so they say, she was overfull and *superboiling* over on the left side" (my italics). The power that came from her left side—unlike Christ who came from her right and ever tended higher—besprinkled with light, fell downward, "and it they call Sinistra, Prunicus, and Sophia, as well as masculo-feminine." This power enters the still waters below and imparts motion to them, while at the same time acquiring a heavy materiality that prevents return to the Mother.

Irenaeus's tale is confirmed somewhat in the Nag Hammadi *Second Treatise of the Great Seth*.[9] There "our sister Sophia—she who is a whore" (Roger A. Bullard's controversial translation of *Pro[u]nikos*) makes the first move, dashing without assistance of the Pleroma to make bodily dwellings from the lower elements. Prunicus remains impetuous and untameable, though she is now lost in the material world, until she forms a plan to regain her lost power, her seed-light, from the archon; this she will accomplish through the celestial man appearing momentarily to the archons. In trying to make man themselves, the archon drains his power into the creature, which now yearns for his true Mother, whom the archon knows not.

As Prunicus, Sophia boldly went where none (from the Pleroma) had gone before, but becomes stranded in a distant world. Seth/Jesus comes as a stranger, or "beams down" to the lower world to rectify Prunicus's errors, to the consternation of the lower powers who loved their trapped human beings "like a glutton loves his lunch."

The idea of the "untamed" is leading us to a simpler epithet for

Sophia: the "WILD ONE." Did she return in the 1950s on a motor-
cycle, disguised as Marlon Brando? For certain images provoke strife.
As Anne Pasquier has observed,[10] *Prouneikos* is etymologically linked
to the Greek *neikos,* meaning "strife" or "dissension." Epiphanius seems
to pick up on this and concludes that the Sethians are troublemak-
ers, stirred up by a pretty face with a lewd look: pimps after whores.
Epiphanius observes how in the Greek myths, beauty provokes agita-
tion. Look no further than to Helen of Troy: one of Helen's incarnations, according to Simon Magus! Epiphanius's "lascivious one" then
connotes his whole disgust at the seductive nature of the "gnosis falsely
so-called." With Prouneikos, he is saying, you can see the whole filthy
face of it: it is not the beautiful radiance of wisdom, but a painted
Jezebel, insatiable with lust, whose only talent is to provoke war and
dissension, as the captive Helen did, for all the powers of the world
were set at boiling point by her, prepared to go to any lengths to possess
her (even the Trojan War).

How very differently the Gnostics envisioned this beauty! For them,
it marked the supremacy of the spirit over the body and caused dissension only among those archons dedicated to keeping humanity on their
treadmill. To think of Prouneikos simply as the "whore," in the sense
of Epiphanius, is a blatant travesty: she is brazen, but not cheap: her
tragedy arises from well-intentioned impetuosity, spirit, and, arguably,
a hint of jealousy, which seems to come out in her abortive mess of a
creation.

She's the *Wild One,* the one that got away. If you want to "get away"
too, the Gnostics seem to say, you'll know the one to follow.

THE WILD ONE

In 2006, with the sensational publication of the Sethian *Gospel of
Judas,*[11] I wrote a study of its contents, its past, and its journey to belated
publication. In this book, I asserted my discovery that the name of the
Sethian Barbelo (or Barbelos) may well have been derived from the

Greek feminine noun *hē barbilos,* which means "the wild peach tree."

While further research continues to vindicate my original ascription, I should not have launched this hypothesis had it not been for what I considered the inadequacy of earlier attempts to penetrate the meaning of Mother (or Higher) Sophia's Sethian and Ophite moniker. Earlier interpretations included the Rev. Wigan Harvey,[12] where Harvey posits Barbelo's derivation from two Syriac words meaning "God in a Tetrad." This seems forced, to say the least: what Tetrad? Barbelo is not fourfold, though one can always find two pairs of aeons (ever-existing aspects of the Pleroma), or coteries of lights surrounding them if one wishes, but "God in a Tetrad" doesn't say anything essential for such an important, ambiguous, and adored figure: the Mother of Heaven. The idea utterly fails to resonate.

An obscure scholar by the name of Matter derived Barbelo from two Hebrew words, denoting "Daughter of the Lord."[13] Well, Barbelo is not really the daughter; she's the Mother and receives the Father's seed of prognosis on request.

While it ought to be abundantly clear that the visual conception of the Gnostic Pleroma and its illegitimate, wild extension beyond its bounds was seen to be a tree, or a series of trees, with fruit and seeds that fall and are scattered, I thought I should run my idea that Barbelo owed her name to the "wild peach tree" past some eminent Coptologists for their response to the shock of the new, bearing in mind that I was positing something unheard of, to my knowledge, in the last eighteen hundred years, and conservatism is justifiably ingrained in academe. I indicated beforehand that my initial inspiration had come from the Valentinian view that Jesus was emanated as the fruit of the Pleroma and that Sophia was instrumental in Ophite and Naassene circles with both the tree and the fruit of the knowledge of good and evil in the Gnostic retelling of the Eden temptation myth.

Hellenist, Coptologist, and scholar of esotericism Dylan M. Burns, Ph.D., at Leipzig University, responded swiftly. He was still partial to Harvey's contention that Barbelo derived from the Aramaic *b'rb'el',* translated into Greek as βαρβα 'Ηλω = εν τετραδι θεος ("in four, there is God"), being a product of the Gnostic Trinity of Father-Mother-Son in Barbeloite cosmogonies. This view is supported by Paul-Hubert Poirier's commentary on the Nag Hammadi text, the *Trimorphic Protennoia*.[14] In the *Trimorphic Protennoia* ("the three-formed First Thought") Barbelo as the Father's First Thought is also identified, as had become a commonplace for Sophia in Alexandria, with the Logos.

I must say I find the leap from three to four most unconvincing, along, to a lesser extent, with the Aramaic transliteration. The Protennoia (First Thought) is Barbelo, and she is plainly *Tri-* not *Tetra-*morphic in the text's own account. There might be the remnant in Barbelo of a pun, of course. It would not take much Semitic language knowledge in a Gentile to see *bar* ("offspring of") and *el* (a "god" or "lord") sitting in *Barbelo*. But that stubborn *b* does not, I think, fall into place by conjuring up a strained transliteration from Aramaic to Greek. I daresay if Irenaeus had directly said Barbelos derived from an agricultural term for "wild peach tree," few would now demur! Wouldn't it be obvious?

And that leads us to the second flaw Professor Burns suspects in my hypothesis; that is, that Irenaeus himself does not mention or seem to know of any simple derivation of Barbelos from *barbilos,* describing Barbelo by the Gnostics' own epithet "the virgin spirit that never grows old."[15]

This virgin spirit was to be identified with the Spirit of God that "moved upon the face of the waters" of the deep (*Bythos*) in Genesis 1:2. Her face moving on the unfathomable depth issues in God's Word: Let there be light. This Sethians took to be the spark that impregnates the Mother with seed of prognosis, the besprinkling, liquid light.

The *root* of Barbelo as Mother is sunk in the waters of the Deep; such is her power and being. That mercurial liquid flows thence everywhere and exists in everything (recall the *Wisdom of Solomon* 12:1: "For thine incorruptible Spirit is in all things"). The *Trimorphic Protennoia* itself states of her: "I am numberless beyond everyone."[16] Numberless, not "God in four." "And he who is hidden within us pays the tributes of his fruit to the Water of Life."[17]

Professor Burns considers that since neither Irenaeus nor Epiphanius themselves draw any connection between Barbelo and *barbilos,* we should take this as decisive. To this objection, I should simply counter that Irenaeus does not appear to know the meaning of *Prouneikos* (or Prunicus) either, nor does he hazard a guess. He wants his audience to think of these names as basically meaningless gibberish, dreamt up in the imaginations of their dotty progenitors: inherently silly. The last thing the heresiologists want is for their readers to think Gnostic reconceptions of Wisdom predated or had been held contemporaneously with the apostles; that would have given them authority. Epiphanius likewise does not want his readers to be drawn in by or seduced into Gnostic logic. We have already seen that his explanation of *Prouneikos* coalesces in the worst possible light: guesswork used to paint Gnostics as debased, dirty, self-condemning, bestially pretentious.

Nevertheless, we have seen that there are some curious giveaways by the heresiologists themselves. They know very well they're dealing with images of trees and fruit. Tertullian pokes fun at the Gnostic Ptolemy for not realizing that "nut trees" grow not in the sky, but on earth: a nasty jibe.[18] Furthermore, I am grateful to Coptologist Hugo Lundhaug for drawing my attention to a coruscating joke of Irenaeus's at Valentinus's expense when he proceeds to parody the Valentinian emanation series in terms of a metamorphosis, indeed apotheosis of fruit:

> It is manifest also, that he himself is the one who has had sufficient audacity to coin these names; so that unless he [Valentinus] had appeared in the world, the truth would still be destitute of a name. But, in that case, nothing hinders any other, in dealing with the same subject, to affix names after such a fashion as the following: There is a certain Proarche, royal, surpassing all thought, a power existing before every other substance, and extended into space in

every direction. But along with it there exists a power which I term a Gourd; and along with this Gourd there exists a power which again I term Utter-Emptiness. This Gourd and Emptiness, since they are one, produced (and yet did not simply produce, so as to be apart from themselves) a fruit, everywhere visible, eatable, and delicious, which fruit-language calls a Cucumber. Along with this Cucumber exists a power of the same essence, which again I call a Melon. These powers, the Gourd, Utter-Emptiness, the Cucumber, and the Melon, brought forth the remaining multitude of the delirious melons of Valentinus.[19]

Irenaeus is saying that the coterie of Valentinian aeons amounts to nothing more than a poorly stocked fruit stall in a marketplace (shifted about perhaps by a *prouneikos*). It is surely telling that Irenaeus, Hippolytus, and Tertullian all make jokes at the expense of the use of varied fruit images familiar to Gnostics. They have seen and heard more of these treatments than have survived; we can only guess as to what Tertullian's Ptolemaic "nut trees" originally referred, Irenaeus's "melons" also. It may be observed that nuts, melons, and cucumbers were common produce, while peaches were luxuries linked to royalty, divine figures, and to faraway Persia. I suggest the heresiologists desired to rob the fruit images of their classy exoticism in the interests of bathos and propaganda. The "peach" may have been suppressed, though we have already seen that sexy peaches (nectarines) were linked in risqué discourse to the image of the *prouneikos*.

Professor Burns did make the valid observation that in Nag Hammadi texts focusing on events in Eden—the *Hypostasis of the Archons* and *On the Origin of the World*—Barbelo is not identified with the fruit of the tree of the knowledge of good and evil. *Barbilos* means the "wild peach tree," not the "wild peach." But, of course, she is in all things. Besides, neither of the aforementioned works features Barbelo by name at all; the mother figure is called Pistis-Sophia.

In the Sethian *Apocryphon of John*, Barbelo's involvement with the

Eden narrative is indeed confined to her part in the revelation of the heavenly Adam to the archons, and to her descent and incarnation at the end of the text (the Pronoia hymn), but my contention is not that Barbelo is necessarily the Edenic tree of the knowledge of good and evil, but that the descent of Barbelo and the passage beyond the Pleroma are made in terms of the germinating seed of the wild peach tree that takes its root in the soul.

Furthermore, I suspect that the image may have found its figurative inspiration in part from Paul's description of the Gentiles as being a "wild olive tree" grafted onto the pure stock of God (Romans 11), combined with the myth of the breakout of seed from the Pleroma through the motions of Sophia-Prouneikos, the Wild One, as I have interpreted her name. As we have seen, Hippolytus may well be parodying the wild peach tree idea when he asserts that the heresies are a wild fig tree sprung from a grateful fig tree of Gentile Christians. (Two contrasting fig trees, of course, figure in Jesus's orthodox parables: one barren, to be destroyed, and one whose fruit prefigures the coming kingdom of God; see Mark 13:28 and Luke 13:6.)

It may also be observed in the stirring narrative that completes the *Secret Book of John,* when Barbelo descends the second time to bring forth herself (as fruit) from those "who belong to the light," she says: "And I ran up to my *root of light* lest they [the archons] be destroyed before the time."[20] This root of light is the root of the tree of gnosis. The narrative climaxes in the scene of the virginal spirit's third descent (doubtless the third day of Jesus's resurrection prophecy), where Barbelo, as the "remembrance of the Pronoia" and the "remembrance of the Pleroma" appears to enter the dead body of Jesus and raise him. Awakening the man from "the deep sleep," she raises him to the "honored place," saying: "Arise and remember that it is you who hearkened, and follow your root, which is I, the merciful one, and guard yourself against the angels of poverty and the demons of chaos and all those who ensnare you, and beware of the deep sleep and the enclosure of the inside of Hades."[21] This is the Gnostics' answer to the canonical

Jesus's question: "Who is my mother?" (*cf.* Matthew 12:48). His mother is Barbelo. Barbelo's resurrection message is, of course, addressed to all Gnostics who have awakened from the horror of the world to the light in them that, drawn forth by remembrance of the root of Barbelo, takes them high and free.

Professor Hugo Lundhaug of Oslo University's theology faculty concurred with Dylan Burns's objections to my reading of Barbelo, but added in support of my etymology that the name *Barbelo* would, in Coptic, have been pronounced "Barbilo," due to itacism during the period of the Nag Hammadi Library's writing (itacism means the pronunciation of the Greek eta as an iota). This means that, in colloquial speech, *Barbilos* would have sounded identical to *Barbelos,* and may have been written either way, depending on how familiar the term was. Such would easily have allowed the word's usage as a proper name to include the *el* ("god") pun within it, if such a pun was ever intended.

It ought to be radiantly clear by now that Barbelo is, for all intents and purposes, symbolized as a tree, drawing sap from the source of life. Proverbs 3:18 portrays Wisdom as a tree, a tree whose branches have saving power, for the tree is watered in the Lord. Alexandrian Wisdom literature abounds, as we have seen, in specifically dendrous images of Wisdom. The Septuagint's Greek of Proverbs 3:18 with regard to the Sophia figure and of Genesis with regard to the tree of life is perfectly consistent. It seems therefore a simple matter to accept that the symbolism is contained in her name.

Additional patristic literary support for my identification comes from heresiologist Hippolytus when he gives us an extract from the Gnostic Justin's secret *Book of Baruch* (*Baruch* means "Blessed"; he is a saving angel). Described as "abominable" by Hippolytus, the text says directly:

> The angels of paradise are allegorically called trees,
> And the tree of life is the third paternal angel,
> And his name is Baruch,

> While the tree of the knowledge of good and evil
> Is the third maternal angel, and he is Naas.
> Moses spoke these things covertly
> Because not everyone can hold the truth.
> (Hippolytus, *Refutatio,* V, 19)

So we see already a Gnostic interpretation of the tree of life as a redemptive figure: an expression of the Divine Nature—and, note, the Baruch myth is specifically anti-Naas (the serpent).

The Gnostic *Book of Baruch* is itself interesting in our context, portraying the curious conflict beween three deities: the Almighty Good principle (identified startlingly with Priapus whose phallic image adorns every temple as the progenitor of all), the Elohim, and Edem (or Israel). *Edem* is a feminine, *Elohim* a masculine, Demiurge. Their union is responsible for the paradise of Eden and the making of humanity, of which Edem gave the soul, Elohim the spirit. In terms of possible punnish resonances with *Barbelo,* apparently unfamiliar to Justin, the names of the maternal angels deriving from Edem are "*Babel,* Achamoth, Naas, *Bel, Belias,* Satan, Sael, Adonaeus, Leviathan, Pharao, Carcamenos, (and) Lathen" (*Refutatio,* V, 21; my italics). In Valentinian cosmogonies, Achamoth is a Lower Sophia and primal mother of humankind, linked positively to the serpent. Justin presents these particular angelic trees negatively, being Edem's brood.

Elohim, by contrast, has a vision of the Good in heaven, and, suitably humbled, decides to separate himself from the lustful, bestial, earthly, common-love Edem. While Elohim learns from the male above him, Edem takes revenge by persecuting humankind through her angels (this may have been a subversive code for the oppression of the Roman Empire, seen as the instrument not of God, as Paul believed, but of the wicked angels). In response to human misery, Elohim sends angelic helpers to humankind: Jesus, Moses, Hercules (yes!), and Baruch to lead humankind back to the Good; Baruch in fact will save Jesus's Spirit from the body on the cross. The contrast is between a high love for wisdom and virtue and a low, bestial love, obsessed with love of the body: common Aphrodite (one thinks of Roman orgia). The paternal angel (from Elohim) is the tree of life; the maternal (from Edem) is Naas, who misleads humankind. Baruch's account reads somewhat like a male homosexual, aesthetic, and anticarnal tract.

We have then ample evidence of tree speculation in Gnostic circles applied to redemptive figures. It is likely that the Gnostic *Book of Baruch* was in part inspired by the Septuagint's deuterocanonical book *Baruch* (meaning "the blessed one"). This book contains stirring words from the "blessed" that lend themselves easily to a Gnostic twist, for they speak of removing the "garment of sorrow and affliction" (for Gnostics, the body) and taking shelter beneath "every fragrant tree":

Young men have seen the light of day, and have dwelt upon the earth; but they have not learned the way to knowledge, nor understood her paths, nor laid hold of her.

Take off the garment of your sorrow and affliction, O Jerusalem, and put on forever the beauty of the glory from God. Put on the robe of the righteousness from God; put on your head the diadem of the glory of the Everlasting. For God will show your splendor everywhere under heaven. For your name will for ever be called by God, "Peace of righteousness and glory of godliness."

Arise, O Jerusalem, stand upon the height and look toward the east, and see your children gathered from west and east, at the word of the Holy One, rejoicing that God has remembered them. For they went forth from you on foot, led away by their enemies; but God will bring them back to you, carried in glory, as on a royal throne.

For God has ordered that every high mountain and the everlasting hills be made low and the valleys filled up, to make level ground, so that Israel may walk safely in the glory of God.

The woods and every fragrant tree have shaded Israel at God's command. For God will lead Israel with joy, in the light of his glory, with the mercy and righteousness that come from him. (*Book of Baruch* 3:20; 5:1–9)

While I think we may safely conclude that Barbelo or Barbelos is typified as a redemptive tree, we have not yet proved that her name is derived from the word given in some Greek circles to a wild peach tree. This we may now attempt.

She is a tree of life to all that lay hold on her. (Proverbs 3:18)

Liddell and Scott's *Greek-English Lexicon* derives its translation of *hē barbilos* as "the wild peach tree" from the *Geoponika*.[22] Edited ca. 920 CE from ancient sources, its twenty books were published in Leipzig in 1781 in four volumes by editor J. N. Niclas.[23] In book 10, chapter 13, we find the Greek words *dōrakina* and *persika* for "peach." The latter word denotes the tradition that peaches were brought to Egypt and Greece from Persia. With the fruit came much mythology surrounding these royal delicacies.

Chapter 13's section on growing peach trees from a stone is attributed to Florentinus, an early third-century Roman writer on farming from Bithynia, roughly contemporaneous with Clement of Alexandria.

The plants also increase if we immediately set the stone after eating the fruit, leaving some part of the fruit on the stone: as we then know that the *duracinum* soon grows old, we ought to graft it on the damson, or on the bitter almond, or on the *barbilus*. The tree which grows from the stone of the peach is indeed, by way of eminence, called the *barbilus*.[24]

It is interesting to note the eminence accorded this plant. A footnote adds that according to Gruterus, the name *durakina* is explained by peaches deriving from Dora, an island in Persia. This could have been a misnomer for the Arab *Durak,* a place where the Tigris and Euphrates met. (Inevitably this reminds one of the story that the Peratae Gnostics were founded by a Euphrates or, according to Clement of Alexandria, came from "beyond the Euphrates," that is, Persia.)

Didymos, a Greek farming writer of whom nothing else is known, contributed a sentence on the grafting of peaches in book 10:17: "The duracinum is grafted on the almond, the damson, and on the plane-tree, from which circumstance, the fruit turns red." I wonder a little if this snippet might possibly connect us to the counterimage of the scarlet woman or whore of Babylon "drunk on the blood [juice?] of the saints." One intuits anyway that we are somehow in the right territory! The woman in question's golden cup is, of course, "full of abominations and the filth of her fornications": an attack that sounds curiously familiar (Revelation 17:1–6).

Chapter 14 of *Geoponika* drew on Demokritos for "making persica carry writing" (in transmitting secrets: an interesting quality in our context). Sharing a name with the early fourth-century BCE Greek philosopher, Demokritos's writings on natural history are generally attributed to the Greco-Egyptian Bolos (or Bolus) of Mendes. Tantalizingly, Bolos's third-century BCE work *Physika & Mystika* shows that a rudimentary alchemy was practiced in Egypt at the time. Bolos quotes from Persian alchemist Ostanes who apparently died trying to produce an elixir to separate his soul from his body: a familiar Gnostic tendency. Ostanes was also the source of an important quotation made by the Egyptian Hermetic alchemist Zosimos of Panopolis in the third century CE in the latter's search for a transforming, alchemical stone in his *Concerning the Art and Its Interpretation*: "Go to the waters of the Nile and there you will find a stone that has a spirit [pneuma]. Take this, divide it, thrust in your hand and draw out its heart; for its soul [psyche] is in its heart." I have had cause to repeat this intriguing fragment before,[25] but it has acquired fresh meaning placed in the context of the peach—to which there is much more than meets the eye—and of the Gnostic interest in divesting the pneuma (spirit) of its garments. The stone of the philosophers, dear friends, may be available at your local produce merchant: everywhere present but nowhere seen.

Can we discover more about the eminence of the *barbilus*? Let's go on a little tour through the catacombs of etymological history: a very dark passage, for sure, but there is light not only at the end of it. First, we consult an old, decaying book: Claude Lancelot and Isaac Louis le Maistre de Say's *The Primitives of the Greek Tongue Containing a Complete Collection of All the Roots or Primitive Words, Together with the Most Considerable Derivatives of the Greek Language.*[26] There, on page 230, we find "βαρβιλος, *hē barbilus,* a wild peach tree." We find a variant—*brabilos,* a seedling peach—while *barbilon* is found in Eustathius of Thessalonica's twelfth-century *Commentary on the Odyssey* (10.242), but the translation is uncertain as Eustathius seems to confuse it with the cornelian cherry, an olive-shaped red tree fruit, fed to Odysseus's crew when they were transformed into pigs by Circe.

Another old book: *An Analysis of the Egyptian Mythology* by James Cowles Prichard, published in 1819.[27] On page 88 of this work, we find the peach in a most suggestive context. Plutarch (45–120 CE) was a Greek historian who penned an important book that gave Greek speakers a way into ancient Egyptian mythology. *Concerning Isis and Osiris,* chapter 68, tells us about the Greco-Egyptian figure Harpocrates (or the infant Horos, son of Isis and Osiris): "by this infant god the Egyptians represented the first shooting up or budding forth of succulent plants. . . . The bud, or opening blossom of the peach tree, was also in a peculiar manner sacred to Harpocrates."

We next consult *De Iside et Osiride in Plutarch's Morals, Translated from the Greek by Several Hands.*[28] Therein Harpocrates is described as "the governor or reducer of the tender, imperfect and inarticulate discourse, which men have about the gods. For which reason, he hath always his finger upon his mouth, as a symbol of talking little and keeping silence. Likewise upon the month of Mesore [about mid-June, the last and twelfth month of the sacred year; to celebrate the birth of the

Nile] they present him with certain pulse [first fruits of lentils] and pronounce these words; *the tongue is Fortune, the tongue is God;* and of all the plants that Egypt produces, they say the peach tree is the most sacred to the Goddess [Isis]; because its fruit resembles the Heart, and its leaf the tongue" (my italics). Footnotes to this text inform us that the pulse represented the "Emblem of Generation" (presumably the phallus is implied), while the tongue that represents "fortune" is "Isis or the Moon, and God, Hermes, or the Sun, that is: The Tongue provides for Body and Soul."

As for the fruit resembling the Heart (the Greek for "peach" in Plutarch is *persean*), the note says: "The Heart and the Tongue are apt symbols of *Alētheia* or Truth," with which latter principle Isis is also identified.

Further observations on page 116 of this ancient tome might strike us as significant in the context of Barbelo, the Mother of Heaven. Isis, we are told, "they sometimes call Muth [Mother], and sometimes again Athyri [Horus's mundane home, as Plato calls it, "the place and receptacle of generation," i.e., the womb], and sometimes Methuer [a compound of two words, one *Full* and the other, the *Cause*].

In a commentary on Alexander Pope's translation of *Homer,*[29] we find under an entry to a god of Silence: "allegorical deity placed by Ariosto is the entrance of the grotto of sleep." The figure is a young man clad in black with the finger of his right hand upon his mouth, calling for silence. His attribute is a branch of the peach tree, sacred to Harpocrates. The next entry is for Harpocrates, the Greco-Egyptian god of silence. His statue was to be found at the entrance to temples; many have survived. Sacred to him were first fruits of vegetables, lentils, and, above all, the peach tree. His mother was Isis, of course, and we may note that in the Valentinian Pleroma, the primal Mother, the First Thought of the incomprehensible Bythos, is called Sigé, "silence." As the Nag Hammadi text *Eugnostos the Blessed* relates: "Sophia, his consort, who was called 'Silence,' because in reflecting without a word she perfected her Greatness."[30]

Imagery and religious philosophy in the heyday of the Gnostics furnishes ample reason for relating the symbolism of Barbelo with that of the peach tree.

However, the significance of the peach tree to Wisdom, the Heavenly Goddess, and to initiation is by no means confined to the Greco-Egyptian religion that dominated Alexandria in this period.

Space does not permit anything remotely like a full review of the significance of the peach and the peach tree, wild and cultivated, in Eastern and Far Eastern folklore, religion, and philosophy, but the following points may assist those wishing to go further into this subject.

The peach is thought to have reached Persia from its homeland in China. In the Chinese *Shi Jing* (*The Book of Odes* or *The Book of Songs*, ca. 1100–600 BCE), peach lore abounds. Perhaps most startling is the fact that in that work the Chinese word for *union* (*cf.* "yoga") is actually pronounced "tao," a word familiar to us as denoting a spiritually enlivening Way through life, with its own peculiar attendant sexual practices to retain and multiply energy, and it also means "peach," the outdated genus *amygdalus*. The Tao also means the heart or wisdom of things, while the person who valued peaches most highly as a kind of divine elixir was the Xian, which can mean an enlightened person, an alchemist, a magician, a sage, a recluse, or an immortal, celestial being.

Folklore preserves the idea of the peach world-tree, a form of the Mother Goddess. Its fruit is charged with her "life substance" (*shen*) and the peach symbolizes the goddess. This ascription need not surprise any who have looked carefully at the peach stone beneath the juicy flesh. The stone looks much akin to the vagina; there's no getting away from it! Not everyone has realized that within that stone is hidden a beautifully smooth, spherical seed, with medicinal properties. Seeds, bark, and leaves contain low cyanide levels, allegedly useful in treating cancerous tumors. They can also help encourage menstruation, while vitamin advantages combat some effects of aging. There are other benefits as well.

In China, people heard of an elixir made in a paradise garden by Queen Mother Wang Mu, a kind of alchemist; her peaches of immortality are fed to the gods at sumptuous banquets. When supplies were low, the story was told of how the queen ground up a special mix, an immortalizing liquor that could take the lucky recipient to the heavens. One wonders if Gnostic magician Marcus had his own supply! Ancient Chinese artwork stretching twelve hundred years before our period shows the peach symbolizing longevity, purity, female sexuality, and truth: it is the yin.

Caravan trains brought the mythology, the peach, and prized peach depictions on objects from China to Persia, thence to Greece circa 400 BCE. Unaware of the Chinese origin, Greeks called peaches *persikon malon,* the "Persian apple": tempting fruit. Naturally, Romans associated the fruit with Venus. It was grown in Egypt, but not altogether successfully elsewhere. Peach pits were discovered at the last stand of Masada in Israel, however, so we know they were grown in the birthplace of Christianity.

The Roman natural historian Pliny, who died in the Vesuvius disaster that hit Pompeii and Herculaneum in 79 CE, wrote about peaches in his day in his *Natural History:*

> As touching peaches in general, the very name in Latin, whereby they are called *Persica,* doth evidently shew that they were brought out of Persia first; and that it is a fruit not ordinary either in Greece or Anatolia, but a mere stranger there. Contrarywise, wild plums (as it is well known) grow everywhere. I marvel therefore so much the more, that *Cato* made no mention thereof, considering that of purpose he shewed the manner, how to preserve and keep divers wild fruits, until new came: for long it was first ere peach trees came into these parts, and much ado there was before they could be brought for to prosper with us, seeing that in the island Rhodes [which was their place of habitation next to Egypt] they bear not at all, but are altogether barren. And whereas it is said, that peaches be

venomous in Persia, and do cause great torments in them who do eat thereof; as also that the kings of Persia in old time caused them to be transported over into Egypt by way of revenge to plague that country; and notwithstanding their poisonous nature, yet through the goodness of that soil they became good and wholesome: all this is nothing but a mere fable and a loud lie. True it is indeed, that the best writers who have taken pains above others to search out the truth, have reported so much concerning the tree *persea;* which is far different from the peach tree *persica,* and beareth fruit like unto Sebesten, of colour red, and willingly would not grow in any country without the Eastern parts. And yet the wiser and more learned scholars do hold, that it was not the tree *persea,* which was brought out of Persia into Egypt, for to annoy and plague the country, but that it was planted first by king Perseus at Memphis. Whereupon it came that Alexander the Great ordained that all victors who had won the prize at any game there, should be crowned with a chaplet of that tree, to honour the memorial of his great grandsire's father. But how ever it be, certain it is that this tree continueth green all the year long, and beareth evermore fruit one under another, new and old together.

It is surely noteworthy that Egyptian folklore preserved a story that when Seth put his brother Osiris's body in a coffin, Isis found it caught in the branches of a persea tree (*Mimusops Schimperi*), favored for its perfume by the king of Byblos (Phoenicia). The persea tree was held in Egypt to be a tree of life, linked to Re and its fruit an earthly correspondent of the sun. The names of those who had ascended were written on its leaves. Threatened by the serpent god of the chaotic underworld, Apophis, the tree was guarded by the lioness-cat goddess, Bast, the "devouring lady." The Hebrew Proverbs were undoubtedly influenced by diverse traditions of Egyptian wisdom, one of which was that the tree of wisdom was feminine.

And we should bear in mind always that Gnostic teachings were intended, and composed, to veil secrets. The heresiologists did not know everything. Besides, contempt for one's subject is not the best path to understanding it.

We sought the Pruneikos and found the wild one. We should hardly be surpised to find she came from a wild but eminent root: a stone of the heart, not a heart of stone—Barbelo: "I am the silence that is incomprehensible . . . I am the voice whose sound is manifold and the word whose appearance is multiple. I am the utterance of my name."[31] She is the "one whose image is great in Egypt" and her name is what she is.

PART II

GNOSTIC LOVE
AND THE SPIRITUAL
REVOLUTION

TWELVE

ALL YOU NEED IS SOPHIA

I wonder if I would have written this book if I hadn't been raised in the 1960s. I was not yet a year old when Yuri Gagarin became the first man to escape the Earth's atmosphere, accomplishing physically what the Gnostics enacted spiritually eighteen hundred years before. The day after the USSR's new hero completed his first orbit of the Earth, a group from Liverpool called the Beatles played their opening night at the Star Club in Hamburg, Germany (April 1961). Truly, there were stars everywhere. By the time I was ten, Neil Armstrong had walked on the moon in a U.S. mission named after the Greek sun god, and the mighty Beatles had split up forever. In all that time, my head was like a great radio-telescopic dish, picking up the zeitgeist with a beaming smile, storing up enough of its spirit to spend the next four decades advancing the era's exceptional spiritual promise in my own sweet way.

Amazing, looking back, how much of the initial shock of the Beatles came from their long hair. This really seemed to get the old guard going. Could it have been the suggested androgyny? All those girls screaming! Letting go . . . bypassing intellect, it all went straight to the unconscious. Dionysiac outsiders were back in town, singing and philosophizing and making love like frenzied Corybants, as if the war had never happened and would never happen again. There was soul music, and spirit, and much divesting of garments. Oh and dream potions that would have made even the Gnostic Marcus's head spin! There were talks about Gnostics among the London Free School hippies, and Syd Barrett felt the heady gusts of a Gnostic, poetic revolution coursing through his body. One of Jimi Hendrix's last songs concerned an angel who came down from heaven, just in time (or, arguably, too late) to rescue him, before he slipped inadvertently over the horizon, having serenaded the first rays of the new rising sun, like the Rosicrucians of 1615, while the Rolling Stones sang, rather desperately and a little too prophetically, about the Devil laying traps for troubadours who die before reaching the goal. Certainly the rising death toll of lost stars would make a Gnostic wonder if the archons weren't singling out the new children of the heart for their cold embrace! Amid gathering paranoia, London's Sufi mystics propounded love and remembrance of wisdom divine. Tantra hit Esalen on the West Coast, and the doors of perception creaked open awhile in Venice, California, just long enough for Jim Morrison, Ray Manzarek, Robbie Krieger, and John Densmore to make a lasting mark. And *she* was about, in miniskirts, on motorcycles, in milk bars and marriages, the wild one displaying her many colors to the monochromatic ghosts of yesterday. And the boys looked like girls and the girls like boys, and it seemed for a second, or a moment. . . . Yes, it seemed. But it didn't happen, did it? No more than the Second Coming dreamt up by the apocalyptists and still hawked around the world to save people from the very thing they think they're looking forward to!

But, as I and as many others have found out since, it had always been happening. She had always been there: reviled and revered, Lady Wisdom, Sophia, Barbelo, Prunicus—the virgin whore, the pure spirit, frothing in fruitful dance; how she appears depends on what you are, and what you are looking for. If you're blind, you'll miss her. If you have seen her, you'll miss her too.

We don't know what really happened to those groups of Barbelites,

Ophites, Naassenes, Valentinians, Simonians, and the rest. To say there were persecutions and repressions goes without saying. We had cause to mention at the beginning of our story that the third century saw the growth of Encratism: a fear of the body and a real hatred of sex. It seems that some Gnostics were not immune to this movement, a movement that had given up on the world, and one that created the first monasteries in the desert of dry soul. Sophia below was to be denied her seeds.

William Blake thought the Dark Ages coincided with the repression of sex and of women; a denial of Christ. The new Western church was a church for barbarians; they who had caused enough damage and would have to be controlled in the manner of the carrot and donkey. In the Middle East, overrun in the eighth century by the tribal armies of Islam, anything that smacked of paganism was wiped out, and women had to be corralled into servitude for their own good. That was not how every Muslim saw it. There were mystics, Gnostics really, who believed that the glorious wisdom of God could be envisioned, enjoyed through divine love, passionate love, even passionate love with a woman. Perhaps their ancestors, before conversion, had been secret Gnostics. But it mattered not; their opponents declared that man was utterly unable to approach God to love him, for God, they asserted as if they knew, was very far beyond humanity; creaturely man could only submit to God's merciful, compassionate, inscrutable, and absolute will. God demanded that men control women, lest women rise and bite them, serpentlike. For challenging the root of such doctrines, the Sufi al Hallaj was crucified in 922 CE, and the Persian mystic Suhrawardi was executed for heresy between 1191 and 1208 in Aleppo, Syria. Sufis still have a hard time in the intolerant parts of the Middle East, but then, as Steven Runciman so helpfully put it in his book on the Albigensian Crusade that wiped out the Cathar church in France in the thirteenth century: "Tolerance is a social, not a religious virtue," a saying that fits very well the attitude of the Catholic Inquisition from that day to this.

RETURN TO THE TROUBADOURS

In 1988, I wrote a novel called *Miraval—A Quest* about the troubadour knight, Raimon, lord of Miraval, a castle some twenty miles
north of Carcassonne in southwestern France, perched just above
the river Orbiel in a verdant paradise. It was intended to encapsu-
late the essence of research on the relations between the twelfth- and
thirteenth-century troubadours of Languedoc and the Gnostic Cathars,
or Church of Good Christians (the *Sancta Gleisa*), research generously
supported by Joost Ritman, founder of the *Bibliotheca Philosophica
Hermetica,* Amsterdam. I think Mr. Ritman was as disappointed as I
was that research did not yield proof for a fascinating idea. That idea
was embraced by members of the Dutch *Lectorium Rosicrucianum,*
influenced by Otto Rahn's prewar (1934) bestselling book *Le Croisade
contre le Gral* (*The Crusade against the Grail*).* The essential idea—a
brainchild of Joséphin Péladan (1858–1918)—held that the Cathars
and the troubadours were one and the same movement, and that troubadour lyric poetry encoded Catharist doctrines, being integral to the
ongoing gnosis through human history. Was there not a mysterious
link between the unattainable lady and lord of the troubadour and the
Sophia of the Unknown God of the Valentinians? Were they not, in
fact, one? Did not the troubadours give melodious voice, covertly, to the
God of the heretics: love (*agapē*)? Was not troubadour chivalrous-erotic
poetry symbolic of the higher love?

My research had concluded no. Since the Cathars, with all the zeal
of the Gnostic (or orthodox) Encratite, embraced only unfleshly *agapē*
as the practicable love-ideal, dismissing eros as being of the Devil, it
was impossible for the Cathar *perfecti,* or leadership, to have identified
with the Fine Love of the troubadours, which while idealistic, courtly,
chivalrous, and largely Platonic, was nevertheless fulfilled through eros.
My novel failed because its inspiration failed.

---

*English translation (2006) published by Inner Traditions.

The reason I think was not only because the above distinction effectively separated the lovers (precluding the expected romantic conclusion), but also that the novel identified an ordinary romantic loss, such as happens when two lovers part and suffer, with the loss of God. By loss of God, I mean a certain pang, an intense nostalgia for a spiritual home that besets some souls as their dreams are materialized by being in the world, suffering remoteness from spiritual being. It makes for wanderers in the night of life. A piece of music, a poem, something elusive in peripheral vision can awaken that sense of the lost, but apparently unobtainable, home. Listen to Claude Debussy, Maurice Ravel, Erik Satie, Richard Wagner (the *Liebestod* from *Tristan,* of course!), John Barry, Burt Bacharach, John Lennon. It's there . . . she's there. Finding loneliness in ourselves, we seek the tantalizing ideal in the soul of another, like the Father of the Gnostics looking into his First Thought as a mirror.

In the story, the lady Azalaïs de Boissézon denigrates the Fine Love (*Fin Amors*) of knight-lover Raimon de Miraval. She believes it is too much of the flesh, or beauty idealized by longing. She says she has found something better. She exchanges his mortal, consoling kisses for the Consolamentum of the perfecti, the severing of the spirit from the world. Miraval loses her, and then loses his castle, taken by the crusaders against the Cathars (these were historic facts). He trudges across the mountains to Aragon, where he dies, somewhat broken. I think something broke in me writing that book; *Miraval* nearly destroyed me.

Looking back, it's easy enough to see why. I identified too closely with my hero-sufferer. I had lived the troubadour life; I had sought the unobtainable in my lady. I had pursued her and it seemed I had lost. I was cut adrift in the world. But the Lady brought me back.

I returned to the troubadours and had another go at trying to understand what made them tick. The results of that search can be found in the troubadour section of my book, *Gnostic Philosophy.* Here a more nuanced picture emerges, inspired in part by the work of Languedoc scholar of Catharism René Nelli (1896–1982)—I enjoyed the privilege of meeting his devoted widow, Suzanne Nelli (d. 2007)—by the fabulous re-creations of the troubadour sound made by Gérard Zuchetto (*Grop Rosamonda*), with whom I shared much time in the Narbonnais; and by conversations with Anne Brenon, director of the Centre Nationale d'Études Cathares, at Villegly, Aude, France.

It became clear that, spiritually speaking, as well as with regard to the cultural intermingling of Troubadour and Cathar at the highest levels of society, there was indeed something Gnostic about the inspiration behind the troubadours' new world of sensibility, their devotion to real flesh and blood women, some of whom would go to the stake as unrepentant heretics, and the troubadours' ability to suffer for the Lady. I had recourse to Jungian archetype theory and was content with a link on the level of the unconscious. The treatment was academically respectable.

Years later, I find myself compelled to think academic rigor alone may have just prevented me from seeing what was plain, first to Joséphin Péladan and then to Denis de Rougemont (1906–1985), whose remarkable book *Love in the Western World* (1940; 1983 Princeton edition) was, I'm sorry to say, only recently brought to my attention.

De Rougemont credits the extraordinary, pioneering figure of Péladan with the (then) novel conviction that troubadours and Cathars were essentially indistinguishable. Troubadours had long been regarded by literary historians as lightweight epicureans of immoral jests, contemptuous of marriage in devotion to courtly eros. It was accepted, however, that their devotion to the *langue d'Oc* (the Occitan language spoken in the "Languedoc") inspired Dante's conviction that this was the proper language for love poetry. Péladan, a sometime eccentric master of esoteric symbolism, saw through the obfuscation that had condemned the troubadours to almost risible status as medieval libertines and recognized with crystal clarity their challenge to the Catholic Church of the West.

De Rougemont's approach was different. He set out to prove that the Western ideal of romantic love, which was supposed to find its fulfillment in marriage or in extramarital affairs, and which was a dominant theme, though cheapened into banality, of movies and books and magazines, was a great myth: indeed, a true myth perverted. He tried to trace the romantic ideal back to the troubadours, back through Persian love poetry and back to the Gnostics. Looking at the troubadours, de Rougemont straightaway recognized, thanks to Péladan, that they saw Fine Love and conventional marriage as incompatible. Troubadour love is always adulterous, forbidden love. Western romantic love was the twisted survivor of a condemned religion. Troubadour love and the Cathars were inseparable cultural phenomena. The troubadours simply could not have reached the idea of the unobtainable Lady, one a man would rather die for than reject, without a consistent spirituality that was open to be applied to real women. The troubadours, he strongly suspected, worshipped Sophia through their love objectified as individual lady-lords, but not contained by the lady's flesh-and-blood image: together, man and woman, they could reach the heights of an unearthly love that the world could not contain, and often would conspire to destroy. Marriage was a tie of bodies and property; love opened the soul to its home beyond the stars!

The only key factor I think de Rougemont was missing was the realization that the early Gnostics had bifurcated into two streams: one Encratite (inherited by the Cathars through Balkan Bogomilism) and one erotic-agapaic-sophianic, inherited in essence by the troubadours, perhaps through Persian, Indian, and Arabic erotic-ideal poetry, influenced by Sufism, Kabbalah, Manichaeism, and Gnostic echoes. You could say that the troubadours and the Cathars were long-lost cousins, raised in the alembic of the widespread twelfth-century spiritual renaissance in the West to see one another, face-to-face, with the added factor that families could include both troubadours and Cathars within them, in amity.

We know, of course, that the Valentinian heresy was particularly prevalent in the Rhône Valley at the time of Irenaeus, where there was a Jewish population and interest in kabbalistic tropes (as there was in the twelfth century). Nine hundred years is a long time for a religion to survive without leaving some archaeological evidence, but then Gnostic religion had never favored material evidence. It still remains something of a mystery why Catharism found such a ready welcome among the nobility of the Languedoc.

First published in 1906, the key work of Péladan's on the subject repays a revisit: *De Parsifal A Don Quichotte*, in particular, its third chapter entitled *Le Secret des Troubadours* ("The Secret of the Troubadours").[1] We should recall that Péladan was not only the promoter of an important idealist art-aesthetic movement (joined to the "Symbolists"), and of the *Ordre de la Rose-Croix Catholique et Esthétique du Temple et du Graal,* but also of the book *L'androgyne* (1891) wherein he subscribes to the Gnostic view that the perfect Adam was androgynous, and that by his fall into matter, Adam's spiritual being has been sundered into male and female in conformity with the divisions of the Fall, often resulting in strife and much mismarriage of incompatible souls. Spiritual man hankers for spiritual unity; this is what he is nostalgic about, deep, deep down. He seeks reunion through woman and vice versa.

Péladan believed that if the right person of the opposite sex came into one's life, it was possible, either through companionable, fraternal, and uplifting Platonic love, or through sexually consummated love characterized by mutual, unselfish devotion to the ideal, that the soul could experience as a prefigurement, the glories of the world to come. Such unions were, however, rare. There seems little doubt that Péladan saw a prefigurement of his idealist and spiritual art of love and magic in the devotion that looked beyond the image (or *ikon* of the lady) to the divine *Hokhmah* (Wisdom = Sophia) above. Thus, he found what he considered the secret of the troubadours: "The lover, in these singular fables, dedicates to his Lady the prowess of the knight and the mortifications of the monk; he brings into the 'sexual cult' the rites of divine love, and the ways of mysticism."[2]

Péladan writes of the thirty-one-point Love-Code of Andreas

Capellanus, of which the first and last rules are: "Marriage is not a legitimate excuse against love."[3] The Cathars also frowned on marriage and procreation; it was all right for the *croyants* (believers), the rank and file, but impossible for the *perfecti* who must renounce marriage and the comforts of the flesh; even the *croyants* must sever earthly ties before death in the rite of the *Consolamentum*.

Péladan observed a case brought before a Court of Love, that alternative law of courteous noble ladies. (Was it not challenging the law of the lord of this world? Péladan asks.) The question brought before the court was this: Could the divorced husband of the countess of Narbonne again become her lover now that she had married again? Péladan asks wryly, "What dramatic author today would dare a similar thesis?" He did not live to see the soap opera where all things are possible when ratings threaten.

"Who has not the right to show his face wears a mask," observes Péladan.[4] Thus, declares Péladan, the *jongleur* appeared inoffensive, a joker who served as propaganda for a deeper, subversive cult. "The heretics therefore become the troubadours in Provence, the *trouvères* in the North, *guillari,* men of joy in Italy, *minnesängers* in Germany, *scaldes* in Norway, minstrels in Wales." He says they constituted a counter-church. This was not a mere literary mirage.[5]

"In a theocratic civilization, independence revealed a character of heresy and the seditious *politique* called itself impious," asserts Péladan. Yet the real purpose of the troubadours, and declared at times in their works, was to *purify* love: lust had to be purged through extended love service to the point of dying, if necessary, or *dying* to the impure, if possible.

Péladan makes the point that the counter-church was a response to the historic situation of the Catholic Church: "Inheriting the Roman Empire, the church wanted, passionately, blindly, to realize spiritual unity in the West." "Man always conceives a different ideal to that which he sees realized. This inquietide, or best this desire for other things constitutes the instinct of the spiritual life. The church exasperated it and a new Christianity was born." Not entirely, new though, Péladan says. Its gnostic composition followed a long line to the past.[6]

For Péladan, the fact that only one troubadour is known to have supported the crusade against the "Albigensians" (Cathars) is powerful testimony that the Troubadours supported the Cathars, nay, were with them, even, as in the case of Raimon de Miraval, to the extent of losing his castle and patrimony to the invaders from the north on their mission from Pope Innocent III. He notes also that after the final fall of Catharism at Montségur in 1244, in a unique occurrence, the Occitan language was "excommunicated" by a Bull of 1245 that forbade its teaching in schools. It was not the Cathars who dignified the Occitan tongue with their poetry; it was the Troubadours. Occitan was, says Péladan, the "idiom of heresy *par excellence*." The Inquisition was created to defeat the Cathar church, and "nothing less than a crusade of extermination would satisfy the Papacy. The Cathar church counted among its faithful the totality of the Troubadours."

This author would not go so far in seeing the Troubadours as simply a kind of literary wing of the Cathars; it would have had to have been a very broad church indeed for that! But they had much in common, and there is little doubt that the spiritual atmosphere generated about the tolerant, goodly natured *bons hommes* and *bonnes femmes* (many of whom were nobility), made curious good sense of the Troubadours' music and song to people familiar with the stories of Tristan, and of Arthur, where high spiritual idealism was combined in narrative with love and lust and adulterous adventure.

I sometimes think of the attitude of the *perfecti* to the Troubadours—their paths must constantly have been crossing—as analogous to that of the faces of Indian gurus at Woodstock and other countercultural events of the 1960s (if you'll forgive me!). The smiling gurus invited onto stages, whether to preach, or to play sitar, or simply to observe, seemed very happy to have distinguished, often educated, middle class ("makers of the future") audiences before them, offering a tolerant oversight of human mores they may have disapproved of. "We'll deal with those later" they seem to say. *These children are waking up; we must help them. First we must encourage the spiritual idealism, then the children will understand that "free love" by itself won't save souls, rather will bind the children even more to the wheel that grinds the soul into submission.* I think of the late Ravi Shankar regarding George Harrison "like my son" and encouraging him to take what he had learned of the mysticism of Indian music to Western audiences not through the sitar, but the familiar guitar in idioms the Western young could accommodate most easily, while pointing them in the direction of deeper and higher things.

Denis de Rougemont saw a greater penetration of Catharist idealism into the actual lyrics of the courtly love songs than I had allowed in my last treatment of the subject. He quotes a number of troubadour and troubadour-influenced poems from the twelfth and thirteenth centuries. Service to the Lady is paramount: "Take my life in homage, Beauty of hard pity, so long as you grant me that by you I shall tend to heaven!" (Uc de Saint Circ); "Each day I grow better and am purified, for I serve and reverence the most suave lady in the world" (Arnaut Daniel); "Submission to the beloved lady is the natural mark of a courtly man" (Arab troubadour, Ibn Dâvoud). Chastity too: "He who is disposed to love with sensual love goes to war with himself, for a fool after he has emptied his purse cuts a poor figure!" (Marcabru. This seems to suggest the possibility of a *coitus interruptus* technique, purified from lust); tyranny of desire can be overcome by persistent desire for that which is greater: "By excess of desire, I think I shall remove her from me, if nothing is to be lost by dint of loving well" (Arnaut Daniel). Godfroi Rudel de Blaye does not even require the physical presence of his lady, for she that is distant is most present, when the physical is absent: "I have a lady friend, but I do not know who she is, for never, by my faith! Have I seen her . . . and I love her well. . . . No joy is so pleasing to me as the possession of that distant love." The Fine Love could even spring forth a fountain of youth. This quotation made Ezra Pound speculate about whether the troubadours practiced some kind of Taoist or Tantric technique for generating a spermatic elixir (internalized or externally consumed), using the Lady as a mantra: "I want to retain (my Lady) in order to refresh my heart and renew my body, so well that I cannot age. . . . He will live a hundred years who succeeds in possessing the joy of his love." And this came from the great nobleman William IX Duke of Acquitaine (1071–1126), often called the first troubadour.

De Rougemont gives numerous examples of troubadour lyrics that could have been inspired by seeing the sacred church of the Cathars as the "Lady," or the Sophia of the Gnostics, or, if those are not admissible, then the troubadour's own spiritual spouse in heaven that his earth-bound soul craves for in his isolation on Earth, and that it is the Lady who serves as a living sacrament of that devotion to the spirit: the same spirit incidentally, venerated by the Cathars. We may also note that both Cathar and Troubadour endeavored not to use sex for having children, and this "saving of seed" may have been influenced by ancient doctrines of the process of "gathering" enacted by the spiritual church that takes only the Holy Spirit from the grip of the Devil's creation. He cites the famous story of Godfroi de Rudel who traveled as far as Tripoli to meet a celebrated lady he had only heard of. She comes to his death-bed and gives him a kiss of peace, whereupon he dies, content. And she, it is said, devoted herself to piety ever after. He has followed the distant image of the faraway love to its conclusion in death, which for him, is that longed-for kiss of peace.

One point here is that Troubadour life offers a philosophy of life, a path. By observing the proofs of love that the Lady must demand, the life becomes meaningful, dynamic: its end out of sight, but not out of mind. Péladan declares that in the primitive poem on which Wagner based his opera *Tristan und Isolde,* Tristan is a missionary of love (a "parfait" according to Péladan) who kills the Irish Morhout who takes the girls and boys away to a convent.[7] His niece Iseult (Isolde in German) at first seeks revenge on Tristan, but is converted. The Lady then effectively intitiates the knight until death does them unite. Péladan sees the long-waited but still initital kiss of the lady when hands are grasped and the knight kneels before his lord, as a consolement, obviously linking it to the Cathar sacrament of *Consolamentum* by laying on of hands. This is the Troubadour answer to marriage.

Formal marriage was the yoke of the Roman church, indifferent utterly to love. Church doctrine declared lust for the wife as a form of adultery. The Roman church had defeated eros, in principle and absolutely: return to eros was return to the Devil. But the Troubadours did not think in terms of eros and agapē; they thought in terms of *Love,* pure, unobtainable, incredible, massive, and amazing love. Péladan notes that for Troubadours, the Lady *is* the doctrine. She is the locus of the cult; she is the altar before which the knight sacrifices himself in service. Through her service, the knight pereives the Holy Grail, for the ideal Lady is the Grail, and are we then wrong to suppose that the true meaning of the Grail is the womb that only the pure may enter into communion with.

In von Eschenbach's *Parzifal,* the Gral is a stone from heaven (*lapsit exillis*), kept secret by the angels from the impure, that only the purest may approach, those purged of the world entirely. The Gral transforms what comes from the world into what is heavenly: eternal life.

> By the power of that stone the phoenix burns to ashes, but the ashes give him life again. Thus does the phoenix molt and change its plumage, which afterwards is bright and shining and as lovely as before.

If the stone is the womb (or Sophia), and the rising phoenix the phallus, as divine symbol of regeneration then . . . The Gral receives the holy blood. Surely, we cannot avoid thinking of what we know of the Gnostic belief that the sperm-seed of the Gnostic combined with the juice (fruit) of the womb is the "blood of Christ," containing the seed of the Logos, poured into the gral in willing self-sacrifice for eternal life's sake: the holiest love sacrament of the Valentinians.

In *Parzifal,* angels must come to Earth to retrieve the "incorruptible" stone, as Prunicus is brought back to the Pleroma when she gets embroiled in the powers of the world. ("For thine incorruptible spirit is in all things" *Wisdom of Solomon* 12:1.)

Well, the question remains open as to whether this mythology and sacred practice was experienced in any way at any level by actual troubadours. Certainly, it is hard to imagine that the idea would not occupy the interest of a Cathar *croyante or parfaite,* since this was not a love of the body, nor an urge of lust, nor a procreative itch of the loins, but the most refined possible conception of love itself, devoted utterly to the kingdom of heaven and the Love beyond: fount of wisdom. And, of course, was so utterly undermining of the Catholic Church that only extermination could satisfy the latter's archontic sense of grievous opposition.

Certainly, Péladan believed that the counter-church held the secret of the Holy Grail. This church, including the Troubadours, "practiced and preached a Christianity more evangelical and above all more Johannite than Rome."[8] Péladan also believed that the "most secret libraries of the Vatican" contained "the true secret of the Troubadours of Provence and of the heretics of Aquitaine. The church has continued by a secular will of silence, the extermination of Innocent III and the abolition of the Templars."[9] Péladan, a Roman Catholic, felt that the times he lived in (1906) no longer understood an anticlerical faith with an independent mysticism, but "the court of historical research will lead fatally the erudite to discover that western freedom of thought first flourished in the Midi of France, and that it inspired the genius of the Middle Ages that appears so orthodox, and that the troubadours were Christian dissidents whose doctrine was immortalized by the greatest of modern poets and of the troubadours, Dante Alighieri."[10]

It seems you will find her there, if you wish to.

THIRTEEN

THE GOLDEN RIDDLE

S ome time in or after 1804, William Blake wrote a mysterious verse. He appended it to a section addressed "To the Christians" of his 100-plate, illuminated epic poem *Jerusalem—the Emanation of the Giant Albion*. It goes like this:

> I give you the end of a golden string,
> Only wind it into a ball:
> It will lead you in at Heaven's gate,
> Built in Jerusalem's wall.

It appears to be a riddle. *What does it mean?*

The late authority on Blake, Kathleen Raine, informed this author in 1986 that she believed the "golden string" referred to the "Excluded Tradition." By this she meant the Gnostic-Neoplatonist-Hermetic-Alchemical-Rosicrucian-Behmenist-Paracelsian-Theosophical spiritual stream—a rattling train of word-freight that adds up to what scholars today call "Western Esotericism": complex, overlapping traditions of spiritual knowledge at last receiving the serious attention they eminently deserve.

I am sure Kathleen would not mind at all if I here stated her interpretation of Blake's golden string does not exhaust its possibilities, though it does set one a-thinking. To find the complete solution to

Blake's riddle we need first to do as William Blake asked: take the end of the string and wind it into a ball. Then we may find that the ball becomes something magical, as Blake undoubtedly conceived it.

When Blake urged winding the golden string into a ball, he was in fact employing an image from a famous poem by Andrew Marvell (1621–1678), a figure from the artistic and philosophical aspect of English revolutionary history of the 1640s and 1650s: a period best known for conflicts that set King and Parliament apart in armed camps. Blake empathized with poets and natural philosophers of the era, men such as John Milton, Andrew Marvell, John Hall, Thomas Henshaw, Thomas and Henry Vaughan, Robert Vaughan, Dr. Robert Childe, Elias Ashmole, John Pordage, Samuel Hartlib, and a bevy of other bright sparks—some royalist some republican—who all inherited spiritual ideals from the Elizabethan Renaissance whose seeds lay partly in the Platonic-Hermetic revolution of the Italian Quattrocento, but the kernel of whose ideas take us back to late antiquity.

"Andy Marvell! What a marvel!" exclaimed David Niven (playing poet "Peter Carter") in The Archers' movie *Stairway to Heaven* (1946). In this justly famed cinematic jewel, the hero decides to spend his last minutes before death in the burning cockpit of his Lancaster bomber as it careers toward inevitable destruction, crying out lines of spiritual poetry, religion, and philosophy to a disembodied female voice in his earphones. The voice belongs to an American girl called June (Midsummer is approaching) stationed with an Air Force squadron in the south of England. The date: May 2, 1945. The setting is World War Two: the night Berlin fell, spelling an end to a crisis for the light of the world. On this night of magic, when one man's mind flies briefly beyond the earthly sphere, June is privileged to hear Carter's last visionary tirade:

> But at my back I always hear
> Time's wingèd chariot hurrying near;

> And yonder all before us lie
> Deserts of vast eternity . . .

The words are Andrew Marvell's. Taking his cue from the marvelous Marvell, Master Bomber Peter Carter declares his belief that a better world takes off "where this one leaves off, or where this one could leave off if we'd listened to Plato and Aristotle and Jesus. With all our little earthly problems solved but with greater ones worth the solving." Having bid his love adieu, he jumps optimistically, even triumphantly, to what he thinks is certain death in sure hope of the continuity of personal identity in eternal life. Of course, this being a movie, he will find his better life on Earth, in an erotic tryst with June in a flower-powered garden of roses and rhododendrons. The lovers' passion is only interrupted when time stops still for the arrival of a being from "another world" come to claim Peter whose "time is up."

Fast-forward twenty years. It is 1965. We are in Paris: a short trip away from "Swinging London." The movie is Charles K. Feldman's production of Woody Allen's script for *What's New, Pussycat?* What's new is that Paris is fast dissolving from black and white *nouvelle vague* existentialism into Technicolor, Art Nouveau-drenched, pleasure-seeking psychedelicism, to the tune of Burt Bacharach's fabulous Satie and Ravel-inspired jazz-pop romances. The scene is Lothario Peter O'Toole's attempted nighttime seduction of neurotic nymphomaniac Paula Prentiss. She wants to recite her versified agitprop "pleas for better housing" as a last ditch, left-wing resistance to letting her "warm lover," played irresistibly by O'Toole, into her knickers. Countering Prentiss's tiresome "free verse" with genuine lyric poetry, O'Toole invokes Marvell. "I know a poem too!" he declares:

> Had we but world enough, and time,
> This coyness, Lady, were no crime

There's no time to dilly-dally: *carpe diem*—or at least the night! Passion is all. Marvell's poem is addressed "To His Coy Mistress," written in the early 1650s. It is the same poem quoted by "Peter Carter" in *Stairway to Heaven* to his disembodied lover-to-be. Quite a poem to leap from World War II to the Swinging Sixties in two utterly contrasting scenes, the first with a celestial subtext, the second sublunary and carnal, but both having one hot thing in common: *passion.*

June is as slayed by the voice of Niven/Carter as was Cerberus by Orpheus's lyre. Paula Prentiss's character attempts a comic suicide rather than admit she's in love—or lust—with young and beautiful Peter O'Toole. "Andy Marvell, what a marvel!" indeed.

And Marvell got brother poet William Blake excited too, with these lines, also from "To His Coy Mistress":

> Let us roll all our strength and all
> Our sweetness up into one ball,
> And tear our pleasures with rough strife
> Thorough the iron gates of life:
> Thus, though we cannot make our sun
> Stand still, yet we will make him run.

Now we have something. Marvell's "To His Coy Mistress" has inspired at least three scenarios of visionary art, all composed at critical moments of history. Can this simply be attributed to the literary quality of a poem apparently about sexual frustration? While such frustration is probably universal, it barely covers the ground.

THE GOLDEN BALL

Let's hear Blake again:

> I give you the end of a golden string,
> Only wind it into a ball:

> It will lead you in at Heaven's gate,
> Built in Jerusalem's wall.

Blake has added his "golden string" to Marvell's gathering-into-a-ball metaphor, before transforming Marvell's "iron gates of life" into "Heaven's gate."

What, we may ask, could break down the iron gates of life, or transform them from being a dark, forbidding, "no trespassers" barrier into the gates of very heaven?

The first clue lies in Blake's golden string itself. What is a golden string? The answer lies in Pindar (518–438 BCE), known in Pythagoras's time as Greece's greatest lyric poet. A worshipper of Apollo, Pindar came to envision his god as civilization's redeemer: the bringer of grace, harmony, wisdom, and the unity behind diverse created things, symbolized by the golden light of the sun.

Apollo's virtues are concentrated in Pindar's first *Pythian Ode* into the image of his "golden" lyre. Plucking Apollo's seven stringed, golden instrument can even enchant and pacify the belligerent Zeus. The seven golden strings express the "music of the spheres." We may note that when Blake's golden string is wound, it forms itself into a light-giving ball or sphere, a personal sun, serving to banish darkness through the explication of love in sexual harmony.

The classical world believed the Earth to be encircled by seven "planets" ("wanderers"): Venus, Mercury, the Moon, Mars, Jupiter, Saturn, and, of course, the Sun. Each planet corresponded to a metal. Mars, for example, corresponded to iron, so iron is linked to war, and the "iron gates of life" represents life as a locus of conflict: civil war. The Sun rules gold, the highest metal. Blake's "golden string" resonates in tune with the Sun, and thus we may hear an echo of Marvell's last lines "To His Coy Mistress":

> Thus, though we cannot make our sun
> Stand still, yet we will make him run.

Blake's golden string expresses Marvell's "all our strength and all Our sweetness," which gathered up, or "charged," into a solar union of love can break through life's iron gates; *cf.* "the gates of hell shall never prevail against it [the "stone"]" (Matthew 16:17–19).

Blake doubtless intuited what Marvell was getting at, or what he thought Marvell was getting at.

But what was Marvell's original meaning?

In search of it, I contacted Marvell specialist Paul Bembridge, fellow lecturer in Western Esotericism and the first man to reveal the depth of Marvell's commitment to "British Rosicrucianism" whose radiant, utopian influence, Bembridge believes, Marvell and others attempted to shed on British republican government after the execution of King Charles I in 1649.[1]

Bembridge first considered the nature of the ball Marvell imagined consisting of "all our strength and all our sweetness"—a blended combination powerfully redolent of blissful sexual intercourse. An initial impression must then be that a ball that could tear through the "iron gates of life" must be a metaphoric cannonball: the idea being that, at least for a magic moment of supreme joy, the couple might momentarily shatter the constraints of devouring time, the sound of whose "wingèd chariot hurrying near" makes the poet's plea so urgent as to suggest delay or "coyness" would constitute naught less than a "crime."

Apart from the suggestion of iron's being ruled by bellicose Mars, Marvell's iron gates of life probably allude to the Neoplatonic belief that the soul enters the physical cosmos through the Gate of Cancer where it loses its memory of divine life, before proceeding to struggle under the weight of inexorable zodiacal Fate bearing down on life's course, before exiting by the Gate of Capricorn, often little wiser for the experience. (One should also bear in mind that Cancer marked the northernmost "gate" of the Sun before its "return"; Cancer used to rule Midsummer, and Midsummer was traditionally held to be the perfect time for souls to enter the world, Apollo-blessed.)

It is, however, unclear whether Marvell's ball is a metaphor, allegory or symbol, or indeed a synthesis of the three. Were we dependent on Marvell's poem alone, we should only know that the ball is somehow love's creation or consummation, a conglobing of loving, will-directed energies. The word *ball* could mean anything round; it did not have to be fully spherical or globular, or represent a plaything. The Earth—flat or spherical—could be described at the time as a "ball." Accounts existed of the alchemical philosopher's stone and of the elixir of life being contained as a ball. The idea of something turning—like a head (the etymological origin of "ball")—is central to the idea of the "ball": something, literally, *revolutionary,* or world-turning.

Marvell was familiar with kabbalistic images of the attributes of the Godhead descending through the emanated tree to the Earth and lower hells as spheres. Marvell was also mindful of images of ball-like planets on their courses, along with the stars' unearthly counterpart on Earth: the globular dew, believed by alchemists to be impregnated with star power through stellar rays. Bembridge focuses on the link between alchemical processes and the pains of love unrequited.

He finds this link in Sir Philip Sydney's last sonnet, "Astrophil and Stella," which undoubtedly describes amorous frustration in terms of a failed alchemical operation. Sydney's personal association with Elizabethan astrologer-magus John Dee would have furnished appropriate practical knowledge to stock the metaphor.

Boiling like lead in a darkened heart, the poet's sorrow is relieved solely by the light afforded by thoughts of Stella ("Star"). But the light compounds frustration, for the "iron doors" of Astrophil's sorrow obscure the poet-lover from "Phoebus's gold" (possession of Stella's radiant, solar love in love's physical fulfillment). The Sun "turns back" from the northern Gate of Cancer. Taking Sydney's idea into Marvell's poem, we see that Marvell's "iron gates of life" likewise evoke the base metal's oppression of the aspirant lover, but the poet aspires yet to blast through to the physical (and by analogy, spiritual) gold (Sun) by virtue of the propitious strength of the magic moment, a consummation both spiritual and physical, devoutly wished: to run with the sun.

Such insight makes good sense of Marvell's lines concerning the lovers tearing their "pleasures" through the iron gates of life to so striking an extent that "though we cannot make our sun/Stand still, yet we will make him run."

What does Marvell mean by making the sun run?

Alchemists of the time believed that variant metals grew imperceptibly over great time periods like vegetables in the earth, the ores' parent principles, sulphur and mercury, being affected by the sun: a photometamorphosis. The ultimate end of the process—transformation into perfected gold—could be speeded up like lightning if the alchemist by art created in the laboratory the philosophers' stone through heat and chemical combination, taking into account solar and zodiacal influences from the macrocosm into the microcosm. Thus, Marvell seems to be saying that should the lovers attend on nature's course alone for their fulfillment, time will surely run out on them, but by making a philosopher's "ball" from their willed ardor, they might yet make the sun "run" in favor of love's consummation: a great purpose fulfilled.

Put another way, if the iron gates of Cancer could be obliterated, then that which made the sun retreat could be inhibited and the sun's natural course come under the influence of the lovers' will.

While we can see here clearly how alchemical symbolism and practice can relate precisely to sexual magic, Bembridge takes the view that Marvell's concern was not confined to the private world of amorous heroes and heroines "breaking through to the other side." Rather, Bembridge believes that Marvell was using the lovers' alchemical potential as an allegory for more universal aspirations in the sphere of national government, that is to say, to join earthly government to the active will of heaven, to set the British Isles under the direct guidance of supernal Wisdom. Was he suggesting the republican government instigate a stupendous act of love? Was he, like the Pole Samuel Hartlib advocating republican support for Sir Francis Bacon's "Great Instauration," the great reformation of knowledge Bacon (1561–1626) proposed as the work of "Six Days" in imitation of the divine Creation, culminating in Adam's re-ascendancy over creation? Notably, the image for this process appeared as the frontispiece to Bacon's *Sylva Sylvarum* ("The Wood of the Woods"; 1627), where we see the divine Name at the center of the Sun. The fiery orb shoots down powerful rays of divine wisdom to enlighten earth's shadowy state. The rays seem to tear roughly through the cloudy vaults that cover the ball of the Earth, bringing Apollonine light to those in darkness.

Bembridge locates Marvell's source of inspiration in the poem called "To his Tutor, Master Pawson. An Ode." Written by John Hall (1626–1656), Marvell's government associate, Hall published it in 1646. While Marvell was writing his poem 'To His Coy Mistress' (Marvell served from 1650 to 1653 as tutor to the daughter of Lord General Thomas Fairfax, lately commander of the parliamentarian army), fellow Cambridge graduate Hall was in the government employ as a brilliant propagandist in a world of "rough strife," pitched in pamphlet and actual war with royalists supporting the late King's son and heir, Prince Charles Stuart.

Hall, like Marvell, was something of a utopian with high hopes for the republic's capacity to enact a golden age of purified science and religion. It is thus significant that in 1647, Hall followed up his "Ode" with a translation of German Johann Valentin Andreae's *Christianae Societas imago,* Hall's translation appearing as *A Modell of a Christian Society.* Samuel Hartlib, Bacon's chief advocate, commissioned the work.

Andreae (1586–1654) wrote at least two of the first so-called Rosicrucian Manifestos: startlingly provocative utopian works published in Germany between 1614 and 1616. The manifestos would stimulate a gnostic spiritual movement that persists to this day. We need to bear this background in mind as we read the signifying words of John Hall's remarkable ode, addressed, when the poet was just twenty, to Cambridge tutor, Master Pawson. I have italicized those lines with the most direct bearing on Marvell's imagery.

Come, let us run
And give the world a girdle with the sun;
For so we shall
Take a full view of this enamelled ball,
Both where it may be seen
Clad in a constant green,
And where it lies
Crusted with ice;
Where't swells with mountains, and shrinks down to
    vales;
Where it permits the usurping sea
To rove with liberty,
And where it pants with drought, and of all liquor
    fails.

And as we go,
We'll mind these atoms that crawl to and fro:
There may we see
One both be soldier and artillery;
Another whose defense
Is only innocence;
One swift as wind,
Or flying hind,
Another slow as is a mounting stone;
Some that love earth, some scorn to dwell
Upon't, but seem to tell
Those that deny there is a heaven, they know of one.

Nor all this while
Shall there escape us e'er a braving pile,
Nor ruin, that
Wastes what it has, to tell its former state.
Yet shall we ne'er descry [discover]

Where bounds of kingdoms lie,
But see them gone
As flights new flown,
And lose themselves in their own breadth, just as
Circlings upon the water, one
Grows great to be undone;
Or as lines in the sand, which as they're drawn do pass.

But objects here
Cloy in the very taste; *O, let us tear*
A passage through
That fleeting vault above; there may we know
Some rosy brethren stray
To a set battalia [distribution of battle forces],
And others scout
Still round about,
Fix'd in their courses, and uncertain too;
But clammy matter doth deny
A clear discovery,
Which those, that are inhabitants, may solely know.

Then let's away,
And journey thither: what should cause our stay?
We'll not be hurl'd
Asleep by drowsy potions of the world.
Let not Wealth tutor out
Our spirits with her gout,
Nor Anger pull
With cramps the soul;
But fairly disengag'd we'll upward fly,
Till that occurring joy affright
Even with its very weight,
And point the haven where we may securely lie.

It is difficult to disagree with Bembridge's view that herein are secreted keys to unlock further the riddle of Marvell's ball. Hall's youthful, poetic vision launches the reader out of the world altogether, without benefit of fiery rocket, pointing himself and us in the direction of Marvell's "deserts of vast eternity," which "yonder all before us lie." He has flown to the starry heights, torn his way through the sky's "fleeting vault" in his mind's exalted vision, seeing all things from a cosmic perspective, imagining himself girdling the planet like the sun but faster, by will of vision, autonomous, revealing (almost) what is known by the "rosy brethren" (the invisible Rose Cross Fraternity) of the eternal life in the spheres of the heavens and their role in our little earthly lives. Hall wants to open free passage of spirit from the heavens to the Earth. To do so will require escaping from the dullness of "clammy matter" where all that is immediate seems most real, to embrace a supra-cosmic vision where the world appears in its relative place as an enameled ball, and life a window of spiritual opportunity—so long, that is, as one is not drugged by the "sleep" or unconsciousness of the world and the worldly (in Gnostic terms, the Demiurge).

Hall's "drowsy potions of the world" precisely invokes the discourse of the second so-called Rosicrucian Manifesto, the *Confessio Fraternitatis* (first published in Latin in 1615 and in English by Thomas Vaughan in 1652) wherein: "what before times hath been seen, heard, and smelt, now finally shall be spoken and uttered forth, when the World shall awake out of her heavy and drowsy sleep, and with an open heart, bare-head, and bare-foot, shall merrily and joyfully meet the new arising Sun."

Christopher McIntosh's recent masterful re-translation of the *Confessio*'s predecessor manifesto (the *Fama*) encouraged me to ask him to re-examine the above passage from the *Confessio*. Christopher offered the following translation from the *Confessio*'s first German version (1615): "that which in earlier times has been seen, heard and smelt shall now finally be spoken ["uttered forth" is repetition], when the world shall awake out of its heavy ["drowsy" is also an English addition]

262 *Gnostic Love and the Spiritual Revolution*

sleep and, with an open heart, bare-headed and barefoot, go towards the newly rising sun."[2] The crucial redundancy of the word "drowsy" in the English translation suggests to me the likelihood that the translator deliberately included the English word with the analogous section of Hall's visionary Ode to Master Pawson in mind.

The 1652 English translations of the *Fama* and *Confessio* are often attributed to Thomas Vaughan (1621–1666). Vaughan, however, as "Eugenius Philalethes," was the publisher, and his introductory note tells us that the *Confessio*'s predecessor the *Fama* was translated by a man unknown, a copy of it being given him by one "more learned than myself," a man who wished to remain anonymous. Vaughan respected his wish: a respect that extended to printing what Vaughan considered the translator's error in confusing "Damcar in Arabia" with Damascus.

Significantly, in the translation of the *Confessio,* "Damcar" also occurs as the place where "Frater R.C." obtains his secrets (in fact the proper place was *Damar* but that error belonged to the original German). This suggests whoever translated the *Fama* may have contributed to translating the *Confessio,* a translation inferior in style to that of the graceful *Fama.* A likelihood that Hall was the *Fama*'s translator emerges, and that it was Hartlib who conveyed the translation to Vaughan. If so, we can explain Hall's preference for anonymity on account of his working for the government where association with an apocalyptic, utopian work with a secret magical agenda was potentially embarrassing. The word "drowsy" then may have entered the text as a "clue" from Vaughan to those "in the know." Alternatively, Hall may already have undertaken a rough or part-translation of the *Confessio* (including his arguably "giveaway" preference for "drowsy" over the German's "heavy" sleep) with or without Vaughan.

The foundation works of Rosicrucianism were printed from existing manuscripts for the first time in English in 1652 as a *parergon,* or "by-product," of the attempts of Vaughan and friends Thomas Henshaw (1618–1700) and Dr. Robert Childe (ca. 1612–1654) to conform themselves to an ideal alchemical fraternity, inspired by Andreae's Wisdom-focused *Image of a Christian Society,* whose translation by John Hall as *A Modell of a Christian Society* was commissioned and published by Hall's (and Vaughan's) friend, the Polish Baconian and "Rosicrucian" activist, Samuel Hartlib (1599–1652).

A Modell of a Christian Society first appeared in 1647 printed by Roger Daniel, printer to the University of Cambridge, with its rubric from Matthew 18:20: "When two or three be gathered together in my name I will be in the midst of them." It takes only a handful of "centered" people to become a heavenly "mustard seed" (Matthew 13:31–2) or radix for God's active will.

Hall, Vaughan, Henshaw, and Childe were not the first English-speakers to be inspired by the Rosicrucian promise. A generation before them, Hartlib himself, along with the Czech educationalist and Moravian church-member Comenius (1592–1650), journeyed to England to exert themselves between 1628 and 1642 enacting a spiritually oriented reformation of learning through cultivating social and political contacts in their host country, efforts largely thwarted by energy-sapping conflict between King and Parliament. Comenius is famous as the promoter of *Pansophia,* an integrated spiritual-arts-science-philosophy educational program. As the name indicates, Comenius found the divine Sophia in everything and wished to point the world's children in the same direction.

Thus it is possible to see Marvell in "To His Coy Mistress," following Hall, pondering a revival of the efforts of the earlier "rosy brethren" to stimulate a divine transformation of society.

The new republic of the early 1650s was, however, riven by infighting between parliament and its army, now dominated by Oliver Cromwell, once Fairfax's subordinate. The dramatically uncertain times and anchorless fluidity generated not only profound frustration but, in the visionary gleam, high expectation or "wishful-thinking" that the new era might yet herald propitious signs for a holy, enlightened nation under Wisdom's care. Apocalypticism of sundry degrees was abroad to stir the blood of many looking for God's will out of the mess. I have used italic for emphasis:

> *Had we but world enough, and time,*
> *This coyness, Lady, were no crime*
>
> Now therefore, while the youthful hue
> Sits on thy skin like morning dew,
> And while thy willing soul transpires
> At every pore with instant fires,
> Now let us sport us while we may,
> And now, like amorous birds of prey,
> Rather at once our time devour
> Than languish in his [time's] slow-chapt
>   [slow-grinding] power.

The youthful Christian republic could boast good men who felt called to enact the divine will. Close to the circle of Hall, Milton and Marvell, Samuel Hartlib was familiar with the new generation of chemist-alchemists, "natural philosophers" and scientific reformers.[3] Marvell himself, however, was wary that just as the Hartlib-Comenius dream of the 1630s and early 1640s had been dashed by the Civil Wars, continued conflict overshadowed the highest hopes: in 1650 Cromwell's army savagely subdued Stuart supporters in Ireland and Scotland while parliament dithered. It would take a tremendous effort of will, and of concerted *love,* to revive the "Rosicrucian" golden-age promise of a union of pure knowledge and spirituality guiding a goodly, Godly nation in the face of prevailing conditions.

Marvell had ample opportunity to weigh up the odds at Nun Appleton House, near York, as tutor to Lord Thomas Fairfax's daughter during the period 1650 to 1653. In the poem "Upon Appleton House, to my Lord Fairfax" Marvell reflected melancholically on the wars' waste that had devastated a once paradisiac garden (the italic words are Marvell's):

> Unhappy! shall we never more
> That sweet *Militia* restore,
> When Gardens only had their Towrs,
> And all the Garrisons were Flowrs,
> When Roses only Arms might bear,
> And Men did rosie Garlands wear?
> Tulips, in several Colours barr'd,
> Were then the *Switzers* of our *Guard*.[4]

The paradise (garden) becomes an image here for a lamented "Rosicrucian" vision when men with "rosie Garlands" populated a radix of true religion like the "Switzer" (Swiss) Guard about the Vatican. Brightly attired, like harlequin-tulips, the "Swiss Guard" consisted of Swiss professionals: mercenary soldiers paid both to protect the Pope and French (Catholic) royalty. Marvell's Protestant "sweet *Militia*" directly echoes Hall's "battalia" of the "rosy brethren" in Hall's ode to his Cambridge master, Dr. Pawson. That is to say, the invisible Rosy Cross brothers had a secret, spiritually militant plan for the restoration of humankind: an *apocatastasis,* or "return to Adamic perfection," before the fall of spiritually aware Man into matter. *This,* Marvell intones, was the Militia required; not mercenary (paid) guards defending the indefensible, nor even, perhaps, Cromwell's controversial military suppression of Catholics in Ireland: on the one hand recognizing the danger of militant, politicized Catholicism (Cromwell's fear) while possibly being disturbed by the army's ruthless response to that danger.

In "To His Coy Mistress," Marvell looks, I think, to the wavering government to set in train a more inspired direction than constant war; the violence should at least have a peaceful, Godly goal. Spiritual-physical science could yet break the bonds of dark matter whose dense "psychology" makes for endless conflict, while opening men and women up to the light of the divine sun.

Marvell's poetic analogy for this breakthrough was, apparently, that of "cosmic" orgasm, breaking the bounds and circumference of earthly bonds, shooting forth beyond the vault of an interior heaven to the very center of spiritual influx (a theme that would grace the *Preface* to Vaughan's *Fame and Confession* edition). In sonic terms, the projection of the ball beyond the Earth is consistent with that triumphant E major heavenly chord that paradoxically slams the coffin shut (and the gates of heaven open) in John Lennon and Paul McCartney's equally melancholic-optimist "A Day in the Life" (1967), composed at another turning-point of Western history when the paradise of flowers was again invoked as an image for the power of social and spiritual renewal in the wake and face of war's devastation.

Who may we ask was intended by Marvell's "coy mistress," she to whom the poem's plea was ostensibly addressed?

THE COY MISTRESS

In order to locate the "mistress" of the poem, we must first reexamine the notion of the "ball" that the poet hopes will be projected with "rough strife" from the strength and sweetness of union with that mistress. In doing so, we catch a luminous glimpse of the heroine of this book.

In order to locate the "mistress" of the poem, we must first reexamine the notion of the "ball" that the poet hopes will be projected with "rough strife" from the strength and sweetness of union with that mistress. In doing so, we may catch a luminous glimpse of the heroine of this book.

Vaughan's publication of the *Fame and Confession of the Fraternity RC* (printed in 1652) opens its address "To the Wise and Understanding Reader" with a literary invocation of the personified divine Wisdom (*Sophia*):

Wisdom (saith Solomon) is to a man an infinite Treasure, for she is the Breath of the Power of God, and a pure Influence that floweth from the Glory of the Almighty; she is the Brightness of Eternal

Light, and an undefiled Mirror of the Majesty of God, and an Image of his Goodness; she teacheth us Soberness and Prudence, Righteousness and Strength; she understands the Subtilty of words, and Solution of dark sentences; she foreknoweth Signs and Wonders, and what shall happen in time to come; with this Treasure was our first Father Adam fully endued [. . .]

No Gnostic would take issue with any of that. Although, asserts Vaughan, Wisdom has been lost due to the "sorrowful fall into sin," the Lord God has sometimes bestowed Wisdom to "some of his Friends." He then makes it clear that the Fraternity of RC may be so described. They may be counted as "true Disciples of Wisdom, and true Followers of the Spherical Art."

The Spherical Art . . . . Could this art have something to do with Marvell's "ball"?

Both the *Fama* and *Confessio* offer tantalizing clues as to the mysterious nature of the "Spherical Art." The *Fama* declares that Wisdom enables one to see what ordinary logic cannot grasp, that Plato, Aristotle, Solomon, and the Bible are in fundamental agreement: "All that same concurreth together, and make a Sphere or Globe, whose total parts are equidistant from the Center, as hereof more at large and more plain shall be spoken of in Christianly Conference." The *Confessio* sees this spherical gift of insight as being at the Rose Cross Brothers' disposal. They can transcend circumferences or boundaries of space and time by standing at "the center," thus being able to see everything as a totality, being equidistant from all manifestation influenced or projected to a superficial circumference from that divine, invisible central point:

Were it not a precious thing that you could always live so, as if you had lived from the beginning of the world, and, moreover, as you should still live to the end thereof? Were it not excellent you dwell in one place, that neither the people which dwell beyond the River Ganges in the Indies could hide anything, nor those which live in Peru might be able to keep secret their counsels from thee?

Indeed, Paul Bembridge would have this passage from the *Confessio* as being the inspiration behind the opening verse of Marvell's poem:

> Had we but World enough, and Time,
> This coyness Lady were no crime.
> We would sit down, and think which way
> To walk, and pass our long Loves Day.
> Thou by the Indian Ganges side.
> Should'st Rubies find: I by the Tide
> Of Humber would complain. I would
> Love you ten years before the Flood:
> And you should if you please refuse
> Till the Conversion of the Jews.

Bembridge reckons Marvell retains the "Ganges" for the mistress, while substituting his native Humber for "Peru" and for himself, while extrapolating from the *Confessio*'s "from the beginning of the world . . . to the end thereof" with biblical approximations: from "ten years before the Flood" until "the Conversion of the Jews" (an event believed to signify the final consummation of history). Such incredible universality of insight, the spherical art, could, Marvell suggests, be attained should the heart and will of the "coy mistress" be won. Bembridge is thus pleased to identify the "Coy Mistress" with a coy *Sophia,* the divine Wisdom of the Rosicrucian Brotherhood: Lady Wisdom Herself, who appears star-bespangled to the storyteller of the so-called third Rosicrucian Manifesto: *The Chemical Wedding of Christian Rosenkreuz* (first published in German in 1616) to invite the troubled Brother "CR" to a spiritual, alchemical wedding, that is, consummation by spiritual resurrection (a truly Valentinian theme).

I should like to add that Marvell might have taken his Mistress's discovery of "Rubies" by the Ganges from Vaughan's *Epistle to the Reader* that introduces the English translation of the *Fama* and *Confessio*. Perhaps with a nod in the direction of Jacob Böhme's work of this name, Vaughan writes of the coming "Aurora": the Great Day when the Phoebus (Sun) of Divine Day-Light will reveal all mysteries from their occulted, obscure places, all the invisible "Treasures of godly Wisdom." This light, Vaughan declares "will be the right kingly *Ruby*, and most excellent shining *Carbuncle* [an object that shines in the dark like a candle or burning coal, or *rose-red ruby*], of which it is said, That he doth shine and give light in darkness, and to be a perfect Medicine of all imperfect Bodies, and to change them into the best Gold, and to cure all Diseases of Men, easing them of all pains and miseries." The rubies will not be offered to the suitor until the end of time ("wisdom is more precious than rubies" Proverbs 8:11). Therefore, the poet is enjoined to a projected acceleration into a "ball" (or Carbuncle?) that could chivy up the slow work of the natural sun or unaided worldly order.

THE SPHERICAL ART

There are other Sophianic clues to consider in Vaughan's alchemical *Preface* to the *Fama* and *Confessio*. Thomas Vaughan is struck by the ability of the "Spherical Art" to demonstrate inner, central conformity of different schools of ancient Wisdom. He compares Philostratus's account of the natural philosophy of magus Appolonius of Tyana (ca. 15–100 CE) with that of the RC Brothers, noting how Appolonius describes with respect the "Brachmans" (Brahmins) of the Ganges (India). But before detailing his observations of the "Brachmans" who by the Ganges have formed secret fraternities of wisdom, in tune with the exalted thoughts of the Jewish Kabbalah (Vaughan calls the Spheres of the kabbalistic *Sephiroth* a "Sphiristical Order," also suggesting the "Spherical Art"), Vaughan tells a fascinating story.

He says that Alexander the Great never reached the holiest, secret places of the Brachmans, which stood on a hill between the Ganges and the River Hyphasis (the Beas River which rises in the Himalayas). He did not seize them, out of respect for their mysteries. However, it may have been respect engendered by fear for we are informed that the Brachmins had perfected, apparently by alchemy, the ability to rest secure within their gated refuge, while defeating the enemy without by means of "Thunder and Lightening" [*sic*]. Vaughan is quick to remind his readers that while the experience of gunpowder would have shocked Appolonius, nothing was now more familiar to his readers (on account of the Civil Wars), nor indeed would such fires and terrors of the sky have surprised the thirteenth-century adept Friar Roger Bacon.

In discoursing on "several wonderful Experiments," Roger Bacon "tells us amongst the rest of a secret Composition, which being form'd into Pills, or little Balls, and then cast up into the Air, would break out into Thunders and Lighetnings, more violent and horrible then those of Nature." Vaughan quotes Bacon to the effect that only a "thumb-measure" of the substance could "cause a horrible report and show a brilliant flash, and this can be done in many ways, by which a city or an army may be destroyed."

Here I think we have the seed of the fiery ball that only the ruby-wisdom of the Ganges could make: a ball to rock the body politic and break the iron doors of worldly blindness. Its composition was a secret wisdom of the east that held a key to blow such a storm in the heavens as could cow even the great Alexander—surely it could do so for Oliver Cromwell and the bickering parliament! But so long as the "Coy Mistress" remained by the "Ganges" and the English poet by the Humber, the magic could not be worked until the end of time. Then, all the secrets would be revealed—unless, that is, the signs of the day were right away seized and the transformative consummation—or "instauration"—hastened.

There is still hope for those who labor in the darkness, for Wisdom occasionally shines forth her fruits upon her disciples: one such fruit being the "Spherical Art" itself.

One must imagine, I think, a crystalline globe. If you "stood" at its center you would not be "standing" by any ordinary concept at all, for the center of a sphere must be a pure point, which by its nature must be invisible. One is reminded of the words attributed to Nicholas of Cusa but which first appeared in medieval commentaries on Hermetic wisdom: "God is an infinite sphere whose center is everywhere and circumference nowhere." Particularize that concept and you have nothing less than an image of God: *mundus imago dei* ("the world is the image of God"), as the Hermetic *Asclepius* has it! Are you a bit lost? Of course you are lost in a sphere, unless you *are* the center, then you can see everything. That's what the perfected adept can do.

Vaughan is at pains in his preface to speak of the difference between the knowledge of the worldly, superficial pedant and the knowledge of the adept. The center is the pure insubstantial substance. The adept must come to this center as he would his own soul's spiritual kernel, the seed that enfolds into the divine being. The "enemy" is the circumference, the mere "skin" or flesh. That is where impurities accrete as on a surface (hence the peril of "superficiality") where reflected essences are mixed.

Our ordinary rational faculties, unenlightened by the glowing light of Wisdom, know only how to deal with impure cards. Confused, the player is tempted to cheat. Only Wisdom can call Man to the Center. Thus the "true Disciples of Wisdom" are the "true Followers of the Spherical Art." Such beings stand at peace, indifferent to affection of one thing over another, but subsist in solitary "darkness of God," which though light to the enlightened is obscurity to the blind (*cf.* the Masonic axiom: "The light of the Master Mason is darkness visible"). She is black to the blind.

The one at the center is in perfect stasis, moving but unmoved, untrammeled by temptation, emotion, lustful attraction. At this one point, the adept finds all things are at his command, for with loving Wisdom he is the invisible center-point of the creation that forever extends from a center to a line, to a circle, to infinity (Elias Ashmole's motto was: EX UNO OMNIA—"From the One, All").

The perfected adept is with God and instrumental in His Will. He STANDS while others are forced to fall by imperfect position, gravity, pulls of the world, fancies, attractions, magnetism; taking each day and making each day, like a sun, but not subject to time's corruption, which works on impure intimacies, magnetisms, but rather loving God through his Wisdom, which is Truth. He is in "yoga," or union, with God (*cf.* John 10:30); he has found the Tao. As the German mystic-gnostic Jacob Böhme observed in his *Aurora* (1612): when Adam stood in his own center he was in Paradise, at one with his Sophia, but becoming enamored of his reflection in the lower sphere, his image was drawn down and bound by inferior powers. Love of Sophia can bring him to his return and the healing of the wound. The Center is essential; it is essence, being that is: the circumference is error. Or as the Master Mason degree still declares like an unheard voice in a desert of incomprehension, unheeded by the stone-less: "At the center of the circle, the Master Mason cannot err."

The Center is with us, always.

THE CONVERSION OF THE JEWS

Marvell's plea to his "Coy Mistress" posits the idea that she might withhold her favors "Till the conversion of the Jews." No matter, the poet seems to say, that will give—or indeed has given—veritable ages (or *aeons?*) for him to reflect on and to appreciate every part of her beauty. Marvell describes her as a very special being, one worthy of the most intense intimacy. But it is the "last age" when she will finally "show her heart":

> I would Love you ten years before the Flood,
> And you should, if you please, refuse
> Till the conversion of the Jews.
> My vegetable love should grow
> Vaster than empires, and more slow;

A hundred years should go to praise
Thine eyes and on thy forehead gaze;
Two hundred to adore each breast,
But thirty thousand to the rest;
An age at least to every part,
And the last age should show your heart.
For, Lady, you deserve this state,
Nor would I love at lower rate.

Marvell was not alone in seeing the Millennium or "last age" as imminent. This was a theme underlying the Rosicrucian Manifestos and was such a hope and expectation among certain figures in British government that it is widely thought to have functioned as an unstated component in Oliver Cromwell's willingness to hear the case of Dutch Rabbi Menasseh Ben Israel who, in 1655–56, persuaded Cromwell of the wisdom of granting government permission for Jews to come to Britain from Amsterdam after over 350 years of exile.

While there were sound mercantilist reasons for depriving the Dutch of some of their economic strength in Britain's favor, the tacit (but not legislated) acceptance of Jews settling once more in Britain in 1656 encouraged many who believed that conversion of the Jews constituted a sign of Christ's "thousand-year" reign on Earth, before or after the Last Judgment. Thus, while return was not conditional on accepting conversion (in fact Jews were instructed not to make proselytes), the simple reappearance of Jewry in Britain could be taken to signify imminent apocalypse, a conception that gave Britain's growing influence in the world the dimension of a divine commission: a Godly nation would serve God's historical plan. Such a plan was based chiefly on St. Paul's fervent hope (Romans 11) that the severed "branches" of the Jews who denied that Jesus was the Messiah would one day see the light and be regrafted by God onto what Paul believed had become the Christian olive tree wherein all the sons of Adam would find salvation.[5] Thus for visionary enthusiasts of the conception, Britain had become a millennial locus with a serious role in God's Book of Life. This conception would play a part in William Blake's philosophy of Britain, as we shall see, where "Jerusalem" will be identified as Albion's bride—and having addressed Valentinian eschatology, we ahall understand what was intended by the bride-bridegroom idea of Albion and Jerusalem, rising into each other's arms for the New Age at the spiritual revolution.

Paul Bembridge has observed how Marvell's millennial enthusiasms emerged as government propaganda in his 1655 poem, *The First Anniversary of the Government under O.C.* (Oliver Cromwell). Marvell here gives Cromwell a role in the (alchemical) "Great Work" that would "precipitate the latest day," referring to the Last Days:

> Sure, the mysterious Work, where none withstand,
> Would forthwith finish under such a hand:
> *Foreshortened time its useless course would stay,*
> And soon precipitate the latest day.

Again we have the theme of foreshortening time (I have added the italics), of precipitating changes through superior knowledge, of trumping merely natural processes. Time is hurrying near and requires decisive responses. However, like John Hall's reservation that "clammy matter doth deny/ A clear discovery," Marvell and his associates did not possess the full benefit of the "Spherical Art," not themselves being perfected *adepti*. There was room for doubt, as these lines from *First Anniversary* immediately following those above demonstrate:

> But a thick cloud about that morning lies,
> And intercepts the beams of mortal eyes,
> That 'tis the most which we determine can,
> If these the times, then this must be the man

Bembridge is I am sure quite right to make a plea for the existence of something called "British Rosicrucianism" in this period, supported by Marvell, Hall, Henshaw, Vaughan, Childe, and Ashmole, building on the work of Andreae, Comenius, and Hartlib. According to Bembridge, British Rosicrucianism was "a heady mix of Neoplatonist and alchemical ideas which converged with millennialism to produce the 'new dawn' politics of the 'Left' at a crucial period in English history. This is the background against which Marvell's 'Coy Mistress' is best read. Superficially a biographical courtship poem, at a deeper level, it is a call for adept action to conjure forth a golden age whose reality was there for those with esoteric eyes to see."[6]

Indeed, perceiving a suspect Rosicrucian strain within 1650s government, those who despised the Cromwellian Protectorate seized upon the "Rosicrucians'" political dreams as accounting for the religious anarchy and uprooting of tradition that characterized the tumults of the eleven-year alien republic. Cromwellian government's ultimate failure to secure broad support from the country became a matter for mockery, and what better way to mock than to accuse it of having toyed with dubious alchemical arts and chaos-inducing "Rosicrucian" magic (like blaming the "Sixties" or the "hippies" for numerous contemporary social ills).

In his Restoration comedy *Characters*, Royalist poet Samuel Butler (1613–1680) placed his "Rosicrucians" in literary stocks and cast rotten vegetable matter at the invisible brethren, though he suggests they were now dwelling in "spheres" above, for having bungled a reformation of government below. They were now:

> carrying on a *thorough Reformation* in the celestial World—They have repaired the old Spheres, that were worn as thin as Cobweb, and fastened the Stars in them with a Screw, by which means they may be taken off, and put on again at Pleasure. . . . But their Intelligence in the upper World is nothing to what they have in the infernal; for they hold exact Correspondence with the Devils. . . . By their Advice the Fiends lately attempted a *Reformation* of their Government, that is, to bring all Things into Confusion, which among them is the greatest Order.[7]

Butler's conception of the "new dawn" politics of British visionary politics was that it precisely lacked that very divine Wisdom to whom Marvell had apparently addressed his plea.

Does it transpire then that Marvell's error, if such it was, was in confusing spiritual and material planes? Was his and his country's "coy mistress" really the government of Britannia? Etymology rather reinforces this view, for while modern readers think of a "mistress" as a woman who engages the erotic interest of a married man—and therefore a "coy" mistress (as we understand the word "coy") must seem a contradiction in terms—*Dr. Johnson's English Dictionary* (Volume 2, 1766) gives *mistress's* primary meaning as "a female *master*" and quotes John Milton's expression "sov'reign mistress" to back this up, followed by Elizabethan playwright Ben Jonson's "Rome now is mistress of the whole world"; while Sir Richard Blackmore has the "lunar orb" as mistress. A mistress, says Dr. Johnson, is a woman who governs "correlative to a subject or servant": a female master. We may think then of Britannia enthroned.

Dr. Johnson's second meaning for "mistress" is a "woman who has some thing in possession"; he cites Edmund Waller: "mistress of the Indies." Thirdly, "mistress" may mean a woman skilled in any thing. Not until the fifth meaning do we come to "mistress" as a "woman beloved and courted," while the sixth and final meaning offers "mistress" as a "term of contemptuous address; a whore, a concubine."

For the word "coy," *Dr. Johnson's Dictionary* (Volume 1, 1785) offers us: "1. Modest, decent; 2. Reserved, not accessible, not easily condescending to familiarity." Johnson notes the verb "To Coy," meaning: "1. to behave with reserve; to reject familiarity. 2. not to condescend willingly; to make difficulty." On this basis, we may indeed impute a mixed metaphor or conflation of planes to Marvell's mistress. She appears to be both the British State, his mistress or master, unsure of the next step to take, *and* Sophia, Lady Wisdom, virgin spirit, who might yet shower Herself upon the country's governance, while gathering in her own, should the "ball" of desire shatter the iron gates that block her solar passage. Certainly, even as Johnson's dictionary definition of "mistress," Sophia has some interesting contrasts in her makeup. She is a female governor who compels service, a woman beloved and courted, and, last, a whore or concubine. By now, astute readers will see just how close the Divine Wisdom is to being "Mistress of the world," and even a sometimes "Coy Mistress," and therefore we shall see just how close Marvell seems truly to have come to his beloved heart's core.

HEAVEN'S GATE

We can now return to Blake's riddle from his epic poem *Jerusalem*. Unlike Marvell, Blake gives us a concrete image for the "ball" created from winding the golden string. The frontispiece to *Jerusalem* (1804–ca. 1820) depicts a young traveler. His left hand touches an opening perpendicular arched door. The thumb and fingers of his right appear to be embedded within a radiating three-dimensional disc (it is unclear if it is a true sphere; it could be, though it more resembles a kind of *lens,* suggesting vision).

When we carefully examine the golden ball, it appears joined to the traveler's hand by a black line (possibly the "end" of the golden string) that is joined to his body and/or garment; Blake considered the body to be but the spirit's fleshly garment.

We should, I think, compare the two cursive fingers within the sunlike ball to the two linear fingers of Blake's famous *Ancient of Days* image, where Blake shows a crouching, bearded, Godlike figure bounding the circumference of the measurable universe with his fingers stretched into the form of a compass. I suspect Blake is here making a direct contrast between the fingers of the hopeful traveler who has allowed himself to be led by the apparently autonomous ball through an obscure gate (or indeed *the* obscure gate) in Jerusalem's wall, to the insistent, metallic fingers of his figure "Urizen" or Reason. Thinking himself the highest God, the figure of Urizen the "Ancient of Days" (measurable by time) bounds the universe, setting a *circum-ference* to the infinite, rendering its appearance *outside* of Man: separating Man from spiritual reality. The golden ball, on the other hand (literally) represents the infinite spiritual imagination: the true center, the antithesis of Urizen's realm, the hell of the false god: the circumference. The traveler is led within, where Jesus said the kingdom of heaven could be found.

The ball is the image's sole source of light, and by its sunlight, the traveler's attention is caught by something we cannot see that he, having been led through the door, can see, in the darkness illuminated by the beams that emanate from the golden ball. We note also that this door has a precise stone threshold. While one of the traveler's feet is still outside it, the other has made the definitive step and thereby become invisible to the worldly perspective of the viewer outside of the wall (us).

And the golden string of which the ball is made? We naturally consider the famous thread of Ariadne that leads Theseus out of the dark labyrinth inhabited by the savage Minotaur in the Greek myth: the dark labyrinth being taken as an analogy for the material world. We may also ponder the idea that the God of the Bible "writes" with his finger. The magus-doctor Paracelsus (1484–1541) whom Blake admired so much, believed the good doctor's essential task was to search for "divine signatures" or signs of divine mind in Nature. These signatures point to the Wisdom of its ultimate source: vestiges of the Logos (the "Word"), scattered like seams or seeds of glittering gold in a dark mine. If one caught hold of a natural observation—the hidden curative power of certain plants for example—and, through empathetic understanding, followed where the discovery led (the essence of experiment being *experience*), the seeker would find the gold of health and a divine blessing. To use Blake's image, if we should follow the spiritual gold, obscured in Nature by our lack of vision, we should activate what Blake called the "Poetic Genius" within. Then we should remember of what we are truly made and where our true home is: we should embrace the lady he calls "Jerusalem" once more, for she is the bride. The Gnostic, after all, is one who has found his or her way home.

More simply, the traveler's fingers have plucked the golden string of Apollo's lyre and entered in the key of the Sun: the outer image of the God within.

Heaven's Gate, Blake tells us, is "built in Jerusalem's wall." Must we travel to the East to find heaven? No indeed, for Blake tells us that "Jerusalem" is the "sister" of Albion which doped-up, "drowsy" England must be awoken to. In Blake, it is not the *Mistress* who is coy, but "Albion," the spirit of England, who in Blake's time will not embrace his "emanation," his divine syzygy, his Bride, Jerusalem. As an unbalanced, disintegrating arch-patriarch, Albion considers himself separate from Jerusalem, who in truth he is joined to. Failure to see this has led to Albion's rupture with America whose spirit has embraced liberty. Albion's anguish of desire cannot be satisfied with earthly attachments, for She is beauty beyond flesh and heart of his heart. But he does not see this for his psyche has been shattered by the usurper, Urizen: the false God: Reason abstracted, the ruler of the circumference and the superficial.

Like Marvell, Blake envisions the salvation of the country, and indeed the world, in terms of the necessary embrace of Albion and Jerusalem (or Christ and Sophia in classical Gnostic terms, and on Earth: the spiritually reborn man and woman). And, like Marvell and the millennialists, Blake sees a final consummation with the Last Judgment (meaning a reunion with God) and its signs—such as the conversion of the Jews (that is, the return of the Jews to "Jerusalem" or spiritual liberty)—in terms of an erotic, orgasmic surrender of pride and separateness.

In the apocalyptic "Night the Ninth" in Blake's unpublished spiritual epic *The Four Zoas,* justice is a sign of the return to the Center:

> The thrones of Kings are shaken, they have lost their robes
>   & crowns
> The poor smite their oppressors, they awake up to the
>   harvest.

Echoing the biblical prophecy of John the Baptist, Blake's great day occurs when Man comes back to "himself," which is to come back to God: to realize that he is one with the infinite, free of the false god. Then, only then, inadequate or oppressive religions will lose their grip on the reintegrated spiritual mind of Man, integrated in its faculties, united to its source where Male and Female are one dynamic life of God, where spiritual reality reveals the error of materiality as a hopeless imitation, where spirit is alive and not a dream, where mere pleasures are transformed into infinite joy, whole once more:

> Thus shall the male & female live the life of Eternity,
> Because the Lamb of God Creates himself a bride & wife
> That we his Children evermore may live in Jerusalem
> Which now descendeth out of heaven, a City, yet a Woman
> Mother of myriads redeem'd & born in her spiritual
>   palaces,
> By a New Spiritual birth Regenerated from Death.

A City, yet a Woman. . . . Note that: *It will lead you in at Heaven's gate, built in Jerusalem's wall.*

A City, for many may live in Her; a woman, for some may know her, really know Her: *She,* the Wisdom of God, is in woman, to be loved and embraced as She loves and gives Herself freely, utterly, ever pure to the pure in heart.

Yes, you have probably got there before me. This is to do with sex, is it not? Not perhaps a sex we have known, but something very great, something that could lift sex itself from the gutter of modern life, and raise us to the heavens and a New Jerusalem.

THY HEAVEN DOORS ARE
MY HELL GATES

Like Marvell, Blake sees the "Last Times" as being both somehow signally present (immanent) and temporally imminent (coming). Blake had taken Emmanuel Swedenborg's doctrine that the Last Times had actually been initiated in heaven in the year 1757, the year of Blake's birth. Crises on Earth reflected the spiritual revolution above and within. But whereas Marvell's poem of the previous century employed sexual imagery to chivy up the divine Millennium—even envisioning a sexual union with Lady Wisdom to explode the "iron gates of life"— Blake undoubtedly saw a divine sexual liberty as a key central characteristic of the New Age, a principle that rather horrified his contemporary, the Platonist Thomas Taylor (1758–1835) for whom love expressed in fleshly passion constituted an anti-Platonic abomination.

In 1790, as reports circulated of Fletcher Christian having taken the King's *Bounty* by mutiny in the South Seas, while, closer to home, the French Revolution and its victims were in full swing, Blake declared in his cannonball of fiery, etched writing *The Marriage of Heaven and Hell:* "a new heaven is begun, and it is now thirty-three years since its advent: the Eternal Hell revives. And lo! Swedenborg is the Angel sitting at the tomb; his writings are the linen clothes folded up. Now is the dominion of Edom, & the return of Adam into Paradise."

The new dawn brings new insight. Contraries, such as Reason and Energy, called by the churches "Good" and "Evil," or Heaven and Hell, are, Blake announces, necessary to human existence. The contraries promote progress; they should properly embrace one another in fructifying intercourse. Enthusiastic passion is necessary for things to change. With a possible eye on the shocking news of mutiny on the South Seas, Blake famously declares: "the lust of the goat is the bounty [free gift] of God." The spiritual and physical worlds, falsely set at odds with one another, are really the "working out" of one dynamic world: that which appears "without" is really within this *unus mundus* (one world).

The Marriage of Heaven and Hell demands we consult Isaiah chapters 34 and 35, for an understanding of what is really happening in—or rather *through*—the world: "For it is the day of the Lord's vengeance, and the year of recompenses for the controversy of Zion [Jerusalem]" (Isaiah 34:8).

And behold! The abolition of nobility in the French Revolution is *predicted:* "They shall call the nobles thereof to the kingdom, but none shall be there, and all her princes shall be nothing" (Isaiah 34:12). And with the fall of nobility and monarchy, Britain ("the island") will be the place where the "wild beasts" meet: "And thorns shall come up in her [France's?] palaces, nettles and brambles in the fortresses thereof: and it shall be an habitation of dragons, and a court for owls. The wild beasts of the desert shall also meet with the wild beasts of the island, and the satyr shall cry to his fellow; the screech owl also shall rest there, and find for herself a place of rest" (Isaiah 34:13–14). Island Britain is where the New Jerusalem will be built: "And the ransomed of the LORD shall return, and come to Zion with songs and everlasting joy upon their heads: they shall obtain joy and gladness, and sorrow and sighing shall flee away" (Isaiah 35:10).

What did Blake mean by: "Now is the dominion of Edom"?

Isaiah 34 announces a judgment of slaughter that is to fall on Idumea, another name for the biblical Edom (meaning "Red"). Edom was linked to Isaac's son Esau, who, born red all over, surrendered his inheritance for a mess of "red pottage" and went to live in Edom (where King Herod came from): "For my sword shall be bathed in heaven: behold, it shall come down upon Idumea, and upon the people of my curse, to judgment" (Isaiah 34:5).

Jewish commentators came to identify Edom with Babylon (which held Jews captive), with Rome (which imposed Idumean monarchy over Israel), and, subsequently, with Christianity. Edom, then, is the Gentile world. But Edom is also an "Adam" (whose name means "red earth") returning to Paradise; and Edom is a desert where, after execution of justice, "waters break out." Where once were dragons, Edom will be "grass with reeds and rushes."

A green and pleasant land . . .

The "dominion of Edom" had even more specific connotations in Blake's time. Suddenly, we shall see how Jewish conversion is tied in to sexual revolution and the culmination of history.

Jacob Frank (1726–1791) proclaimed himself successor to Jewish pseudo-messiah Sabbatai Zvi (1626–ca.1676), astonishing Polish Catholic leaders in the 1750s by his devotion to the kabbalistic text, the *Zohar* (or "Book of Splendour"), which in Frank's view allowed for a Trinity, over the Talmud's authority, and encouraged a reconciliation of Frank's many Jewish followers with the church.

In the apocalyptic year 1757 (Blake's birthdate), a debate between Talmudists and anti-Talmudists or "Zoharists" was presided over by the bishop of Kamenetz-Podolsk. Heeding the bishop's judgment that the anti-Talmudists had won the debate, Jacob Frank appeared in Iwana, Poland, claiming, as Zvi's successor, to be a man in receipt of heavenly messages. There followed a rush of interest among Catholic and Protestant leaders to accept the reconciled Jews into their communion. In London, the Moravian Church (whose members had included Blake's mother until her second marriage to Blake's father) was alerted to the dramatic, apocalyptically suggestive events in Poland.

By the time Blake finished *The Marriage of Heaven and Hell* (1793), some 26,000 Jews had been baptized in Poland. Frank enjoined his followers to adopt the "religion of Edom" (Christianity), as a step toward a religion he called "das," meaning "knowledge": that is to say, *gnosis.* Seeing themselves as free of the Law of Rabbinic Judaism, embracing a spiritual journey on the "highway" established in the redeemed Edom of Isaiah chapter 35: "the way of holiness" (Isaiah 35:8–9), they adopted a "way" distinguished by love, song, "joy and gladness," and, notably, a nonrepressive attitude to the human body, when, that is, its energies were directed to a heavenly ascent. The suggestion of a sexual religion in the service of the Holy Spirit was strong.

It is the transformed "Edom" bathed pure by the sword of heaven ("nor shall my sword sleep in my hand" as the famous hymn "Jerusalem" has it) that Blake celebrates in *The Marriage of Heaven and Hell*, a marriage made possible by marrying the contraries, attributable to divine will, for God's ultimate being is limitless. Blake writes in *The Marriage* [consummation] *of Heaven and Hell*:

> For the cherub with his flaming sword is hereby commanded to leave his guard at [the] tree of life, and when he does, the whole creation will be consumed and appear infinite and holy, whereas it now appears finite and corrupt.

> *This will come to pass by an improvement of sensual enjoyment.*

> But first the notion that man has a body distinct from his soul is to be expunged; this I shall do by printing in the infernal method by corrosives, which in Hell are salutary and medicinal, melting apparent surfaces away, and displaying the infinite which was hid.

> If the doors of perception were cleansed everything would appear to man as it is, infinite.

> For man has closed himself up, till he sees all things through narrow chinks of his cavern.

> *This will come to pass by an improvement in sensual enjoyment.*

The New Age requires two definite signs for its enactment: Jewish acceptance of Jesus, and a sexual revolution in the melting into union of the fundamental sex-negative religious doctrine of body-soul dualism. The new heaven and new Earth result from an improvement of sensual enjoyment.

There was, and is, need of it.

Wherever in the world men appear most ready to react violently to circumstances, we find repression of women and sex-negative taboo-inflicting culture. Misogyny is at the root of much murderous psychosis, the perennial, absolutist division of woman into the "pure" and the "whore": the fruitful one, the wild one, is of course, both.

The full recovery of humanity (*apocatastasis*) requires the relationship between body and soul to be properly understood. Blake's *Marriage of Heaven and Hell* offers guidance: "Man has no Body distinct from his Soul for that calld Body is a portion of Soul discernd by the five Senses. the chief inlets of Soul in this age." What we call body is a portion of the soul discerned by the five senses.

Remarkable.

Are the senses physical or psychological?

It is, according to Blake and the "golden string" of tradition he followed, the mind that creates the sensation of material existence. Sensual existence can be heightened until the senses are found rooted in a higher plane, when "we shall see things as they are: infinite."

Blake called on the Jews of his time to recognize their own esoteric tradition: the kabbalistic doctrine of the Adam Kadmon, the original image of Man (the Gnostic *Anthrōpos* or *Phōs* = "Light"), the image of God, the Man who contains the universe in himself. Blake identified this figure with Albion, and he identified him with *"Jesus the Imagination,"* for the imagination links us to the Pleroma through music, poetry, and painting: together they constitute the "golden string" vibrating with the sexual energy of Wisdom. And Blake addresses his call to Christians too, for he is of the view that the church worships the false god and ignores the true, insofar as it has condemned the joy of sex.

In the scattered verses of a probably unfinished poem called "The Everlasting Gospel," composed in the second decade of the nineteenth century, Blake makes his call to the Christians who, unbeknown to themselves, had abandoned Jesus:

> The Vision of Christ that thou dost see
> Is my Visions Greatest Enemy
> Thine has a great hook nose like thine
> Mine has a snub nose like mine
> Thine is the Friend of All Mankind
> Mine speaks in parables to the Blind
> Thine loves the same world that mine hates
> Thy Heaven doors are my Hell Gates.

The reference to the "hook nose" might be a jibe at the expense of the Duke of Wellington, victor of Waterloo (1815), famous for his great hooked nose ("Old Hookey" he was called) who once said: "Educate people without religion and you make them but clever devils"—a comment Blake would have objected to, insofar as what children learned of religion from the national church at that time was often less likely to open their hearts than to frighten them. And note that last line: *Thy Heaven doors are my Hell Gates*. Do we not hear an echo here of the breaking down of Marvell's "iron gates of life" (the Gate of Cancer where souls enter the material cosmos and forget their spiritual origin)? For by a neat inversion we may also have: "Thy Hell Gates are my Heaven's doors," for Heaven and Hell have been united in Blake's vision: married. *Everything that lives is holy,* declares Blake the prophet. If the Gates to Heaven are righteous obedience to the Mosaic Law, subjection to Reason, condemnation of the body, then they are Hell's Gates and so invite that contrary "Energy," which is "Eternal Delight." And if the vagina and penis are declared sinful and dirty, then they are in truth symbols of divine, eternal delight and should be respected as such.

And so the golden string, wound into a ball, leads us in at Heaven's Gate built in Jerusalem's wall. For "Jerusalem is a City, yet a woman," and in her wall or circumference is a gateway. She has the keys to the kingdom, and her womb is the Gate of Heaven to the spiritually free.

To ignore Her is to sleep the sleep of death; to embrace Her is to find God.

The Golden Ball will, if we will, lead us. It is the substance of a true Spiritual Revolution that, by its fundamental nature, involves each and every living one of us. For the ball is still spinning, casting its beams into the darkness.

Notes

ONE. THE "FILTHY GNOSTICKES"

1. Versluis, "Baader, Benedict, Franz Xaver von," in Hanegraaff and Brill, *Dictionary of Gnosis and Western Esotericism,* 148–54.
2. Lennon, "The Mysterious Smell of Roses," in *Skywriting by Word of Mouth, and Other Stories.*

TWO. HERESY STARTS IN EDEN

1. Irenaeus, *Adversus Omnes Haereses,* I.13, 7.
2. Blair, *The Kaleidoscope of Truth, Types and Archetypes in Clement of Alexandria,* 13.

THREE. HOW TO BE A SUPERMAN

1. Eusebius, *Ecclesiastical History,* vol. 2, ch. 13.
2. Josephus, *Antiquities of the Jews,* ch. 4, 18.

FOUR. AFTER SIMON, THE DELUGE

1. Justin Martyr, *Apology,* 1.26, 56.
2. Irenaeus, *Adversus Haereses,* I.23.
3. Ibid., I.3.

4. Tertullian, *De Praescriptione Haereticorum* (*On the Prescription of Heretics*), (a "prescription" was a Roman legal means of denying a plaintiff a court hearing); sections 41 and 43.

5. Tertulliana, *Q.S.Fl. Tertuliana Adversus Omnes Haereses,* 6.

6. Hippolytus, *Refutatio,* VII, 21.

7. Justin Martyr, *Dialogue with Trypho,* ch. 35.

8. Irenaeus, *Adversus Haereses,* I.

9. Ibid., I, ch. 28, 2.

10. Hippolytus, *Refutatio,* VII, 16.

FIVE. THE DIRTY PEOPLE

1. Irenaeus, *Adversus Haereses,* I.30, 15.

2. Clement of Alexandria, *Strōmateis,* VII, 17.

3. Hippolytus, *Refutatio,* V, 2.

4. Tertullian, *De Praescriptione Haereticorum,* 1.

5. Irenaeus, *Adversus Haereses,* I.25, 3.

6. Ibid., I.29.

7. Ibid., I.29, 3; my italics.

8. Ibid., I, 30, 9.

9. Ibid., I.30, 15.

10. Ibid., I.30, 7.

11. Ibid., I, 30, 9.

12. Ibid., I, 30, 12.

13. Hippolytus, *Refutatio,* V, 15–17.

14. Nag Hammadi Library, VII, I, 40.

15. Ibid., VII, I, 1.

16. Nag Hammadi Library, *Asklepios,* VI, 8, 66.

17. Nag Hammadi Library, III, 2, 60.

18. Clement of Alexandria, *Strōmateis,* VII.

19. Julius Africanus, *The Writings of Julius Africanus,* ix.

20. "Sexuality and Sexual Symbolism in Hermetic and Gnostic Thought and Practice, Second to Fourth Centuries," in Hanegraaff and Kripal, *Hidden Intercourse: Eros and Sexuality in the History of Western Esotericism,* 12ff.

21. Nag Hammadi Library, *Gospel of Thomas,* II, 2, logion 113.

22. Epiphanius, *Panarion,* 25, 2:4.
23. Ibid., 25, 3:2.
24. Ibid., 26, 8:2.
25. Nag Hammadi Library, *Gospel of Thomas,* II, 2, logia 21–22.
26. "Sexuality and Sexual Symbolism in Hermetic and Gnostic Thought and Practice, second to fourth centuries," in Hanegraaff and Kripal, *Hidden Intercourse,* 16.

SIX. TANTRA—REMARKABLE PARALLELS

1. Urban, "The Yoga of Sex, Tantra, Orientalism and Sex Magic in the Ordo Templi Orientis," in Hanegraaff and Kripal, *Hidden Intercourse,* 402.
2. Arthur Avalon [Sir John Woodroffe], ed., *Kularnava Tantra,* II.4. II.117; quoted in Urban, "The Yoga of Sex, Tantra, Orientalism and Sex Magic," in Hanegraaff and Kripal, *Hidden Intercourse.*
3. Quoted in Dasgupta, *An Introduction to Tantric Buddhism,* 142.
4. Quoted in Urban, "The Yoga of Sex, Tantra, Orientalism and Sex Magic," in Hanegraaff and Kripal, *Hidden Intercourse,* 402.
5. Agamavagisha, *Brihat Tantrasana,* 703.
6. Kripal, *Kālī's Child,* University of Chicago Press, 1998, 28.
7. Crowley, *Magical Record of the Beast 666,* 248.
8. Djurdjevic, "The Great Beast as a Tantric," in Bogdan and Starr, *Aleister Crowley and Western Esotericism,* 126.
9. Sanderson, *Purity and Power,* 200–201; quoted in Urban, "The Yoga of Sex," in Hanegraaff and Kripal, *Hidden Intercourse,* 409.
10. Urban, "The Yoga of Sex," in Hanegraaff and Kripal, *Hidden Intercourse,* 406.
11. Djurdjevic, in Bogdan and Starr, *Aleister Crowley and Western Esotericism,* 115.
12. Walter O. Kaelber cited by Djurdjevic in Bogdan and Starr, *Aleister Crowley and Western Esotericism,* 116.
13. Ibid., 118.
14. Nag Hammadi Library, *Apocalypse of Peter,* VII, 3, 81–83; *The Second Treatise of the Great Seth,* VII, 2, 55–56.
15. Kripal, *Kālī's Child,* 28.

16. Carrithers et al., "Purity and Power among the Brahmans of Kashmir," in *The Category of the Person: Anthropology, Philosophy, History*, 198.

SEVEN. BE MY VALENTINE

1. Irenaeus, *Adversus Haereses*, III, 11.9.
2. Helderman, *Die Anapausis im Evangelium Veritatis*.
3. Tertullian, *De Praescriptione Haereticorum*, vii.
4. Nag Hammadi Library, I, 3, 18.
5. Ibid., I, 3, 16.
6. Quispel, "Reviews," *Vigiliae Christianae*, 39 (1985), 394.
7. Ibid.
8. Nag Hammadi Library, *The Thunder, Perfect Mind*, VI, 2, 13.

EIGHT. A QUESTION OF SEED

1. Irenaeus, *Adversus Haereses*, I.6, 4.
2. Ibid., I.7, 1.
3. Quispel, "Reviews," 394.
4. Bentley Layton translation.
5. Nag Hammadi Library, *Gospel of the Egyptians*, III, 2, 42, 62.
6. Ibid., *Gospel of Philip*, II, 3, 67, translated by Wesley W. Isenberg.
7. Ibid., II, 3, 69.
8. Ibid., II, 3, 70.
9. Ibid.
10. Irenaeus, *Adversus Haereses*, I, 15, 6.
11. Ibid., I, 21, 3.
12. Ibid., I, 21, 2.
13. Tertullian, *De Praescriptione Haereticorum*, 7; 36.
14. Tertullian, *Adv. Val.* XXXII.
15. Eusebius, *Ecclesiastical History*, 5, 28, 6.
16. Clement of Alexandria, *Excerpta ex Theodato*, 76.
17. DeConick, "Conceiving Spirits" in Hanegraaff and Kripal, *Hidden Intercourse*, 23ff.
18. Ibid., 23.

19. Ibid., 25.
20. Ibid., 31.

NINE. THE VALENTINIAN MARRIAGE

1. DeConick, "Conceiving Spirits," Hanegraaff and Kripal, *Hidden Intercourse*, 32.
2. Nag Hammadi Library, *Gospel of Truth*, I, 3, 20–21.
3. Ibid., I, 23–24.
4. Tertullian, *Q.S.Fl. Tertulliana Adversus Valentinianos*, NHL XI, 2.
5. Nag Hammadi Library, *The Exegesis on the Soul*, II, 6, 127.
6. Ibid., II, 6, 133–34.

TEN. IN SEARCH OF THE MYSTERY OF PROUNEIKOS AND BARBELO IN ALEXANDRIA

1. Nag Hammadi Library, *Apocryphon of John*, II, 1, 9, 25.
2. Ibid. *The Thunder, Perfect Mind*, VI, 2, 13.
3. Henry Chadwick, "Philo of Alexandria."
4. Philo, *De confusione linguarum*, in *Philo*, 41, 62, 146.

ELEVEN. THE LASCIVIOUS ONE

1. Cephalas, Anth. P. 12.209, *cf.* A.B. [*Anecdota Bekkeri*, or *Anaecdota Graeca*] 3:1415; Photius's *Lexicon*. &c.
2. Pasquier, "Pruneikos: A Colorful Expression," in King, *Images of the Feminine in Gnosticism*, 47.
3. Cited by Liddell and Scott, *A Greek-English Lexicon*, and sourced as: "*Cod. Paris*. 2630."
4. Pasquier, "Prouneikos: A Colorful Expression," in King, *Images of the Feminine in Gnosticism*, 48ff.
5. Photius, *Lexicon*, ed. Naber, 116.
6. Schmidt, *Hesychii Alexandrini Lexicon*, 1:405.3 citing Pasquier, in King, *Images of the Feminine in Gnosticism*, 49.
7. Pasquier, "Prouneikos: A Colorful Expression," in King, *Images of the Feminine in Gnosticism*, 48.

8. Bekker, *Anecdota Graeca,* 3:1415.

9. Nag Hammadi Library, *Second Treatise of the Great Seth,* VII, 2, 50:25–30.

10. Pasquier, in "Prouneikos: A Colorful Expression," in King, *Images of the Feminine in Gnosticism,* 63.

11. Churton, *Kiss of Death.*

12. Harvey, 2 vols., in edition of Irenaeus's *Adversus Haereses,* CUP, 1857.

13. Reference to the obscure scholar called "Matter" in *Ante Nicene Fathers,* vol. 1, 353.

14. Nag Hammadi Library, *Trimorphic Protennoia,* XIII.1; Paul-Hubert Poirier, commentary in Nag Hammadi Library "Textes" 32, Laval University Press, Quebec, 2006, 225–26.

15. Irenaeus, *Adversus Haereses,* I, 29.

16. Nag Hammadi Library *Trimorphic Protennoia,* XIII, 1, 35:25.

17. Ibid., XIII, 1, 37:35.

18. Tertullian, *Adversus Valentinianos,* XX.

19. Irenaeus, *Adversus Haereses,* I, 11, 4.

20. Nag Hammadi Library, *The Apocryphon of John,* II, 1, 30:30.

21. Nag Hammadi Library, *The Apocryphon of John,* II, 1, 31:14–20.

22. Liddell and Scott, *Geoponika,* book 10:13, in *A Greek-English Lexicon.*

23. *Geoponicorum,* [= "Agricultural Pursuits"] *sive De re rustica libri XX.*

24. Cassianus Bassus and Owen, "Concerning the Planting of the Duracina, and the Care of Them." *Agricultural Pursuits, Translated from the Greek by Rev T. Owen, MA,* vol. 2.

25. See Churton, *Golden Builders.*

26. Lancelot and Louis le Maistre de Say, *The Primitives of the Greek Tongue.*

27. Prichard, *An Analysis of the Egyptian Mythology.*

28. Plutarch, *De Iside et Osiride,* volume IV; *De Iside et Osiride.*

29. *Classical Manual,* 226–27.

30. Nag Hammadi Library, *Eugnostos the Blessed,* III, 3, 88, 5–15.

31. Ibid., *The Thunder, Perfected Mind,* VI, 2, 149–216.

TWELVE. ALL YOU NEED IS SOPHIA

1. Péladan, *De Parsifal à Don Quichotte,* 1906, 53.

2. Péladan, *De Parsifal à Don Quichotte,* 2011, 50.

3. Ibid.

4. Ibid., 52.

5. Ibid., 53.

6. Ibid., 54.

7. Ibid., 56.

8. Ibid., 58.

9. Ibid., 59.

10. Ibid.

THIRTEEN. THE GOLDEN RIDDLE

1. Bembridge, "The Rosicrucian Resurgence at the Court of Cromwell," 219–45.

2. E-mail from Christopher McIntosh to the author June 8, 2014. McIntosh's new translation of the *Fama Fraternitatis,* celebrating 400 years since its first publication can be found in *Fama Fraternitatis,* English translation by Christopher McIntosh and Donate Pahnke McIntosh (Vanadis Texts, 2014). Donate McIntosh has also produced a modern German version (also Vandis Texts, 2014).

3. See Abraham, *Marvell and Alchemy.*

4. Marvell, "Upon Appleton House, to my Lord Fairfax," verse 43.

5. Marvell's millennial sympathies are explored in Margarita Stocker's *Apocalyptic Marvell.*

6. E-mail from Paul Bembridge to the author, March 3, 2014.

7. Davies, *Characters,* 148–49.

BIBLIOGRAPHY

Abraham, Lyndy. *Marvell and Alchemy*. Brookfield, Vt.: Scolar Press, 1990.

Agamavagisha. *Brihat Tantrasana*. In Urban, Hugh. "The Yoga of Sex, Tantra, Orientalism and Sex Magic in the Ordo Templi Orientis." *Hidden Intercourse: Eros and Sexuality in the History of Western Esotericism*, Edited by J. Hanegraaff and Jeffrey J. Kripal, New York: Fordham University Press, 2011.

Agrippa, Henry Cornelius. *Of the Vanity and Uncertainty of Arts and Sciences*. Amsterdam: BPH Library, 1569.

Ante Nicene Fathers, vol. 1. (Inc. Justin, *Apology*; *Dialogue with Trypho*; Irenaeus, *Adversus Haereses*). Grand Rapids, Mich.: W. B. Eerdman's, 1981.

Avalon, Arthur [Sir John Woodroffe], ed. *Kularnava Tantra*. Translated by M. P. Pandit. Madras, India: Ganesh & Co., 1973.

Bekker, August Immanuel. *Anecdota Graeca*, 3 vols. Berlin: G. Reimeri, 1814–1821.

Bembridge, Paul. "The Rosicrucian Resurgence at the Court of Cromwell." In Ralph White, ed., *The Rosicrucian Enlightenment Revisited*. Hudson, N.Y.: Books, 1999.

Blair, Eric Arthur. *The Kaleidoscope of Truth, Types and Archetypes in Clement of Alexandria*. Worthington, Sussex, UK: Churchman Publishing Ltd., 1986.

Bogdan, Henrick, and Martin P. Starr, eds. *Aleister Crowley and Western Esotericism*. New York: Oxford University Press, 2012.

The Book of Enoch. Translated by Robert Henry Charles. London: SPCK, 1994.

The Books of Jeu and the Untitled Text in the Bruce Codex ("Nag Hammadi Studies," XIII). Edited by Carl Schmidt. Translated by Violet Macdermot. Leiden, The Netherlands: E. J. Brill, 1997.

Butler, Samuel. *Characters*. Edited by Charles W. Davies. London: Case Western Reserve University Press, 1970.

Carrithers, Michael, et al., eds. "Purity and Power among the Brahmans of Kashmir." *The Category of the Person: Anthropology, Philosophy, History*. Cambridge: Cambridge University Press, 1985.

Casey, Robert Pierce, ed. *The Excerpta ex Theodoto of Clement of Alexandria* (Studies and Documents 1). London: Christophers, 1934 (see also www .gnosis.org/library/excr.htm). (accessed 4-15-15)

Cassianus Bassus, Constantine, and Thomas Owen. "Concerning the Planting of the Duracina, and the Care of Them." In *Agricultural Pursuits* [*Geoponicorum*]. Translated from the Greek by Rev T. Owen, MA, vol. 2. London: Printed for the author and sold by J. White, 63 Fleet Street, 1806.

Chadwick, Henry. "Philo of Alexandria." In *The Cambridge History of Later Greek and Early Medieval Philosophy*. Cambridge, UK: Cambridge University Press, 1967.

Churton, Tobias. *The Golden Builders*. York Beach, Maine: Weiser, 2004.

———. *Gnostic Philosophy*. Rochester, Vt.: Inner Traditions, 2005.

———. *L'Ultimo Vangelo*. Milan: Cairo Publishing, 2006. English version: *Kiss of Death: The True History of the Gospel of Judas*. London: Watkins, 2008.

———. *The Missing Family of Jesus*. London: Watkins, 2010.

———. *The Mysteries of John the Baptist*. Rochester, Vt.: Inner Traditions, 2013.

Classical Manual (commentary on Alexander Pope's translation of *Homer*). London: A. J. Valpy, 1827.

Clement of Alexandria. *Excerpta ex Theodoto*. London: Christophers, 1934.

———. *Strōmateis*, Books 1–7. (Fathers of the Church, Book 85). Washington D.C.: Catholic University of America Press, 1992 (see also www .earlychristianwritings.com). (accessed 4-15-15)

Crowley, Aleister. *Magical Record of the Beast 666*. Edited by John Symonds and Kenneth Grant. London: Duckworth, 1973.

Dasgupta, Shashi Bhushan. *An Introduction to Tantric Buddhism.* Berkeley, Calif.: Shambhala, 1974.

Davies, Charles W., ed. *Characters.* Cleveland & London: Case Western Reserve University Press, 1970.

DeConick, April D. "Conceiving Spirits: The Mystery of Valentinian Sex." In Hugh Urban, *Hidden Intercourse: Eros and Sexuality in the History of Western Esotericism.* Edited by Wouter J. Hanegraaff and Jeffrey J. Kripal. New York: Fordham University Press, 2011.

Djurdjevic, Gordan. "The Great Beast as a Tantric Hero: The Role of Yoga and Tantra in Aleister Crowley's Magick." In Henrik Bogdan and Martin P. Starr, eds., *Aleister Crowley and Western Esotericism.* Oxford, UK: Oxford University Press, 2012.

Epiphanius. *The Panarion of Epiphanius of Salamis,* Book 1, Sections 1–46 (Nag Hammadi and Manichaean Studies). Translated by Frank Williams. Leiden: E. J. Brill, 2008.

Eusebius. *Ecclesiastical History,* 2 vols. Translated by Kirsopp Lake. London: Loeb Classical Library, 1973.

Eustathius of Thessalonica. *Commentary on the Odyssey: Eustathii Archiepiscopi Thessalonicensis Commentarii ad Homeri Odysseam.* Cambridge, UK: Cambridge University Press, 2010.

Fama Fraternitatis. Translated by Christopher McIntosh and Donate Pahnke McIntosh. Bremen, Germany: Vanadis Texts, 2014.

Ferreiro, Alberto. *Simon Magus in Patristic, Medieval and Early Modern Traditions* (vol. 125 of Studies in the History of Christian Traditions). Leiden: E. J. Brill, 2005.

Hanegraaff, Wouter J., and E. J. Brill, eds. *Dictionary of Gnosis and Western Esotericism.* Leiden: E. J. Brill, 2006.

Hanegraff, Wouter J., and Jeffrey J. Krepal, eds. *Hidden Intercourse: Eros and Sexuality in the History of Western Esotericism.* New York: Fordham University Press, 2011.

Helderman, Jan. *Die Anapausis im Evangelium Veritatis* ("Nag Hammadi Studies"). Leiden: E. J. Brill, 1984.

Η ΚΑΙΝΗ ΔΙΑΘΗΚΗ [The New Testament, in Greek]. London: The British and Foreign Bible Society, 1965.

Hippolytus, *Refutatio* ("Refutation of all Heresies" Books I–X (Books II and III missing); including extracts from the Gnostic Justin's *Book of Baruch* in *Ante-Nicene Fathers*, vol. 5. Edited by Alexander Roberts, James Donaldson, and A. Cleveland Coxe. Translated by J. H. MacMahon. Buffalo, N.Y.: Christian Literature Publishing Co., 1886.

Holy Bible, King James Version. Oxford, UK: Oxford University Press, 1969.

Irenaeus. *Adversus Omnes Haereses*. Rome: Forzani et Sacii, 1907.

Jonas, Hans. *Gnosis und Spätantiker Geist, 1934–154*. (*Gnosis and the Spirit of Late Antiquity, 1934–1954*). Göttingen, Ger.: Vandenhoeck & Ruprecht, 1964.

Josephus, Flavius. *Antiquities of the Jews*. Translated by William Whiston. Edinburgh: William P. Nimmo, 1865.

Julius Africanus. *The Writings of Julius Africanus*. Edited by Alexander Roberts and James Donaldson. Edinburgh: T & T Clark, 1867.

Justin Martyr. *Apology; Dialogue with Trypho*. In *Ante Nicene Fathers*, vol. 1. Grand Rapids, Mich.: W. B. Eerdmans, 1981.

Kaelber Walter O. Cited in Bogdan, Henrick, and Martin P. Starr. *Aleister Crowley and Western Esotericism*, New York: Oxford University Press, 2012.

Kelly, John Norman Davidson. *Early Christian Doctrines*. London: A & C Black, 1977.

King, Karen L., ed. *Images of the Feminine in Gnosticism*. Harrisburg, Penn.: Trinity Press, 2000.

Kripal, Jeffrey J. *Kālī's Child, The Mystical and the Erotic in the Life and Teachings of Ramakrishna*. Chicago: University of Chicago Press, 1998.

Lancelot, Claude and Isaac Louis le Maistre de Say. *The primitives of the Greek tongue containing a Complete Collection of all the Roots or Primitive Words, Together with the most considerable Derivatives of the Greek Language*. Printed for J. Nourse at the Lamb, opposite Katherine-Street in the Strand; and G.Hawkins at Milton's Head near Temple Bar, Fleet Street, MDCCXLVIII [1748].

Lennon, John. *Skywriting by Word of Mouth, and Other Stories*. London: Jonathan Cape, 1981.

Liddell, Henry George, and Robert Scott. *A Greek-English Lexicon*. Oxford, UK: Oxford University Press, 1901.

Marvell, Andrew. "Upon Appleton House, to my Lord Fairfax." 1681.

Mead, George Robert Stowe. *Pistis Sophia: The Gnostic Tradition of Mary Magdalene, Jesus and His Disciples*. London: A&D Publishing, 2009.

Newton, Sir Isaac. *Observations upon the Prophecies of Daniel and the Apocalypse of St. John. In Two Parts.* London: J. Darby & T. Browne, 1733.

Oldenbourg, Zoé. *Massacre at Montségur.* New York: Barnes & Noble, 1990.

Pasquier, Anne. "Pruneikos: A Colorful Expression to Designate Wisdom in Gnostic Texts." In Karen L. King, *Images of the Feminine in Gnosticism.* Harrisburg, Penn.: Trinity Press, 2000.

Péladan, Joséphin. *De Parsifal à Don Quichotte.* Rue St André-des-Arts: E. Sansot & Cie, 1906.

———. *De Parsifal à Don Quichotte; Le Secret des Troubadours; Le Clé de Rabelais; Le Secret des Corporations.* Introduction by Emmanuel Dufour-Kowalski. Lausanne, Switzerland: Editions Delphica, 2011.

Philo of Alexandria. *De Confusione Linguarum.* In *Philo.* Loeb Classical Library, 10 vols. Translated by F. H. Colson and Rev. G. H. Whitaker. London: Heinemann, 1973.

Photius. *Lexicon.* Edited by S. A. Naber. Leiden: E. J. Brill, 1864.

Pliny. *Natural History*, 2 vols. London: Loeb Classical Library, 1989.

Plotinus. *Enneads.* Edited and translated by Stephen MacKenna. Burdett, N.Y.: Larson Publications Classic Reprint Series, 1992.

Poirier, Paul-Hubert. Nag Hammadi Library "Textes." Quebec: Laval University Press, 2006.

Plutarch, *De Iside et Osiride* in *Plutarch's Morals, Translated from the Greek by Several Hands,* vol. 4. London: printed by Thomas Bradyll, to be sold by most booksellers in London and Westminster. MDCCIV [1704].

———. *De Iside et Osiride.* Translated by Robert Midgley and William Baxter, Philalethes.

Prichard, James Cowles. *An Analysis of the Egyptian Mythology.* London: Printed for John and Arthur Arch, Cornhill, 1819.

Quispel, Gilles. "Reviews." *Vigiliae Christianae,* 39 (1985), 393–416.

Rahn, Otto. *The Crusade against the Grail.* Rochester, Vt.: Inner Traditions, 2006.

Roberts, Alexander, James Donaldson, and A. Cleveland Coxe, eds. *Against all Heresies.* In *Ante-Nicene Fathers,* vol. 3. Translated by S. Thelwall. Buffalo, N.Y.: Christian Literature Publishing Co., 1885.

———. *Ante-Nicene Fathers,* vol. 5. Translated by J. H. MacMahon. Buffalo, N.Y.: Christian Literature Publishing Co., 1886.

Robinson, James M., ed. *The Nag Hammadi Library in English.* Leiden: E. J. Brill, 1984.

Robinson, Marnia. *Cupid's Poisoned Arrow.* Berkeley, Calif.: North Atlantic Books, 2009.

de Rougemont, Denis. *Love in the Western World.* Princeton, N.J.: Princeton University Press, 1983.

Rudolph, Kurt. *Gnosis.* Translated by Wilson R. McLachlan. San Francisco: Harper & Row, 1985.

Schmidt, Moritz. *Hesychii Alexandrini Lexicon,* 1:405.3. In Pasquier, Anna. *Images of the Feminine in Gnosticism.* Edited by Karen L. King. Harrisburg, Penn.: Trinity Press, 2000.

Stocker, Margarita. *Apocalyptic Marvell: The Second Coming in Seventeenth Century Poetry.* Athens, Ohio: Ohio University Press, 1986.

Tertullian. *Q.S.Fl. Tertulliana Adversus Valentinianos.* Text, translation, and commentary by Mark T. Riley. Dissertation, Stanford University, 1971 (see www.csus.edu/indiv/r/rileymt). (accessed 4-15-15)

———. *De Praescriptione Haereticorum.* www.tertullian.org/works/de_ practscriptione_haereticorum.htm. (accessed 4-15-15)

Urban, Hugh. "The Yoga of Sex, Tantra, Orientalism and Sex Magic in the Ordo Templi Orientis." *Hidden Intercourse: Eros and Sexuality in the History of Western Esotericism,* Edited by J. Hanegraaff and Jeffrey J. Kripal. New York: Fordham University Press 2011.

INDEX